THE NOT-SO-SECRET LIVES OF
REAL
"MORMON" WIVES

THE NOT-SO-SECRET LIVES OF
REAL
"MORMON" WIVES

OWEN, BÖHME, CONDIE, HONG MERRILL,
DOWDELL, EGAN, JACKSON-STOWELL, MELAZZO

CFI
An imprint of Cedar Fort, Inc.
Springville, Utah

Paperback ISBN 13: 978-1-4621-4930-8
eBook ISBN 13: 978-1-4621-4931-5

Published by CFI, an imprint of Cedar Fort, Inc.
2373 W. 700 S., Suite 100, Springville, UT 84663
Distributed by Cedar Fort, Inc., www.cedarfort.com

Library of Congress Control Number: 2024949761

Cover design by Shawnda Craig
Cover design © 2024 Cedar Fort, Inc.
Edited and Typeset by Liz Kazandzhy

Printed in the United States of America

10 9 8 7 6 5 4 3 2 1

Printed on acid-free paper

To my mother, to my sister, to my wife, to my daughter, to all the women who define the word *woman* by making their lives joyful expressions of themselves. Thank you for making the world that much brighter!

CONTENTS

INTRODUCTION

IN MY CAR, DRIVING SEVENTY-FIVE MILES PER HOUR DOWN I-15 WAS the last place I expected to receive revelation for the publisher I work for—let alone from a billboard featuring eight sexily clad women proclaiming to be "Mormon wives" living "secret lives"—but that's exactly how inspiration struck.

Of course, I'd been aware of the TV show before this moment. As a member of The Church of Jesus Christ of Latter-day Saints, I find that it's seemingly impossible to miss references to the Church—usually making fun of it—in modern media.

When *Ocean's Eleven* came out, I recall being in a crowded theater in Salt Lake City, Utah, as the "Mormon" twins were introduced. I assume most of the moviegoers were Latter-day Saints—who made up 66 percent of Utah's population in 2001—and yet the theater erupted with laughter, even though the twins were not remotely representative of our culture or people.

The same thing happened at a theater for the movie *Two Weeks Notice* when the friend of Sandra Bullock's character (Lucy) tells her that Hugh Grant's character (George) asked her to an event too, along with another woman, and Lucy replies, "How many women does a man need to take to dinner? Maybe in Utah."

In my experience, no one has a better sense of humor about ignorant, mocking references to the Church than Church members—or, for that matter, the Church itself.

Take *The Book of Mormon Musical,* for example. How did the Church respond? By taking an ad out in the bill of the play that said, "You've seen the musical—now read the book." It was funny and clever and brilliant in many ways.

Even the term *Mormon,* the name we're often known for all over the world, was initially given to members of the Church in the 1800s as a derogatory term. And what did we do with it? We turned it into a positive. (That said, it's not what we prefer—we respectfully ask to be referred to as members of The Church of Jesus Christ of Latter-day Saints.)

Clearly, we're notoriously good at laughing at ourselves. And when the *Secret Lives* show recently came out, that was my response too. Honestly, I didn't give it much thought—except to remember some responses from friends on social media:

"Our church doesn't teach us to be swingers. Just wanted to clear that up in case anyone was confused." That comment had 186 reactions to it on social media. Of those, 104 were laughing reactions. Again, the responses were from mostly members, though there were a few nonmembers in there as well. Other responses were:

- "That's right—if we want to swing, we don't need lessons."
- "Oh, that's what I've been doing wrong. Oops!"
- "I had to look this up because I didn't know what swinging meant. Lol!"
- "Always did love a good rope swing, especially if it went out over the water and ended up in a really great flip."

All of these were from women in the Church with a great sense of humor. It also shows how absurd the mainstream Latter-day Saint community thought the show's claims were.

Even though I'd seen mostly humorous reactions to the show, I noticed others of a more serious nature starting to seep through as well. For example, another friend made a lovely anniversary post dedicated to a lifelong love and friendship with her husband and included the hashtag #realwomenofthechurchofjesuschristoflatterdaysaints.

But these weren't the things I was ruminating on during my I-15 drive. Instead, like many do on a commute, I was thinking about work.

A large part of my job with Cedar Fort Publishing & Media is to find authors, projects, and books to publish. I spend hours every week researching people and projects that might be a good fit for our company. I also spend a lot of time in prayer asking Heavenly Father for guidance, and that day was no exception.

You see, a lesson I've learned many times in my life—and have learned well—is found in Proverbs 3:5–6: "Trust in the Lord with all thine heart; and lean not unto thine own understanding. In all thy ways acknowledge him, and he shall direct thy paths." I learned it when I served a year-and-a-half mission in New York City and was required to learn Spanish fluently (which I eventually did). I learned it when I had to approach and talk peaceably to people about my beliefs, whether or not they wanted to be peaceable with me. I learned it when I was sick or depressed or felt alone in the world. And I've learned it as a single woman, now in her forties, in my career as an author, and recently as the acquisitions manager for Cedar Fort.

I've also learned the truth of Matthew 21:22: "And all things, whatsoever ye shall ask in prayer, believing, ye shall receive." And in *The Book of Mormon: Another Testament of Jesus Christ*, Alma 34:24–25 reads, "Cry unto him over the crops of your fields, that ye may prosper in them. Cry over the flocks of your fields, that they may increase."

It just so happened that the morning before I saw the billboard on the freeway, I had done just that. I knelt by my bed in fervent prayer, asking Heavenly Father to bless me to know what project I could bring into our company—something that would help the company prosper and that would be important and timely to readers. I'll admit, I felt a certain amount of desperation in my prayer, because for some time, I'd been coming up empty for really poignant projects or even responses from people who might have worthwhile projects for us. And while I'd been praying for weeks for help, it was in that morning prayer that I truly felt what I was asking for.

So there I was, driving down I-15, listening to an amazing podcast about the ten virgins and the wedding feast, thinking, "I should contact so-and-so to do a project," when the digital billboard at the exit near University Parkway in Provo switched to an ad for *The Secret Lives of Mormon Wives*.

At first, I smirked, remembering the funny commentary from friends that I mentioned earlier. But then the words "The *Not-So-*Secret Lives of *Real* Mormon Wives" popped into my head.

My mind whirled, my stomach lurched, and my heart started thudding in my chest. This was it! This was what I had been praying for—there was no doubt in my mind.

I couldn't stop thinking about it. Ten minutes later, I parked in front of our office, grabbed all my things, and with my "idea motors" still running, I headed straight to the office of my boss, Bryce Mortimer, the CEO of Cedar Fort, and told him my vision.

He smiled. "Yes!" Sure, he's a smiley guy, but I felt like this was an *extra* sunny smile—you know, the kind that says "You did good."

Yeah, I did!

Then he added, "Go. Let's make this happen."

"Great!" I replied. "There's a spot open on the schedule for March." This would be perfect.

Bryce shook his head. "I'd like to get this out by November."

That's when my motors came to a (temporary!) screeching halt. It was Monday, September 23, 2024.

November? Like in two months November? Yeah, right. My stomach took a steep nosedive like I was on the first drop of a roller coaster.

"Oh, okay," I said, trying to work through the logistics in my mind. I'd worked with the company for a little over a year at this point, and as far as I knew, we'd never had a turnaround of two months before—let alone with the eight authors I envisioned. "Well, uh . . . I guess I'll go get started."

(I found out a month later that Bryce had been praying for his employees too—praying that we'd be inspired with ideas—and that he'd had that same scripture in Alma in mind that I had. How cool is that?)

Feeling very excited, but also slightly gobsmacked, I grabbed everything I had hauled into Bryce's office—my lunch cooler, my backpack, my coat, and two thirty-two-ounce water bottles—headed over to my office, and plopped down in my chair, still holding everything in my arms.

"You all right there?" asked Sam, our ever-observant vice president of sales and marketing. I'm sure I looked pretty shell-shocked.

"Uh . . ." Part of me was wondering what I'd gotten myself into, while the other part was incredibly excited and remembered that I'd prayed for this. Philippians 4:13 also came to mind: "I can do all things through Christ which strengtheneth me."

"Yes?" I replied, clearly not convinced of my own answer.

Sam laughed, his lighthearted nature coming through. "Uh-huh . . ."

"Yes," I said with a bit more authority in my voice. And then I told him my idea—an idea I'd end up repeating to almost everyone in the office that day.

Not everyone was convinced right away, but by the end of that first day, after I'd gotten the first five yeses—from five remarkable women—others were starting to believe in it too.

My requirements for participants were strict. They had to be married and members of the Church. Easy enough, I thought. But then it got trickier. To be a proper mirror of the show, they also had to be (a) successful in their own right, (b) beautiful, and (c) interested in the project.

Turns out it wasn't that hard to find women who fit my criteria after all. So many amazing women wanted to participate—wanted their voices to be heard.

That night, my sister Erin and some of my friends gave me lists of women to contact.

First thing Tuesday morning, our editor in chief came into my office with his phone held aloft. "Ms. Emily"—that's what he calls all ladies (*Ms.*), and if that's not the most endearing thing ever, I don't know what is—"I talked to my wife last night, and she sent me with a list of names of women she thinks would be great for this project, and as a dutiful husband, I'm passing the message along."

My heart filled with warmth. He told his wife, and she'd given him homework for me!

That was just the start of the snowball that's taken over this project.

Later, Sam's wife hobbled in on crutches while Sam was in a meeting with Bryce—she'd just had knee surgery. She took a seat in Sam's chair. We'd never met, but she turned to me and spoke as if we'd been lifelong friends. "So, have you considered contacting . . ." and she proceeded to list off a bunch of names.

Sam had talked about the project with his wife too, and she'd taken it upon herself to help me! I couldn't believe how awesome that was.

And they weren't the only ones.

Each time I asked one of our "not-so-secret wives" and got a yes, I also got a story about how grateful they were to be included and how much they wanted to represent this project and their beliefs in a "real" way—to show the world what women in the Church are really like.

As the week went on, what had originally been something funny to me turned into something deeply personal as I listened to all these women, in and out of the project—entrepreneurs, stay-at-home moms, philanthropists, wives of employees, my friends, my sister, and so many others—express their frustrations with how women in the Church, specifically, are being represented in the media, and they shared their excitement to do something positive and uplifting—an antithesis.

With the popular media and books that have been released in recent years (the *Secret Lives* show, a new thriller movie featuring sister missionaries, various documentaries, and more), women in the Church have become tired of being represented as either repressed nuns—cloistered and held under the thumbs of their husbands, wearing ugly blue trench coats, and walking in front of temples—or as extremely sexually promiscuous and breaking molds within the Church for being "different."

We're seen as monoliths, when in reality, we're all different—from our marriages, or lack thereof, to our careers, to our countries of origin. But one thing we have in common is our love for Jesus Christ.

To me, this project is a miracle. Within one week, we had our eight women and set them to work doing something that many had never done before—writing a story. And not just any story, but a story about themselves in narrative form. These women are moms, wives, social media influencers, philanthropists, moguls, and industry leaders, but only three of them were writers, and of those three, only one had done narrative nonfiction. And we asked them to write something amazing . . . in a month. And you know what? They did it! I'm not an overly emotional person, but every story in this book has touched me deeply.

There have also been many other miracles along the way in making this project happen—including arranging a photo shoot in ten days with eight extremely busy women!—and I feel privileged to have witnessed them from the inside. But for everyone else, you're not missing out—because you'll find countless miracles recorded in the coming pages.

What we have for you here isn't a callout, though it probably seems that way from the cover and title. What this really is, is the lives and testimonies of eight amazing women who wanted to show the world the other side—their version of what it means to be a successful woman, "Mormon" wife, and member of The Church of Jesus Christ of Latter-day Saints.

You won't see these women talking about the show or any other inaccurate representations of us in the media. (Only I get to do that. Ha!) You'll only see them talking about their own lives and testimonies. And that's what makes this book, in my humble opinion, so phenomenal. Is it salacious? No. Is it funny? Heartbreaking? Tear-jerking? Thought-provoking? Powerful? I think so.

These women are living the truths taught in the Book of Mormon, in 2 Nephi 25:26, which says, "We talk of Christ, we rejoice in Christ, we preach of Christ, we prophesy of Christ, and we write according to our prophecies, that our children may know to what source they may look for a remission of their sins."

So grab a warm drink, find your favorite blanket, and cuddle up next to the fire because you're in for a treat. Not only will you be entertained, but you'll also finally see a true representation of what it means to be a successful "Mormon" wife.

Love,
Emily Clark

1

FERNANDA BÖHME
The Fashion Mogul

JOURNEY TO AMERICA

"Someday you will go to the United States of America," our highly intuitive maid told my mom. It was 1986 in Rio de Janeiro, Brazil. My family had never even thought of going to America. Why would we? What for? Our lives were here.

My mom laughed. "You're crazy—that would never happen."

The maid continued, "You will work like slaves for many years, but one day, your daughters will be very successful entrepreneurs at a young age."

My mom looked at her in complete shock, her eyebrows shooting to her hairline.

How could she know such a thing? She couldn't. It was crazy. After all, my sister and I were toddlers, still in diapers at the time.

Yet six years later, our family of five—my mom, dad, sister, my younger brother, and I—found ourselves on an airplane with a one-way ticket to Utah. There was no turning back. My dad was convinced it was an opportunity of a lifetime to further his education at Brigham Young University (BYU) and also give us a chance for a better future.

We were members of the Igreja de Jesus Cristo dos Santos dos Últimos Dias (*The Church of Jesus Christ of Latter-day Saints* translated into Portuguese). We were members before I knew Utah existed on the map. We left everything we knew—our extended family, our culture, our language, our life in a big city surrounded by the jungle.

As the plane landed on a brisk spring day in Salt Lake City, the white-capped mountains were dramatically contrasted by the almost royal blue skies and desert landscape that was so different from where I came from. *Wow*, I thought. *It's like I've gone to another planet!* Everything was different. Everything. From the small airport to the clean streets to the quiet neighborhoods.

As we drove out of the airport, I thought, *Where is everyone?* Why are there no people walking around? The first night, it was so quiet I couldn't sleep. Where was all the busy, loud traffic?

We lived in a high-rise in Rio, and now, in Provo, Utah, we lived close to the ground in student housing, high in the mountains. This place was far from the loud, bustling city I was accustomed to.

The first day of school was like climbing Mount Everest. I was eight years old, spoke zero English, and had jet-black hair that was so different from the pale shades of blond and brown that surrounded me. The kids at my school stared at me for hours on end, and like a Jaguar on exhibit, I didn't want to show my spots.

Surrounded by tons of other kids, I went through the cafeteria alone and was served up food I'd never seen in my life. *Corn dogs and apple pie? Kids drink plain milk with no chocolate? This is absurd!*

And those weren't my only trials. I was also excluded from all the activities because I was the new ESL student (English as a Second Language), along with my sister, Vivien, who was a grade up.

Our first winter here hit me like a blizzard, swooping in unexpectedly and rattling me. I'd never seen such weather. At first, the snow delighted me, but soon that delight faded with the increase of the icy-cold chill. One day, as snow fell in great big flakes, my parents took us to a thrift store called Deseret Industries to get ourselves some warm coats.

Our first Christmas morning was . . . well . . . there were no gifts under the tree. My dad was a full-time student at BYU, finances were extremely tight, and the mentality was that of "be grateful you're even in this country." But at around 7 a.m., we opened the door to a blizzard-filled sky and found that someone had dropped off a basket with toys, food, and other pleasantries.

"Who would do this for us?" I asked.

My family had no idea either, but that didn't stop my little brother from guessing. "Angels?"

Whether it was the kind from heaven or just people doing God's work, we all had to agree. To this day, I still don't know, but it was a kind act I would always remember. Could it have been someone from the local congregation?

We had been members of the "Mormon" church since Brazil. That was one thing we were very grateful for—the local ward where we attended church took us in as their own family. (*Ward* means a local congregation in the Church.)

This is something amazing about the "Mormon" church. If you were to be dropped off anywhere on the globe, the members of the local wards would take you in as their own.

The Church also has the largest group of organized women in the world, an organization called the Relief Society (*Sociedade de Socorro* in Portuguese). Millions of women spread their light throughout the world. It's powerful, and never had I felt that power, warmth, and welcoming so strongly as I did that Christmas morning. Perhaps we weren't invisible after all.

Soon finances got even tighter as the money we came with ran out and my parents had to find work. Every nationality has their work cut out for them when they come to the US. For the Brazilians, it's cleaning buildings.

My parents started to clean buildings and left us three kids alone at home. It was September, and the skies got dark earlier. I swung on the playground swing set outside while my siblings stayed inside our apartment. Lights shone through our neighbors' windows, showcasing, like a TV show, what was happening inside each apartment. Families were having dinner together and winding down for bedtime.

It was pitch dark, and as I gripped the metal ropes of the swing, I thought, *This is your life now, and you're on your own. You face the world alone.* Heavy thoughts for an eight-year-old.

I eventually went inside late that evening, hungry, and waited till midnight for my parents to come home.

That night solidified something in my mind: If I wanted anything, I had to work for it.

I soon learned from a few friends we'd made that you could take out the trash for people in our complex if you knocked on their door and asked, and they'd pay you 25 to 50 cents to do it. The dumpsters were far away, so it became a profitable little business for my siblings and me because most people didn't want to make that trek.

That change got us our snacks and drinks, so we were happy.

But that wasn't the end of my drive—my desire to seek more. Later, I went on to win a school fundraiser because I knew how to knock on every door in the community. I was very competitive. Even on Halloween, we had to get more candy than any other kid in Provo. There was so much candy it filled our entire tiny living room! We didn't care if we woke people up in their pajamas—we were still knocking on doors till midnight. We spent the next several weeks eating our candy and building pyramids and fortresses out of thousands of smarties.

The Not So "American Dream"

I believe that my parents, at this point, were overwhelmed in a new country, with a language they struggled to learn, raising three kids, and broke. We were in what you call "survival mode." We, as kids, had to be the adults in the home, translating everything from the phone bill to rent. My parents got assigned more buildings to clean, and soon we were going with them. Every day after school, we would come home, eat, and leave.

These were massive office buildings, some even several stories high. My sister and I would get the trash from every cubicle. Occasionally, we would find a nickel or dime on the ground, and that would be our vending machine budget for the night. You see, my parents worked for minimum wage, and we worked, well . . . for free. It didn't matter if you were tired or hungry.

After cleaning three to four giant buildings every night, we'd head home exhausted, knowing that tomorrow would bring more of the same. If you were hungry, there was no McDonald's drive-through in between buildings. You'd wait till you got home, but even then the options were slim to none.

Most of the time, the Church fed us. The Church has its own food manufacturing capabilities with its own grocery stores to help people who are going through hard times. This system also provides relief, in the form of food and other supplies, to areas around the world affected by natural disasters. While we were so grateful for this organization that kept our bellies full, we were facing a different kind of disaster.

Six days a week, we did the same thing: go to school, come home and eat, go to work cleaning multiple buildings. Repeat. Again and again and again.

One particular time, as I was taking out the garbage under a cubicle, I found a family photo taken in Hawaii. I stopped and thought about my long-lost childhood back in Brazil—going to the beach on weekends and taking an occasional walk in the mornings along the shoreline before school started.

While lost in those thoughts, staring at the photo, I recognized a colleague from elementary school in the picture and my face heated. *I would be completely mortified if my friends ever found out I clean buildings till midnight every day.*

A little self-consciousness aside, I didn't usually feel sorry for myself—but I did wonder if those days would ever end.

Day after day, year after year, it went on for almost a decade.

For a family of five, we lived under the poverty line. Even back-to-school shopping was not an option. We got hand-me-downs from the kids who got hand-me-downs. My sister, Vivien, and I wanted to be part of dance lessons and other groups, but that would require payment, so that was a no as well.

As we were preparing for the last day of school field day, the elementary school invited a local dance teacher to choreograph the final performance. After several days of practice, the dance teacher approached me and remarked, "You're a very talented dancer. What academy are you part of?"

I froze. I didn't know what to say. I'd never received such a compliment. Even if we could pay for dance classes, we had to clean buildings every night and didn't have time for anything else. "I don't belong to any dance groups," I answered.

"Well, you should look into it," she replied. "In fact, you should join our academy."

The embarrassment of sharing my harsh reality with the dance teacher was beyond what I could handle. I thanked her and quickly disappeared into the crowd of kids, pretending to be uninterested.

Years later, in junior high, I wanted to join the orchestra, so I got a babysitting job to pay for the lessons and made monthly payments to rent a violin. I was thirteen and thought it was time to do something new. I had severe ADD, as many creatives do, but I was determined to learn to play, and I practiced for hours every week when I wasn't cleaning buildings at night. My practice chart was always the highest among my peers in the junior high orchestra.

Violin wasn't my only hobby. I also collected *Vogue* magazines. In between the Bach concertos, I would memorize every designer's collection.

At sixteen years old, I took a sewing class at the local fabric store and sewed a replica of the Balenciaga two-piece silver Lycra swimsuit. Shopping for clothing was not a regular activity given our circumstances, but I somehow always dressed differently. I never enjoyed the selections offered at the local mall, but I valued couture as the global designers' "It" items to have. I loved the art expression and the dramatic photo shoots. I studied fashion magazines meticulously at Barnes and Noble and the Borders store.

When it was time for prom, I thought the dresses at the local mall were just blah. So I got inspiration from *Vogue* magazine's photo of Gisele Bündchen wearing a leather skirt outfit. My mom, who could sew and make a pattern, helped me put together this very avant-garde snake pleather dress with a zipper all the way up to a mock neck. We worked all night, but at 1 a.m., the sewing machine broke. We couldn't finish the dress.

"Sorry," my mom said, giving me a regretful shrug. "You're going to have to go to prom in one of your church dresses."

I sobbed at the tragedy. Buying a dress at the store was too expensive for me, and besides, prom was the very next day. I prayed for a miracle, but nothing happened, and the machine still didn't work. It was a Saturday and we had state band and orchestra concerts all day.

I cried all the way home on the bus that afternoon because prom was just a couple of hours away and I didn't have a dress to wear.

A band colleague named Malorie noticed me and asked, "What's wrong? Why are you upset?"

Between sniffles, I said, "I don't have a dress to wear for prom. Our sewing machine broke last night and the dress is unfinished." I wiped the tears off my cheeks.

Her face brightened, and she pushed a lock of her blond hair behind her ear. "You know, my mom is a seamstress! I'll ask her if you can come over and she can finish your dress."

A weight lifted from my chest as hope filled my heart. "Really?"

She nodded. "Grab your dress and bring it over."

Right after the bus ride, I ran home, grabbed the pieces, and went straight to her house. Malorie's mom, Jennifer, quickly sewed the dress in her atelier as I stared on with so much gratitude.

Jennifer handed me her daughter's dress to finish the beading while she finished mine. "So . . . who cut this pattern?" she asked.

"I designed it, and my mom cut the pattern. It's really on the low end," I answered, rather embarrassed thinking it wasn't up to par.

"Let me tell you, Fernanda—this is not just some basic entry-level construction. This dress is actually quite complex and takes skill. I think you and your mom know way more than you're telling me," Jennifer said with a wink.

I smiled. *Perhaps we underestimated ourselves.*

Jennifer finished the dress in no time and handed it to me with a big smile.

"Thank you! Thank you!" I hugged it to my chest.

"My pleasure," Jennifer said.

I couldn't believe how quickly she'd been able to pull it together for me! I sprinted home to finish getting ready. It was indeed a miracle from above and showed me that the Lord truly cares about the small details in our lives.

Near the end of my high school years, I decided I wanted to attend the University of Utah for music. My violin teacher, a renowned Korean violinist, agreed to mentor me. Months later, he let me go and told me to pursue fashion. Apparently, I came better dressed than musically prepared . . . or so he thought.

I was so confused. I didn't know which way to go.

My high school counselor said, "You can't be a fashion designer, an interior designer, a photographer, a stylist, a graphic artist, *and* a violinist. It's just not possible. Pick one thing to do for the rest of your life."

I was shattered. My brain was running a million miles a minute *and* in several directions. I had too much creativity and no outlet for all my plans. *But of course*, I thought, *as the poor immigrant kid at school, my future options will be slim.* It wasn't like my dad was networking at the country club. We always lived in what you call "low-income" apartment communities, so it wasn't likely I'd get to be an intern in some fancy company doing fancy, important tasks.

At the end of my high school years, and the beginning of my music college days at the University of Utah, I got a job working at a credit repair law firm downtown in Salt Lake through a band buddy from school. I worked there for many years, always finding new ways of improving my tasks, and then I moved on to improving my department as a whole and cutting costs in the six-digit range for the company.

One day, the law firm director told my boss, "I need your department to recommend the sharpest employee. We have a new position and would like to recruit from within."

After my name was submitted, there was some confusion.

"I think there's been a mistake," the director said to my boss. "Fernanda works in the mail room. Out of the entire department of analysts, IT, and data services employees, there's no way that your sharpest employee works there."

My boss assured the director that there was no confusion.

I moved up, but I wanted to do more—perhaps something creative on my own. I wanted to move to New York City, attend FIT (the Fashion Institute of Technology), and have the city life I always dreamed of. That dream consisted of listening to Buddha Bar, a compilation of chill lounge and world music, while wearing Versace down Fifth Avenue.

That dream got slashed quickly as I once again reminded myself of my reality. Instead, I joined the Salt Lake Community College Fashion Institute. I took full credits and made monthly payments to get an associate's degree with an emphasis in fashion. I worked two jobs, went to school full-time, played in the local orchestra, and played the saxophone in a bossa nova jazz group. Whatever I did, I was going non-stop.

When I was twenty-two, my sister, Vivien, approached me with an idea to open a fashion line with modest pieces that didn't exist on the market. I thought, *No way! I don't want to touch retail.* Besides, we had no money and no connections to make that happen.

Still, I thought about it for a while and realized that perhaps if I didn't take the chance, I would be stuck at my job forever—or worse, watching others doing something creative while I only dreamed about it. By 2007, a year later, I had obtained an American Express credit card, and that's how we got our initial funding.

My sister and I attended a Vegas trade show and met a few vendors that fit our "look." It was very intimidating to have thousands of people walking very fast all around us who knew exactly where they were going, literally and figuratively. We, on the other hand, were lost—not sure who to visit, passing out business cards that said "BÖHME," and hoping for the best. It was a learning curve to talk the talk and walk the walk.

Months later, I got on a plane to Los Angeles and walked the streets by myself through the homeless shelters where the showrooms were to get inventory from the Korean vendors . . . another learning curve that made our once figurative dreams literal.

A Leap of Faith

By October 2007, it was time to open our first store. An older guy who worked at the mall saw Vivien and me staring at the closed shop that we were contemplating taking.

He walked over. "Whatever it is you're thinking of doing, it's a *yes*," he said and left.

Vivien and I looked at each other and decided it was a sign from above.

The mall took our credit card for rent, and we were given a three-month temp lease for the holidays. I still worked my full-time job because we couldn't pay rent by ourselves. We had four days to remodel the old Merle Norman 600-square-foot store.

One morning, at 8 a.m. on the dot, I walked into our store lugging two large bags from Home Depot. I was so overwhelmed because I'd never done a remodel before. We couldn't afford to hire anyone, so we had to do it ourselves.

I went to Target and asked the manager if I could have their giant snowflake foam core chandelier displays that were hanging from the ceiling after they were done with them. He said, "I'll leave them in the back of the building for you to grab. Don't tell anyone we had this conversation—I'm not allowed to give them away after they've been used." I grabbed them later and hung them in our store. It was all starting to come together.

We put up a billboard ad on the freeway and even printed nice black shopping bags. After four days of no sleep, I was so tired that I felt like my soul had left my body. But it was time to open the doors.

People walked by, foreheads scrunched in confusion, as they stared at the store name in all caps and black and white letters: "BÖHME."

"Keep walking! It looks expensive," people said in hushed whispers. "We can't afford that."

"Let's find something cheaper."

What? I thought. Did our build-out look too fancy? Perhaps it did. We had a black-and-white leopard rug, black-painted shelving, shiny chrome mannequins, and giant white snowflake chandeliers hanging. We even had white leather chairs and offered Fiji water to our good customers.

But we'd forgotten one thing . . . we were from another country. We look different, we think different, and we act different.

The entire situation was disheartening, but we didn't know what else to do.

A man walked in at 5 a.m. on Black Friday, after we'd been open for about three weeks. "I think you guys are gonna be big," he said. "I want to be a part of this."

We were shocked.

He was a big-shot entrepreneur, and the building where he worked was one of the buildings we had cleaned in our janitorial days as kids. We quickly found out that introducing anything in 2007 was difficult, especially in a non-culturally diverse place such as Murray, Utah, where our store was located. I mean, people were still wearing Abercrombie & Fitch across their chest and American Eagle jeans. It was basically Olive Garden or bust! How dare anyone shop or eat anywhere that wasn't a national chain, much less a boutique that looks and feels European for such a casual market?

Well, we decided that if the local community didn't accept our modest, edgy style, at least the Playboy bunnies from California liked our unique pieces and moderate prices.

The three-month temp lease came and went, and it was time to close. I was done being the most unpopular shop in the mall with the most difficult name to pronounce. I now had a huge credit card debt, excess inventory I didn't know what to do with, and a bad taste in my mouth from the whole experience. I was exhausted and beyond done. I was going back to my old life of data services at the credit repair firm where at least I could expect a steady paycheck.

The disappointment of trying again was too much, and I didn't have the funds or the energy to move forward. But a few months later, we were approached by the mall in Orem, Utah, to open up another location. They were looking for something fresh and had eyed our store in Murray.

I said absolutely not. It was beyond my experience and expertise. I'd learned that lesson well.

That night, I prayed on my knees, sobbing, and asked if this was the path for me. It was just too difficult and painful to keep failing. I then heard a voice, clear as a bell, speak to my heart and mind, "Get up and go back to work. You are not alone, for there are angels on the other side that will help you make this a success."

This was all I needed to move forward—faith and trust in God. So we opened that shop, and in the days, months, and years that followed, success came that we couldn't have dreamed of. Our days in hand-me-downs were long gone, and we had access to more clothing than we could hope to wear in a lifetime. And instead of wandering aimlessly at vendor shows, we now walked in and saw how everyone alerted each other as if Elvis or some other icon had just entered the building.

If there's one thing I have learned over my years, it's that angels play a huge part in our lives—and they don't always get the credit for the miracles they perform. We have access to them through our divine inheritance. There are crucial times in our lives when the Lord carefully plans and sends angels to guide us and shine a light amidst life's dark tunnels.

Family Struggles

"911 dispatch. What's your emergency?"

"Our daughter ran away!" I cried out in terror. "We've been driving around but haven't found her." My husband Michael drove our SUV down the darkened streets. There were no street lights. I held the phone tight to my ear and covered the other with my free hand—for what reason I wasn't sure. There was no sound other than the hum of the car engine and my heavy breathing. Even Michael seemed to be holding his breath.

"What's your location?" the operator asked.

"We're in a small community in the middle of a desert in Ivins. It's pitch-black outside! There's nothing around us!"

"When was the last time you saw her? And how old is she?"

"She's seven years old. It's been about thirty minutes. We noticed the door was open, and that was at 10:15 p.m. She's autistic and non-verbal. She won't answer to her name."

Typing sounds came through the line. "We're sending an officer right away. Can you describe her to me?"

"She has short blond hair. She's wearing pink pajamas. We've driven around but can't find her!"

"Stay calm—we have help on the way." The operator stopped speaking, and more indistinct voices came through the line. "Ma'am," he continued. "It looks like someone has called in and reported a child wandering around. They said she was trying to get in the pool and knocked on their window. They're holding her there. She's safe."

Relief engulfed me—stronger than the pitch-black darkness we'd found ourselves in. "Thank God. Yes, that's Zara!"

Seven years earlier, a doctor placed a beautiful little baby on my chest and announced, "Congratulations on a healthy, nine-pound baby girl!" She was blond and looked identical to my husband, whose hair was so blond it was almost white. She immediately clawed out of the nurse's swaddle blanket—it was her way or the highway. (It still is!) After a twenty-four-hour labor process, I passed out from exhaustion.

I met my husband Michael at a gas station in 2007—around the same time Vivien and I were figuring out our business. Seven years later, on the same day of August 10, our first child, Zara, was born.

Michael has helped me navigate through many years of ups and downs and has played a vital role in supporting me through the bright and dark days. That fact only increased with the birth of our first baby.

I immediately started to notice that Zara was what they call a "colic baby." She screamed from about 7 p.m. until 2 a.m. every single night. She didn't nurse, wouldn't take a bottle, and of course refused to sleep. Exhausted, I didn't know what to do and could barely think. I had to go back to work in just under two weeks, and even then, I still worked from bed as I recovered.

It was difficult being a working mother of a newborn who still needed to fulfill all her responsibilities.

When Zara was fourteen months old, I came back from a women's conference in Istanbul, Turkey, on an assignment from the US Chamber of Commerce. I was so excited to see Zara, but she didn't acknowledge my return. It was as if I didn't exist. After being referred to many pediatricians who recommended early childhood intervention, we discovered they were unable to give her an official diagnosis. I finally found a clinic through Google that specialized in child psychiatry and we were able to make an appointment at Wasatch Pediatric Neuropsychology.

"This too shall pass" became my motto.

The year 2016 was a tumultuous year for my company. One day, a VP of leasing at a large mall corporation flew in from Chicago to meet with us. "You'll be out of business in thirty days," he said with a smirk. "You're behind on rent, and I don't see how you guys are going to pull out of this without bankruptcy."

We'd brought in too many well-known brands, and if you're in the wholesale business, you know the margins are razor-thin.

"Give us one more chance," I pleaded. "We've grown to several of your locations over the last ten years. All we ask for is six months to turn this around."

He left the office, leaving us with little to no expectations that we would ever make it out alive. He said his boss would reach out and make the decision of how long to give us. As for me, I was racked with nerves.

Later that day, I got a call. "Hello, this is Dr. Julien Smith from Wasatch Pediatric Neuropsychology. Is this a good time to chat?"

"Yeah, sure," I said.

"I'd prefer that you get your husband on the phone if possible," she replied. My already frayed nerves began to spark with anticipation. Why did she need us both on the line?

I linked Michael in a three-way call.

"I'm very sorry to have to tell you this, but your daughter has autism, and she's nonverbal"—words no parent wants to hear.

I swallowed the tears and thought, *More bad news.*

Could the week get any worse? Turns out it could.

The next day, I went to Cottonwood Heights to have a meeting about a lot I had purchased to build a simple house on.

After a two-and-a-half-year battle with the city, the city engineer broke the news. "I'm sorry to inform you that the lot you purchased is an unbuildable property."

"Why didn't you tell me before I dumped all this money into engineering reports to show you?" I asked, feeling irritation building in my core. It had been three years of wrestling with the city, providing every documentation and report requested. Turns out they had made up their minds years ago with the answer but thought it was far more amusing to watch me jump through all the hoops and prolong the process.

"It's not our business to tell you how to do it—we just approve or deny it," he said flatly.

So basically all the money I had spent on engineering and seismic analysis was for nothing. At this point, I was used to getting bad news—it was business as usual. And to put a cherry on top, I was to give birth to my second child that same week. I was tipping the scale at 200 pounds, a 75-pound increase in a matter of months.

That night, I closed the door to Zara's bedroom in our tiny little townhouse we were renting. I cried on the floor in front of her toddler crib. "My business is failing, and on paper, we're out of business. My child has severe autism. I've lost all our money. And now I have to birth another baby who could also have autism."

I remember drawing plans on the back of an envelope for a dream home that I would never see come to life. Every worst-case scenario crept into my mind. I prayed, "Lord, I'm overwhelmed with fear of the future, and I'm not sure what else I can do." If there was such thing as rock bottom, I'd just hit mine.

The next day, I attended the downtown Salt Lake Temple. The temple is a place that, for me, brings peace and allows me to realign my priorities and to "think celestial"—or more heavenly—with a broader perspective of a higher purpose. It's a place to meditate and receive personal revelation, which is what I needed now. At nine months pregnant, and very emotional, I couldn't stop the tears from flowing.

After I left and was standing outside Temple Square, staring at the new mall across the street—the beautiful City Creek Center with its indoor/outdoor features, stone pathways, stream running down the center, fountains, trees, and the glass retractable awning—I heard a voice from above: "Not only will you not go out of business, but you will open a new store in that center." City Creek was Utah's newest shopping destination.

Impossible! I thought. *We just closed four of our twenty-two stores! How's that even a possibility?*

It took some time, but lo and behold, four years later, we opened our flagship store at City Creek. It was our biggest one yet, with large windows open to Main Street. It took exactly seven semi-trucks, which had to park in underground parking, to build and furnish the new store.

No expenses were spared, and we even had an employee lounge with Italian marble. Everything was custom-made to perfection. It wasn't just a store—it was a sensory experience. At the grand opening, long lines went down the corridor of the center. It was a hit! Our customers couldn't get enough of it.

The years leading up to this event were difficult, yet we managed to change our product mix, customize new design selections, focus more on our online business, and grow our sales. We were able to get ourselves out of the hole and become profitable again. The property in Cottonwood Heights eventually sold (which we came to find out was only doors away from the home of Post Malone, an American rapper). I eventually found another plot of land and built that same house I had drawn on the back of an envelope. The house ended up on the cover of *Build Magazine*, and it was far better than I had dreamed of.

Verses 9 and 11 of Matthew 7 say, "What man is there of you, whom if his son ask bread, will he give him a stone? . . . How much more shall your Father which is in heaven give good things to them that ask him?" I learned that if things don't go according to your plan, it's because the Lord has far greater plans for you. His timing means having faith that He's baking the bread in the oven, and if you open it too soon, it won't be ready.

By then, Ford, my second child, was already four years old and I'd had another son, Rome, who was almost three years old.

Ford ended up being a very bright and gifted child. He named every country on the globe only by shape by the time he was three years old.

Zara was my oldest, so I didn't know what "normal development" was. When Ford read the word *photosynthesis* by age two, Michael assured me it wasn't normal for children that age to read, but I didn't believe him.

One day, his preschool teacher took me aside and said, "Your son isn't an average boy. None of the children here know their letters or their colors, but Ford is reading the teacher's manual and can quickly recall information."

In my mind, all the other children were doing what he was doing.

"Your son has a rare photographic memory," the teacher concluded.

Okay, I thought. *That explains why he can tell me the detailed inner workings of the human body and name every capital of the world.* One day, he was sitting in his high chair with his sippy cup and a blankie, happily rattling off, "Titan, Io, Europa, Ganymede, Callisto, Triton, Charon, Phobos, and Deimos—these moons belong to the planets of the solar system. And also, today the moon is waxing gibbous."

I gasped and called Michael right away. "You're not going to believe this . . ." I could hardly repeat and explain the boy's astronomical language.

"Yes, Fernanda, I told you it wasn't normal for a two-year-old to learn and understand these things. But now do you believe me?" he asked with a grin.

Ford continues to tutor me on a daily basis about world facts, medical statistics, and astronomy discoveries.

Rome, my youngest, would be best described as the daring Evel Knievel. He trains at the Woodward skate park every day after school, with dreams of being sponsored someday. He's a natural problem solver with great attention to detail.

Zara, over the years, has only developed a few words. It's challenging enough to raise a regular child, let alone one with a disability that results in little to no communication.

My friends wonder, "How do you manage to meet her needs if she can't communicate?"

"It's a new learning curve every day," I reply. "We do our best to figure it out by process of elimination."

Still, I always get asked, "Has having a child with a disability put a strain on your marriage?"

Michael and I have chosen to have a "unite and conquer" mindset as opposed to "divide and conquer." We've learned so much as a couple and as a family in navigating through it all. Zara has a great sense of humor. Everywhere she goes, she carries a light.

The Present: 2024

A text came through on my phone: "Are you almost here?"

"Here where?" I replied from bed in my house in Park City.

"The photo shoot for the cover of the *Utah Business* magazine. . . . We're all here waiting for you." The photo shoot was in Salt Lake City, a good forty-five minutes away.

Oh no! What a nightmare. I asked them to wait, rolled out of bed, and frantically got ready. I threw on one of my dress design samples that just arrived that morning from our overseas manufacturer, hopped in my car, and flew down the freeway, praying I wouldn't get pulled over.

As I drove, I thought about how far I had come in my career. After seventeen years of business, now at forty years of age, with twenty-plus store locations in seven states, getting written up in Forbes, being awarded fastest-growing company on the Inc. 500 top women-run businesses and SBA of the year, and not to mention getting a visit requested by the former vice president, Mike Pence (which he regrettably canceled due to getting COVID that week), I still sometimes think, *What is my higher purpose?*

But then I remember: We employ hundreds of women, not to mention supply jobs to countless people across the globe who sew and supply our products, which are carefully designed and curated. Although it's a vain industry with trends changing every couple of weeks, at the end of the day, it's an industry that puts food on the table for individuals and their families. It also puts smiles on the faces of women as they look and feel confident in our clothing as they step out in the world. And that's something to be proud of.

Find Your Frequency

How do you know you're successful? It's easy to casually say someone is successful because of their career or status. But to me, saying someone is successful means absolutely nothing. You can't truly measure worldly success because there will always be someone who makes a buck more than you.

True success is when you align your purpose with the Creator and fill the measure of your creation. It's easy to compare journeys, but I know we have individual experiences and battles to conquer in this life that mold and polish our spirits and help us become who we're meant to be. I believe that if we listen to those whispers from the Spirit, we will be guided to do something much bigger than we anticipate. I've seen it in my own life, time and time again.

When you tune into your frequency—the one that's unique to you—it's powerful. You become unstoppable. Untouchable.

When I talk about this, I sometimes get asked, "How does one find their frequency?"

The truth is, you already have it—you were born with it. The question should be, What's keeping you from finding it? You have gifts and talents that come pre-wired from above.

I always think it's counterproductive to feel insecure or diminished because you don't have a list of gifts and assets that someone else has. The secret is that you too have a "Ferrari engine" inside your mind and have a list of gifts and abilities unique to you that others may not have.

Anxiety is another form of physical manifestation that something needs attention. Whether it's a warning, an indication of big things to come, or a hint that change is needed, it's not to be ignored. Those are signs that our souls communicate to our body from time to time.

A friend who's a stay-at-home mother said to me, "Fernanda, that's nice you have a career, but I raise my kiddos, and I don't feel very successful."

I quickly answered, "The most influential person on the planet never had a successful money-making business. He was poor in worldly standards and didn't have much at all. His name was Jesus of Nazareth, and in fact, He did have a business! It was the business of his Father who sent Him to earth to redeem us. He died on the cross and perhaps thought at the time that He had an unsuccessful mission, but His earthly mission was by far the most remarkable of anyone. Now as for you," I told my friend, "it's a very Christlike thing to put aside a career, for example, and your personal time to take care of heaven-sent children who can change the world tomorrow."

In the end, it's a matter of quieting the world and listening to your soul. I believe the soul holds the answers that are within you. When they say "trust your gut," it means trust a light—an insight you have no physical proof for but you know deep inside is true. What we do matters, and understanding our higher purpose is the vision.

The world is constantly pulling our attention to its inferior version of value. Fashion trends come and go, money comes and goes, things come and go, but if there's one thing that can't be taken away from me, it's my faith and trust in Jesus Christ and in His gospel that has been restored to the earth.

Now what does the future hold for me? Well . . . I feel like I'm just getting started!

2

Shayla Egan
The Emergency Preparedness Influencer

Preparedness and Pastries

Some people hear about emergency preparation and erroneously believe that all preppers are getting ready for doomsday or a zombie apocalypse. But as members of The Church of Jesus Christ of Latter-day Saints, preparedness looks different.

As a young girl, my parents taught our family the importance of preparing. Bug-out bags, food storage, and earthquake drills were always a part of our Monday family home evenings (a weekly family night in which the Church encouraged families to spend time together learning about Jesus Christ and his gospel). My parents and family members have taught me that there's more to preparedness than having a bunker stashed with food.

"Shayla, Shantae, Jordan!" my mother called out from downstairs.

Holding on to the wooden railing, I quickly jumped in front and blocked the stairway to beat my older siblings down the steps. We were always competitive with each other, even though we were only nine (Jordan), eight (Shantae), and seven (me). There are five kids in the family, and I was the middle child.

My mother sat on the blue floral couch in the center of the living room, her brown permed hair resting just above her shoulders, with her shimmery pink lipstick matching her rosy cheeks. She stared out the window at our driveway.

"Looks like it's snowing again." She sighed. This was the third time it snowed this week, and it didn't seem like it would slow down anytime soon. "Will you and your siblings get your snow clothes on? Sister Webb will need to have her driveway shoveled."

Sister Webb was a widow of several years who lived down the street from our house.

I ran over to the small closet that was situated near the front door of our home. Bracing myself, I slowly turned the doorknob as coats, hats, and snow pants avalanched down onto my head—the result of quickly shoving all our snow clothes into the closet when we got home from school earlier that day.

We put our snow gear on and grabbed our small red shovels to head to Sister Webb's home.

I put my snow shovel behind me, trying to make a flat trail on the unshoveled sidewalk. Glancing over my shoulder, I caught my brother, Jordan, with his tongue out, trying to catch the snowflakes falling from the sky. I laughed and tried to catch my own.

"Shayla and I will shovel the sidewalk and pathway," Shantae said. "Jordan, you work on the driveway."

My brother let out an irritated groan and rolled his light blue eyes, his glasses sliding to the tip of his nose, but reluctantly, he obeyed her orders despite being the oldest child in the family.

I pushed the shovel through the heavy snow, my hands turning red from the cold, as I attempted to get the job done as fast as possible. Jordan threw a snowball at Shantae and then at me. He appeared delighted as he successfully annoyed his younger sisters. I glanced back over to see his large glasses fogging up from the heavy breathing.

"Almost got you," he grinned.

A large creak came from the house, and we glanced up to see Sister Webb walking out the door with a plate of steaming cups.

"Weren't you kids here yesterday?" She giggled and walked to her front steps. Sister Webb had on a floral blue dress with an off-white handmade shawl wrapped around her shoulders. Her wavy blond hair curled under her chin, and her rectangular-shaped glasses wrapped around her ears. "Thank you for being so kind and shoveling my driveway. Would you like some hot chocolate?"

Everyone knew that Sister Webb made the best hot chocolate in the neighborhood. For that reason, shoveling her driveway wasn't a chore.

Quickly throwing our shovels down, my siblings and I hustled to grab a cup of her delicious hot cocoa.

"Now, if you kids need anything, just come knock on my door," she said with a wink. Her face gleamed as she went back inside her home.

My siblings and I drank our hot chocolate and finished our job.

It was almost dark when we walked through our front door. The smell of fresh sugar cookies filled our home as the Christmas song "Santa Claus Is Coming to Town" played in the background. My younger brother and sister, Jantzen and Mckenzie, sat on the kitchen table decorating plate after plate of Christmas-shaped cookies.

As fast as I could, I threw off my wet boots and coat to join them.

"We're making gifts for the neighbors." My mom pulled another pan of hot cookies from the oven. "So no licking the butter knives." She abruptly glanced at my little brother, Jantzen, who already had a cookie partially hanging from his mouth.

Dad walked in the garage door wearing his dark gray suit. "Smells good in here."

My father was in the ward bishopric (a leadership position in the congregation). He oversaw helping neighbors in the area and sought out opportunities to serve others who were in and out of our religion.

Plates were lined up on our kitchen counter as we carefully placed our decorated cookies onto the dishware, trying not to smudge the frosting.

"We should have twenty-three total," my mother said as Shantae and I counted the plates.

Jordan grabbed one of the dishes. "I call going to the Millgates!" he shouted as he sprinted toward the door.

"Well, I get the Lindstroms." Shantae giggled and followed behind him.

Holding the plates of cookies in our hands, we headed out once again to distribute the holiday treats around the neighborhood.

My parents jumped into the car with the younger kids as Jordan, Shantae, and I made our way down the snowy road. We ran back and forth from the porches to the vehicle window, grabbing the cookies my mother handed through it.

Turning the corner, I noticed a home with no lights on the porch.

"Do we go there?" I asked my father while pointing at the dimmed house.

"Yes," he said with a smile. "How about I come with you?"

He parked the car near the sidewalk and hopped out.

Holding the plate of cookies, I looked up at the house as we made our way to the door. The white paint was faded, and heavy curtains hung over the windows, letting just a little light seep around the edges. It was a home I always passed, but I never saw people come in or out of it.

My father placed his hand on my back as I knocked three times. Dogs barked in the background as loud footsteps came toward the door.

The smell of cigarette smoke overwhelmed me, and I crinkled my nose. An older gentleman opened the door, surprised to see us standing on his doorstep.

"Merry Christmas." I held out the plate of cookies.

"Scott, is this your daughter?" The man grinned at me and reached for the cookies. "These look delicious. Did you make them yourself?"

I nodded and glanced at my feet.

A woman from inside the home peeked around the corner. "Oh, that is the sweetest thing! Thank you and Merry Christmas!"

My heart began to swell seeing the joy in their faces followed by their cheerful smiles.

All this happiness from a plate of cookies?

I started to see why my father wanted us to stop at this house.

Laughter and kind exchanges filled the air. Eventually, my dad gave them a wave and we turned to leave.

"Dad, who are those people?" I asked him while we slowly walked down the steps. "I haven't seen them at church before."

My father, with a gentle smile, replied, "Well, that's because they don't go to our church."

"Why?" I questioned.

"I'm not sure. But they're some of the kindest people I know."

I stood there collecting my thoughts. My father crouched down to his knees and looked me in the eye. "Shayla, there are a lot of good people who don't believe what we believe, and that's okay. We can still be friends with them and serve them."

"Well, that's very nice you brought them cookies," I said with a smile.

My father let out a laugh while standing back up. Wrapping his arm around my shoulder, we walked back to the car to finish our deliveries.

I quickly glanced back at the dark house. A warm feeling filled my chest, knowing that I brought goodness into someone's life.

I learned something that day from my parents: Serving others, both in and out of our religion, is how we become more like the Savior.

ANGELS AND OFF-RAMPS

I didn't just witness a miracle—I lived one. And it forever changed how I viewed the world.

Pulling my long, dirty-blond hair into a tight ponytail, I opened the front door and grabbed my gym bag. "Bye, mom!" I shouted before stepping outside.

"Choose the right! Know what you stand for!" my mother called back.

That was a common phrase my parents would use every time my siblings and I left our home. I walked to the curb as my carpool for soccer pulled up to the driveway. It was the time of year when the sky started getting darker earlier. Even in late afternoon like now, it felt closer to dusk.

"I'm driving today," called out my soccer teammate, Sarah, as I reached the car.

"You're driving?" I came to a halt and glanced up from the door handle to my friends, my heart picking up speed as her words lodged in my mind.

Sarah had just turned sixteen and was new to driving. She was a cool girl, stylish with beautiful blond hair. Her personality was contagious and fun to be around.

"I'm so tired," yawned Brittany as she walked around the car and slipped into the front passenger seat of her car. Brittany was a year older than me and Sarah, and she was petite and cutesy. Just like Sarah, Brittany ran with the popular crowd at her high school. (I went to a different school, so our friend groups were different.) Without fail, her hair and nails were done to perfection. She was always eager to share the latest drama about her boyfriend.

I stood on the pavement, staring at both girls as trepidation filled my core.

Brittany is always the designated driver, I thought to myself. *She owns the car and has a driver's license.*

"Is this safe?" I asked, finally voicing my concerns. "Do Sarah's parents know that she's driving us to practice today?"

Questions began swirling in my mind as unease filled me.

"Shayla." Breaking my train of thought, I glanced at Sarah as she leaned on the driver's door. With a smirk on her face, she motioned me to get into the car with a roll of her hand. "Get in," she said impatiently.

I took a deep breath and reluctantly opened the car door. *I'm sure everything will be fine*, I tried to convince myself.

Brittany's vehicle was on the small side, and it constantly felt like a puzzle trying to fit myself and my bag into the back seat along with Brittany's and Sarah's belongings. As I analyzed the space situation, or lack thereof, I decided to shove my bag in first while I squeezed myself behind the passenger seat. With some persistence, I was finally able to shut the car door.

"I'm gonna take a power nap." Brittany snuggled herself into her seat, kicking her feet up on the dashboard. "This morning's practice was exhausting." Because we were on a competitive soccer team, we had practices multiple times a day—one in the morning and one in the evening.

Sarah nodded as she cranked up the air conditioner while placing a homemade, burned CD into the dashboard.

I sat in the back in silence, watching the Hawaiian flower lei swing from the rearview mirror.

Dread began to overwhelm my mind, knowing that it was conditioning day at soccer practice. I peeked over the seat to check the time on the dashboard. It was 4:00.

"Great. Rush hour," I whispered under my breath.

We had thirty minutes until practice began. I let out a sigh, leaning back in my seat while Sarah quietly sang along to the music. I stared out my window looking at other cars passing on the busy highway.

"Maybe I'll take a nap as well," I decided.

Turning to my side, I shoved my belongings above the other bags and uncomfortably adjusted my seat belt. Slowly, I leaned my head on the pile of luggage and drifted off to sleep.

Shayla.

I poked my head up. "Did someone say my name?"

With tired eyes, I tried to focus on Sarah, curious to see what she needed. But the car fell silent, even with the tunes quietly playing. *Maybe I misheard.* Confusion filled my mind, but seeing that no one needed me, I closed my tired eyes and began to doze off again.

Shayla!

With more urgency, I leaned up, knowing that someone called my name for sure this time. Sarah or Brittany must have been trying to get my attention. From my seat, I only had a sliver view of Brittany's head resting on the car window in the seat directly in front of me. She was fast asleep. To my left, Sarah's blond ponytail peeked over the mountain of bags, but her face was out of my sight. Only the song—"Hollaback Girl"—softly played in the background.

Was I hearing things? I turned my focus to the road ahead and immediately my heart thudded nearly out of my chest. Our car was drifting, heading straight toward a cement barrier.

Alarm bells began to swirl all around me and I yelled, "Sarah!"

She jolted in panic, noticing too that our car was headed toward the side barrier. She grabbed the steering wheel and quickly yanked it in the opposite direction, causing the car to overcorrect. The fast motion jerked me back into my seat as our car began spinning across the busy lanes of traffic.

"Brittany, get your seatbelt on!" Sarah cried as the car continued to spin. It seemed as if Brittany was flying in the air as Sarah attempted to pull her down and buckle her in. Outside the windows, cars swerved around us, horns honked, and then, without warning, we jerked to a stop. The motion flung my body forward, and I lurched to a stop as I got caught on the seatbelt.

Tire smoke began to fill the air around us, and the acrid smell of burning rubber filled the car. My heart wouldn't stop pounding.

"Are we okay?" I asked no one in particular.

A deep, loud, and persistent horn filled our ears. I quickly turned my attention toward the direction of the noise. Our car was facing east on a northbound highway, and a large semitruck was heading directly toward my window seat. We only had seconds before impact.

We're going to die, my mind whispered.

Immediately, an image popped into my thoughts. It was of a beautiful white temple that I had dreamed of entering one day ever since I was a little girl. Flowers surrounded the building as the stained glass windows shimmered in the sunlight. The top of the temple had a spire pointing toward the heavens. It was the Mt. Timpanogos temple my parents had taken me to when I was young and that I had since yearned to enter someday.

Time seemed to slow, and I prayed. *Please bless that my brothers and sisters will go to the temple one day, get married, and have families.* I felt an overwhelming sense of peace.

Loud screams filled the car as my gaze homed in on the silver bars on the front of the semitruck that was about to make impact.

With my heart racing, I leaned away and placed my hands over my head, bracing for the deadly collision.

One second went by . . .

Three seconds went by . . .

Five seconds went by . . .

Then I heard a still, small voice, "Look up."

Slowly lowering my arms, I lifted my head. Our car was driving off the freeway exit ramp.

"What just happened?" screamed Sarah. Her hands were in a death grip on the wheel and turning white.

"Oh my gosh, oh my gosh, oh my gosh" were the only words Brittany could seem to get out, with one arm braced on the window and the other on the dashboard.

What had just happened? I blinked and tried to force a breath, but my mind and body still seemed to be in survival mode.

Sarah pulled off at the nearest parking lot so she could inspect the car.

My heart still beat irregularly, seeming to etch a painful tattoo against my chest. I couldn't comprehend what had just happened. No one was hurt, no cars crashed, and we were still alive.

"How are we still alive?" I asked Brittany while she paced back and forth in front of the car. Biting her nails, she looked at Sarah. "Did you turn the wheel at the last second, Sarah?"

Sarah's hands still shook. "No. I don't know. Maybe? I can't remember!"

We all sat there for a moment, unsure if we were okay or needed help. "I think the car looks okay. Maybe we should just go to practice." I didn't know what else to do, and this seemed the most logical step. I took a deep breath.

Both girls nodded.

"Well, I'm driving now," demanded Brittany.

Sarah seemed to have no problem with that.

As I shut my car door, Sarah turned from her seat toward me and said in a loud voice, "I know why we were saved. Because of you, Shayla."

I looked at her in shock. *Me?* And then the memory of the voice came back into my mind. *Was it the Holy Ghost who called my name?*

Sarah continued, "Because you go to church and seminary—that's why we were saved." (Seminary is a religious class we take in high school.)

I let out a chuckle. "No, Sarah, it's not because of me. I think angels were protecting all of us today."

Before this happened, I'd believed in angels—that they were guiding us through our mortal lives. After this experience, I knew it. And I would never forget the terrifying lesson I'd learned in the middle of rush hour traffic on an eight-lane freeway.

One, Two, Three (123)

A cold breeze blew against my cheeks, which I'm sure were rosy red by now, as I jogged through a snowy trail. I looked down at my watch.

Ten miles in—only five more to go.

It was 2023, and life was the happiest it'd ever been. I was married to a wonderful husband, Connor, and had four beautiful daughters: Evelyn, Hartley, Ila, and Goldie. I'd also received inspiration to do two things I hadn't anticipated. I'd received distinct promptings from the Spirit to (1) start a social media page for the purposes of teaching spiritual and temporal preparation, and (2) run the Boston Marathon taking place in April.

I carefully navigated the path, avoiding the ice patches that covered the ground. Today felt different. My heart was feeling heavy, but I couldn't pinpoint why.

Maybe I'm feeling this way because the last time I ran the Boston Marathon was for Jody and Grandma Hartley.

My dear friend Jody and my grandmother, Grandma Hartley, had been diagnosed with ALS a few years prior and had both since passed away. Their presence heavily lingered in my mind as I continued down the dirt- and snow-covered ground.

Perhaps that's why my heart is aching—because I miss them, I thought.

Yes, I missed them dearly. But that wasn't it.

What am I not seeing?

I stopped at the top of the hill, glancing over the snow-covered valley. The brown weeds slightly peeked through the frozen white dust. Closing my eyes, I exhaled into the bitter cold air. At that moment, a whisper of a thought popped into my mind.

Run for another person.

I opened my eyes, questioning the idea.

You need to run for someone in need.

My brain started scrambling through people I knew, but no particular person came to mind. I needed to run for someone else, but who?

Chills ran down my spine as I began trekking back down the hill, but the thought remained.

Who do I need to run for?

Later that night, I sat on my bed with a warm pink blanket wrapped around my shoulders. A journal and scriptures lay across my lap as I sat engaged in my studies. I felt a distinct nudge on my shoulder.

"It's late, my dear," my husband yawned from his place next to me in bed. "Try to get some sleep." I was surprised to see his normally bright hazel eyes so bleary.

I leaned over to my bed stand, tapping on my phone to check the clock: 1:23 a.m.

"Wow," I gasped. I didn't realize how quickly time flew. No wonder Connor was so tired.

1:23 a.m. is too late, I thought. *I need to remember that I shouldn't study past ten.*

Gathering my belongings, I set the books on my nightstand and fell asleep.

* * *

The next morning, I dropped my children off at school. Needing some essentials from the store, I quickly grabbed my purse and headed off to Costco. Luckily the store wasn't too far from home.

Pushing my heavy grocery cart, I looked at my list.

"Milk, eggs, bottled water, snacks for kids." I read out loud the items left on my list.

I abruptly gathered the items, filling up my cart, and made my way to check out.

"How's your day, ma'am?" asked the women at the register. "Find everything you need?"

"Yes, thank you." I smiled.

She clicked her long nails on the register. "Okay, your total will be 123 dollars."

Looking down at my wallet, my head shot up as the image of my bedside clock from last night popped into my head.

"Pardon?"

"Your total is 123 dollars. No change—how fun!" The woman grinned.

One hundred and twenty-three? What a strange number. Shrugging the thought off, I paid for my groceries and went to my car.

Backing out of my parking spot, I pulled up behind a pickup waiting for the light to turn green. My gaze landed on the license plate on the truck in front of me. The numbers read 123. Squinting my eyes, I reread the printed numbers.

"Well, this is interesting," I chuckled.

Pulling into my driveway, I took the groceries inside. I put them away and went to get ready for another run.

"Shayla, your new running sunglasses came in the mail," Connor called from downstairs.

Feeling giddy, I ran into my husband's home office, swiping the package out of his hand. Tearing off the top, I pulled out my brand-new blue polarized glasses. I placed them over my eyes, seeing how the colors in the room changed to bright pink.

Connor chuckled at my enthusiasm, rubbing his scruffy, cinnamon-colored beard.

"Wow," I gasped. These would be perfect for my upcoming marathon. I kissed my husband on the forehead and headed straight out the door.

"You look great, honey," he said with a wink. "Have a good run."

I let out a laugh. "Thanks, babe. Love you."

Walking toward the road, I took a deep breath. "You got this," I whispered to myself, trying to stay motivated for the speed workout I was about to endure. "It's only seven miles today—easy. You do this all the time."

Swinging my arms back and forth, I pushed my watch to start the time and then took off.

Mile one—done.

Mile two—easy.

Running around the park, I contemplated if I wanted to keep running laps or change directions to another park down the street.

A change of scenery seems nice.

I turned down a path I took regularly as I headed to the new park. A few steps in, a mailbox down the hill caught my eye. Focusing on it closely, the numbers began to stand out: *123*.

"No way," I gasped. "That's not possible."

I ran this route regularly and had never seen those numbers. Quickly, I pulled down my sunglasses to confirm what I was seeing. But to my surprise, the numbers changed. The mailbox read *423*, not *123*.

I placed my glasses back on and realized that the front of the four was fading, so when I had my polarized lenses on, the numbers *123* boldly stood out.

Was this a sign?

Do people see numbers?

What does this mean?

I pulled out my phone and called my husband.

"Honey, you won't believe this," I cried out, trying to catch my breath.

"What?" he asked.

He quietly listened as I filled him in about my day and how I'd seen those specific numbers multiple times. He's always a great listener.

I could hear him take a moment to ponder.

Waiting impatiently for his reply, I asked, "Well, what do you think?"

"You're right—that *is* weird." He hummed deep in his throat.

"Do you think it means something?"

He was quiet for another moment. "Finish your run, and we'll look it up when you get home."

Nodding my head, I said goodbye and hung up. As I headed down the road, another thought popped into my mind.

Pray about it.

This idea wouldn't leave my mind. I hadn't prayed while running before, especially during a speed workout. I reached the end of the road and turned into the park.

Through tired breaths, I began to speak aloud. "Dear Heavenly Father, why am I seeing these numbers? Is there something You need me to know? What can I do to serve You?"

Only a small moment went by when these exact words flowed into my heart: *Not yet.*

"Not yet?" I huffed. "What do you mean *not yet*?"

Again, the words came.

The time is not yet. Go home and record what you've experienced today.

"Go home?" I questioned. As a runner, I would never go home until the workout was finished. But with the impression I undeniably felt, I knew I needed to heed these words.

As fast as my feet could carry me, I made my way home. Storming through the front door, I went to my room and grabbed the journal resting on my nightstand. Immediately, I began writing down my experiences.

My phone rang, my parents' number flashing across the screen.

"Hi, mom," I began. "I have a story for you." I started explaining what had been happening, and only a minute into my story, my mother stopped me.

"Shayla, those are called soul echoes."

Confused, I asked, "What's that?"

"Soul echoes happen when angels are trying to communicate with you from the other side. These messages can come in numbers, phrases, or objects. When you see them repeatedly, you know angels are trying to reach you."

I sat, confounded. "Soul echoes," I quietly muttered. I'd never heard that before, and it wasn't Church doctrine as far as I knew, but in my heart, it made sense.

* * *

Weeks went by, and the numbers continued to show up—on street signs and billboards and license plates and more.

March came—only a month away from the Boston Marathon—and I still didn't have a clue for whom I was going to run.

I looked at the calendar to find that I'd scheduled an eighteen-mile run for the day.

"No looking at my phone today," I promised myself as I began my long run.

I always brought my phone with me in case of emergencies, but I needed to resist the urge to look at it. My social media presence was still new but quickly gaining traction—it was amazing to me how many people were interested in what I had to say about emergency preparedness—and I'd gotten into the habit of checking it out a few times a day to respond to comments, look for relevant topics, and stay on top of trends. I'd even started making friends who went out of their way to encourage me in my marathon training. I hadn't expected all this but felt uplifted by what was happening with it.

The kids were at the pool with their dad, and I wanted to quickly get the run done so I could join them. Miles went by, and storm clouds began drifting over my head. A raindrop fell on my face. In the distance, a pavilion stood on the side of the trail.

I'll stop there to refuel and wait for the rain to ease up, I decided.

At the pavilion, I found a metal table where I could stretch my legs. My pocket began to buzz, and without a thought, I pulled out my phone. It was an update from a girl I'd just started following on social media.

Her husband was recently diagnosed with stage 4 melanoma cancer and was in the hospital again. Immediately, I had the answer I had been searching for—he was the one I needed to run for in Boston. Noticing the rain was starting to die down, I slid my phone back into my pocket and finished my run.

Kelsey Oldroyd and I had only spoken a handful of times over social media. She was a busy mother of four young boys and a loving wife who was supporting her husband while he battled cancer.

I made my way into my house. My stomach churned as I debated whether I should message Kelsey or not.

Maybe I shouldn't do this.

She's going to think I'm dumb for asking.

I don't even know her.

But I couldn't ignore my prompting. I took a deep breath and began typing.

"Hey Kelsey, I know this is so random, but do you have video chat? If so, could I by chance message you?"

Sent.

I hadn't even made it up the stairs before Kelsey responded "YES" in large letters along with her phone number.

Excited, I walked into the office and began recording a video message.

"Hi, Kelsey. I'm Shayla." I smiled and explained how I wanted to run the Boston Marathon in honor of her husband, Brian. I gave her details and explained what I would be doing during the race. I wanted her to know that I greatly admired and respected her brave husband. My eyes started to water up as I told her about my experience running the Boston Marathon in the past for loved ones who had passed on. When I was finished, I sent the message.

Done.

Wiping the warm tears from my cheeks, I went about my day.

An hour went by, and I started to worry that I hadn't heard from her yet. More intrusive thoughts came to me as I continued going about my day.

She probably thinks you're weird.

Maybe you shouldn't have sent her the message.

I bet she's ignoring you because she doesn't even know you.

Butterflies filled my stomach as worries overwhelmed my mind, but then a notification popped up on my phone. It was Kelsey responding to my video message.

My nerves were getting the best of me as my trembling hands pressed "play" on my phone screen.

"Hi, Shayla" Kelsey began.

She got choked up and wiped her eyes as she gratefully accepted my invitation. I felt in that moment that I was called to run for this special family.

A few more weeks passed, and only fourteen days remained until the Boston Marathon. I woke up not feeling like myself. My body ached, my nose and ears were swollen shut, and I began coughing. I felt like all my energy had left my body. Knowing that the marathon was drawing close, I wanted to get out and run. But as I leaned up from my bed, my chest began to tighten. My body was too sick.

A few days went by, and I only felt like it was getting worse.

Running out of options, I decided to get on my social media platform, asking followers what I could possibly do to get my body feeling better before the marathon. What happened next astonished me.

Homemade meals were brought to my home. Essential oils, spices, and tips on how to get my body healthy were given to me. People knew how important this race was to me and to the Oldroyd family. My heart was filled with gratitude for the service my family, friends, followers, and neighbors showed me.

Marathon week finally came. Even though I was feeling slightly better, the sickness still lingered in my body. I knew how hard I trained for this marathon, and I didn't want to let Brian down, so I prepared for my trip.

* * *

The plane landed, and we made our way to the Boston Marathon check-in. Four of my friends joined together as we stood in line for our bibs and then proceeded into the race shop.

My running buddies, Heather and Liz, wrapped their arms in mine with enthusiasm as we began looking through the marathon merchandise. The race wasn't until tomorrow, so today was free time. I searched for a shirt for Brian, frantically texting Kelsey to find out his size. The crowds were large, but that's what made the experience so exciting.

I quickly went through check-out and made my way to the place where runners from all around the world would sign their names on a wall. Grabbing a marker, I searched for a spot to sign.

Brian and Kelsey Oldroyd

I pulled out my phone to take a video.

"I signed it," I said loudly over the busy crowd.

I pointed to the spot where I scribbled their names. It wasn't pretty, but it was a memory I wanted to create for Brian.

I finished my night eating pasta and bread (because carbs are what runners eat before the big race) and then talking about race strategies with my friends I was sharing a hotel room with. Heather, Liz, and I all sat down on the old tan carpet, carefully laying out our running gear and making sure we had everything ready for the next morning.

I took a picture for my social media page, letting my followers know I was ready to go. Messages and responses began rolling in. Ten, twenty, then fifty messages with excitement and encouraging words filled my post.

We're so excited for you!

Good luck! Go crush it!

You are incredible.

A large smile sat permanently on my face as I read the uplifting messages. I placed my phone down on the nightstand and slowly drifted off to sleep.

The next morning, we woke up early. Rain was in the forecast, which none of the runners were enthusiastic about. I grabbed a permanent marker out of my suitcase and started to write Brian's name all down my arms.

B-R-I-A-N

I then proceeded to write his name on the center of my white, long-sleeved racing shirt. Slipping on the shirt, I then layered on my raincoat. Again, I wrote Brian's name down my coat sleeves. This was to inform the crowd so that when they saw me running in the race, they could cheer Brian's name. I put my hair in two thick braids as Heather sat across the room doing the same with her dark blond hair.

A long mirror hung on the hotel wall where we exited the room. I quickly snapped a picture for Kelsey. "For Brian," I typed out on the text.

We made our way to the buses that would drive all the marathon participants to the starting line. The buses were overly crowded, and Heather, Liz, and I had to separate to find seats. Fortunately, I was able to find a spot next to another runner. I pulled out my bagel, banana, and peanut butter as the bus made its way to the starting line. The girl sitting next to me looked out the window, watching the raindrops slide down the glass.

"Are you ready?" I smiled, initiating conversation.

She nodded. "Yes. This is my first time running the Boston Marathon." She then proceeded to talk to me about her life. Her tense shoulders began to relax as we continued our conversation.

"Oh, that's amazing," I replied. I began to explain my story about running for Brian when she grabbed my arm and said, "My last name is Bryan!" And with the biggest grin on her face, she said, "It looks like two people will be running for Brian today."

I knew it was no coincidence that we sat together.

As we stepped down the stairs of the bus, rain continued to pour from the sky. Large pop-up tents were scattered on a big green field with enlarged screens showing that the professionals had already started to race. A microphone was blaring in the background, directing runners where they needed to go.

"Blue bibs, please proceed to the starting line," called out the announcer.

It was my time. Turning to my friends, we all gathered and headed to the start. Some runners placed garbage bags around their feet to keep their socks and shoes dry until the race started. Rain kept drizzling, but it didn't bother me—I was too excited to care.

I pulled out my phone to send another video.

"We're almost to the starting line!" I yelled while doing a silly dance. Heather and two other friends joined in the fun.

A horn blared and runners began crossing the starting line. Volunteers stood on the sides, cheering on the participants as we took off in mass down the road.

We lost sight of Liz as she sped through the crowded runners. Heather and I, matching in our turquoise rain jackets, decided to stick together.

The first few miles were fun. We laughed, made jokes, and took in the scenery. This is what made me love Boston so much. The rain began to subside, so I took off my rain jacket and threw it to the side by a volunteer station.

Staring straight ahead, I could hear the first cheers and clinging bells from the upcoming town. We'd be running through eight towns and cities today: Hopkinton, Ashland, Framingham, Natick, Wellesley, Newton, Brookline, and Boston.

Pressing the record button on my phone, I began chanting, "Cheer for Brian!" Immediately, Brian's name began to be called out.

"Go Brian!"

"You got this, Brian."

"We love you, Brian."

"Looking good, Brian."

I even got some funny comments from people who said, "She doesn't look like a Brian," which made me chuckle as I kept an even pace.

After the first town, there was a small break until we reached the next one.

Once again, I cried out, "Cheer for Brian! He's fighting cancer!"

Heather and other runners around me began to join in as we passed through the loud crowds: "Cheer for our friend Brian!"

There would be moments when I could hear echoes of Brian's name reverberating all around me from the crowd. Emotions overcame me.

Looking up at the sky, I began to pray, "Dear God, please, if You can, let Brian hear these cheers."

Mile ten came quickly, and I could tell my body was finished. My sickness was coming back with a vengeance, and my legs began to ache. I continued giving all my energy to filming and encouraging everyone to chant Brian's name.

"Sixteen more miles—you got this," I told myself. "For Brian."

We continued the race, taking pictures in famous areas, and stopping for cold treats from kids handing them out on the sidelines. Brian's name was repeatedly shouted as we made it to mile seventeen.

"We got this!" I called out to Heather.

Her bright blue eyes gleamed, and she nodded her head as we made our way down the road.

Then suddenly, out of the blue, a sharp electrical shock shot up my left leg, almost making me fall to the ground. Stumbling, I caught myself on Heather's shoulder.

"Are you okay?" She grabbed my arms to support me as worry tinted her voice.

The pain felt as if I had torn my calf muscle in half.

"I don't know. Maybe I need more salt?" I replied.

Confused about what was happening, I grabbed my salt packet and pickle juice, quickly swallowed them, and proceeded to keep running. Less than a minute later, another electrical shock shot up my leg.

Not knowing what to do next, I noticed a white aid tent not too far ahead. Speedily, I hobbled up to the tent with Heather at my side.

I asked for some ointment to put on my calf in hopes that the pain would subside.

"Please, let this help," I pleaded out loud.

The helpers handed me a Popsicle stick with the ointment on top. I hastily rubbed it on my calf, and Heather and I jumped back into the race. A mile passed, and my calf began to tighten once more. Something was terribly wrong.

I said a little prayer in my heart, asking God to help me finish the race. With Heather by my side, we kept on carrying on. At times, we had to speed walk due to the intense pain in my calf. I wanted to be done. My body was aching, my chest was tensing up, and my calf felt torn.

But then I began to think of Brian, his battle with cancer, and the faith he had. Thinking about his trials helped push me through my own much less substantial ones. Mile after mile, I thought of what he was going through—chemo, extreme fatigue, and sickness, among other physical symptoms, along with all the mental and emotional trials he must be facing, the greatest of which must be the idea of having to leave his family alone without him. What I was going through was nothing compared to that.

As I turned the last corner, the finish line came into view in the distance, and my heart jumped in my chest, rejoicing.

I grabbed my phone again, yelling to Brian, "Brian, this is for you! We did it!"

The crowd roared around me as tears began to swell in my eyes. I tried to figure out the words I wanted to say.

"I love you," I sobbed. "Everyone is cheering for you."

Holding Heather's hand high in the air, I crossed the finish line. The race was over.

Taking my time to catch my breath, I moved my aching legs toward the booth where volunteers were handing out medals to the runners who crossed the finish line.

"You're an official Boston Finisher!" the woman said, placing a medal around my neck.

"This is for my friend, Brian," I replied to her, holding the medal in the air.

This was the moment I dreamt about—what I had trained for—and I knew that God had His hand in it all.

I wanted to wait a week to recover before going to see Kelsey and Brian. I was excited to meet them in person, give them the biggest hugs, and share stories about the race. But Brian was in the hospital, so it was hard to coordinate a good time to visit.

Almost two weeks after the marathon, Kelsey sent a message to loved ones explaining that doctors found significant cancer growth in Brian's body and that he would be going into hospice care.

My heart shattered for them. I sent a message to Kelsey, telling her that I loved her and Brian and that they would be in my prayers during this difficult time. Less than two days later, Brian passed away in his home surrounded by family.

I was sitting on my bed working on a project when the text came announcing Brian's passing. My eyes filled with tears. All I could think about was Kelsey. I wanted to be there for her, hug her, and tell her that everything was going to be okay. My heart ached for Brian's wife, children, parents, and siblings.

Connor walked over and wrapped his arms around me to comfort me as grief sank in. We both had grown to love the Oldroyd family and had hoped for a better outcome. Hartley, my ten-year-old daughter, came into the bedroom to see what was happening. I broke the news to her, and she too began to cry.

"But Mom," she said with her large blue eyes peering into mine, "I prayed for him."

"Me too, honey. We all did."

We gathered the rest of the family together in our living room to say a prayer for the Oldroyds. We wanted to help them seek comfort, peace, and relief during this challenging time.

I never had the opportunity to meet Brian in person, but I had an overwhelming feeling that he and I were friends before we came to earth. I had never felt that way with anyone else, but I knew he and Kelsey were special.

Brian's viewing and funeral were a few days later. I decided to attend his viewing even though I didn't personally know anyone there. As Connor and I pulled up to the entrance, there was a line of people wrapped around the entire building. Immediately, I knew how loved the Oldroyds were by everyone who knew them. As I walked up the path, a woman in line waved her hand high in the air, beckoning me to come stand next to her.

"Hi, Shayla," she started. "You don't know me, but I'm one of Kelsey's friends. I've been following your running journey for Brian, so I know who you are."

I felt relief being able to talk to someone while waiting in line. One hour passed, and the line slowly inched closer to where the Oldroyds were standing.

My heart was racing, unsure if Kelsey would even recognize me. We entered another room. It was filled with long tables of pictures of Brian covered in flowers and deer antlers. Brian was a hunter and loved to go looking for shed antlers with his sons.

I enjoyed seeing glimpses of Brian's life and learning who he was and what he valued. We turned another corner, and I caught a glimpse of Kelsey. Instantly, I was taken aback by her beauty. Her long dark curls were gently tucked behind her ears. She had on a beautiful floral dress that made her smile shine brightly. But even beyond that, there was something about her—a glow, as if angels were there carrying her during this difficult time.

We began to circle around the room, inching closer to the front. I peeped my head to the side, attempting to get a glimpse of the Oldroyd family. Brian's brother, Mitch, stood at the front of the line. He looked so much like Brian; the only difference was that Brian had a shaved head. I had to do a double take to make sure it wasn't Brian I was seeing.

My turn was finally here. Walking up, I reached my hand out to shake his and said, "I'm Shayla. You probably don't know me."

Mitch stopped me and with a kind smile said, "I know who you are. Thank you for what you did for my brother. It meant a lot to him and to our family."

I could feel my eyes swell up, but I tried to hold the tears back as I responded, "Of course. I love Brian and Kelsey."

Brian's sister leaned over and said, "Shayla! I'm so happy you are here. Thank you so much for what you did for our family."

Brian's other sister joined in as they both gave me hugs.

An overwhelming sense of joy filled my soul as I spoke to Brian's siblings. I was telling them more about the race, and then I heard my name.

"SHAYLA!"

I turned just in time to see Kelsey right before she embraced me. We wrapped our arms around each other as she picked me up and swung me around. Tears began to flow from both of us as we stood there in a tight hug.

I leaned back, looked up at her, and cried, "I love you."

She repeated the same, and we hugged again. We stood there together like lifelong friends.

Trying to gather her thoughts, Kelsey said, "I'm so sorry you didn't get to meet Brian. He really wanted to see you in person."

I shook my head and replied, "It's okay. I had an impression that Brian and I were friends in heaven before we came to earth. He is so special."

Kelsey's beautiful smile lit up the room as we spoke about Boston. Brian's parents came over to join in on the conversation. I was taken aback by the overwhelming kindness and Christlike love given me by the Oldroyds. I felt undeserving of the attention, but I came to know that's exactly the type of people they were—always thinking of others instead of themselves.

I left that viewing with a thankful heart and gratitude that I was able to share the light of Christ with this family during a time of grief.

Brian's funeral was the next day. Connor grabbed my hand and guided me through the chapel, passing the long, white-sheeted tables filled with flowers, antlers, and paper funeral programs with Brian's smiling face on the cover. Walking into the crowded space, we found two empty seats on the side toward the back. The chapel was overflowing, filled with people who knew and loved Brian.

The audience stood as Kelsey and her four young boys walked into the room following Brian's casket. Other family members followed as they moved down the aisle to their seats. The funeral began with the song "There Is Sunshine in My Soul Today," specifically chosen by Brian.

One by one, family members began to stand and speak about Brian, childhood memories, his beliefs, and the life he established. There wasn't a dry eye in the room while we listened to his legacy.

Kelsey then stood up to speak. I was in awe of her strength and how she was able to keep her emotions together while she spoke of the life she created with her husband. I could feel that angels from heaven had entered the room, and it felt as if the earth was being lifted heavenward.

Mitch spoke next. He told a story about when he and Brian were kids. They never wanted to say "I love you" to each other because they considered themselves "tough boys." So together they decided to come up with a code. The code was 123, which meant "I love you." Before going to bed each night, they would say "123" to each other.

And then . . . it clicked.

I squeezed Connor's arm and turned to him.

"That's it!" I bounced in my seat as I whispered to him.

Connor looked at me with his brows furrowed, waiting for me to explain.

"One, two, three! I was seeing these numbers because of Brian."

Angels from heaven were sending me these "soul echoes," as my mother had called them, knowing that I was meant to run for Brian.

I sat there in shock, with more tears uncontrollably streaming down my face. God answers prayers, and many times it's through people. It was confirmed to me in that moment that angels were watching over Brian's family when they needed comfort.

Kelsey and I have remained close since, calling each other "soul sisters" and sending "123" whenever we get the chance.

In my experience as a member of The Church of Jesus Christ of Latter-day Saints, preparation isn't just about food and water storage. It's also about gaining a special relationship with Jesus Christ by serving others, praying, attending church, and making covenants in the temple. When there are storms in life—whether they be spiritual or physical storms—if we take the time to prepare now, we can face those storms with greater strength and confidence. Preparation equips us with the tools, resilience, and faith needed to weather any challenge.

Both spiritual and temporal preparedness are principles that Latter-day Saints continuously strive to practice. Some say that sounds like a lot of hard work, and it is. But when we strive each day to be like Jesus Christ, He will make our burdens light and lead us back home to Him and our loved ones.

3

ALLISON HONG MERRILL
The Writer

1. 山雨欲來風滿樓

Columbia, Maryland—November 2023

When the applause gradually quieted down, I set the crystal trophy on the pulpit. My clammy palms left streaks on the hard-won prize, but the words etched on the surface were still clearly visible: *Allison Hong Merrill, Writer, Woman of Impact, Best Title for Fortitude and Resilience.*

Even though this wasn't the first time I received recognition for my work at an award ceremony, I was nauseated. Maybe my sequin dress was the culprit—it was slightly suffocating and scratchy and made me sweaty. I bowed to the audience and then reflexively patted my backside for the hundredth time that evening to make sure the ankle-length skirt didn't somehow get tucked in my underpants. Now that I had the floor, my heartbeats turned erratic. What if I choked on my saliva? What if a pool of wet stains gathered under my pits? What if someone laughed at my accented English and grammatical errors?

I scanned the conference room. A middle-aged man in an athletic-cut, black-tie suit was leaning against the doorframe and pointing a phone camera at me. A wave of warmth rose in my chest and my face reddened. Even if the whole audience yawned and just pulled out their phones for mindless scrolling, at least one person would keep his eyes on me and listen as I delivered my acceptance speech.

"I come from a bowing culture," I said into the microphone, surprised at the muffled voice that came out as a nervous mumble. I adjusted my pitch and spoke louder. "Born and raised in Taiwan, I learned to express gratitude by bowing. . . ."

2. 遊牧客家

Provo, Utah—February 2019

Across the dining table, the old man took a long gulp and then released a satisfied "Aah," complete with a loud burp. "Wow, this is . . ." He looked at the mini can in his hand and chuckled. "You sure it's not beer?"

"No, root beer is soda," I said, quickly swallowing the oyster-sauced mushroom in my mouth. I pointed my chopsticks at him. "So . . . are you from China?" As soon as those words slipped off my lips, I felt silly. He spoke Mandarin with the distinctive, authentic Beijing accent—although he might argue *I* was the one who "had an accent." Also, the sheer fact that we were both invited to this house party proved that we had a shared tie with Cathay. The hostess had gathered the Chinese immigrants in town to celebrate Chinese New Year.

The old man nodded and smiled, his mouth full of partly-chewed beef. Tiny bubbles formed along his gums, covering his crooked, yellowed teeth. "You're not—right? I can tell."

"No, um, yes—my ancestors were from Dunhuang. You know, uh . . . the cave temples." I didn't know how to describe my ancestral home. I had never been to that mystic place. I had only read that it was a battlefield during one of Genghis Khan's conquests, and I had only seen pictures of the Silk Road that ran through it. Now I wanted this stranger to tell me what he knew about my nomadic forefathers' roaming grounds.

"Oh, poor people," he said. The Chinese word he used for *poor* didn't mean people with ill fortune; it meant people with little or no worldly possessions. My progenitors had (almost) nothing—that's what he implied.

There were poor people like my family of origin—who had lived in a fishing slum for generations—who didn't know how to find a better way of life. And then there were poor people like my ancestors—who had lived in the Taklamakan Desert for centuries—who didn't know how to find a better way of life except to leave.

So the latter group emigrated from the Eurasian Stepped, Daur, Mongolia, and Tibet, crossing the Yangtze River and the Yellow River, sailing across the China Seas, all the way to the southeastern coastal province of Guangdong. They married the southern frontier minority tribes, mostly the Hmong. The locals tolerated them but didn't welcome them, dubbing these outsiders *Hakka*, meaning "guests who are just passing by."

True to their nomadic nature, in the seventeenth century, a family from the Hakka clan packed up again and headed to Taiwan, settling on the farthest point east, at the land's end, on the ocean's edge, across the road from the Pacific.

Today, it takes a little more than nineteen hours to fly the 1,919 miles from Dunhuang, China, to Hualien, Taiwan. My clansmen traveled that distance by horse, then by boat, for months and maybe years, ending their journey silently in my body, my bones, and my blood.

"You don't look so poor," the old man said. "Your parents must be rich enough to send you to America, the beautiful nation."

I let the piece of chicken linger on my tongue a little longer, savoring the taste. I also let his words linger in my mind a little longer, marinating in the truth.

3. 自生自滅

Hualien, Taiwan—Early 1970s

My two-year-old sister, Dee, wailed, her face distorted. She rubbed her little eyes with her filthy hands, mixing dirt with the tears on her tiny cheeks. Saliva dangled from her lips—swollen from marathon-crying—and soiled the front of her cotton shirt. She trailed behind me everywhere in the house, wobbling with great difficulty.

Her thin, white cotton pants were bulging and had turned brown. She stank of sweat, urine, and poop. Flies followed her the way she followed me, and one of them landed on her eye, making her scream: "Ma! Ma!"

Maybe she thought I would lead her to our mother. Perhaps she thought I could be her substitute mom just for a brief moment—cleaning her, feeding her, holding her. But I was only four at the time and couldn't be anything other than my helpless self.

In the house, there were no toys, books, or food. But there was a huge window in our family bedroom that stretched so high that the top frame touched the ceiling. The window looked out to the front gate. When Mama came back, that's where I would see her first. So I climbed up the window seat, knelt on the wood surface, and stared out.

Dee stood on her tippy-toes and reached up to me, pulling my cotton pants that I had wet the night before. Dee's and my clean clothes were in the backyard, hung on a line, high in the sky. Most of the things we wanted or needed were above us, beyond reach: the latch at the top of the front gate, the TV, our parents.

Dee stopped crying, but her cheeks were still wet, her eyes still red, her lips still fat. She wanted to get on the window seat too, so I climbed down to hold her up. The squishy content in her pants was now pressing against my chest, creating a pool of brown stain on my shirt and a strong foul odor on my body. In this moment, I not only carried Dee in my arms, but I also carried our shared misery in my heart.

She wriggled loose and stood on the window seat, banging her little hands on the dirty window screen and making a dust cloud that looked like black cotton candy floating in the air. I opened my mouth to catch it as it rained down. It tasted slightly salty.

"Mmm . . . You try it," I pushed her head toward the window screen, but she resisted. Maybe she didn't know how to enjoy the salty cotton candy, so I demonstrated.

"Look," I said, licking the screen. "Eat this."

My saliva formed a thin, web-like film across the tiny mesh squares. I swallowed the overpowering, salty dust in one giant gulp and nodded at her. "Oh, wow! It's so good! You want it?"

Instantly she charged at the screen, her tongue sticking out, savoring the dust with such vigor as if the screen were a dinner plate with delicious residual sauce. She clapped as her saliva popped one mesh square after another. I pointed at the disappearing saliva and cheered, "Oh, the lights are going out! One, two, three, four, five! All of your lights went out! Quick, make more!"

So Dee licked the screen again, creating a new film of saliva across the screen. Her face was caked with dust, but she was laughing now. She laughed hysterically, heartily, and repeatedly. I almost couldn't hear my stomach growl.

4. 飽經滄桑

About my mama:

1. A stay-at-home parent
2. Left Dee and me home alone on an almost daily basis (when I wasn't old enough for kindergarten)
3. Never once told me where she was going, what she was doing, or when she would return
4. A ferocious warrior in marital fights
5. Never actually won any marital fights
6. Married to a former Taiwanese frogman, the equivalent of a US Navy SEAL
7. Never maintained a regular workout routine and was never athletic but could sprint at lightning speed, out the door, and into the alleyway whenever my father chased after her in a drunken rage with a butcher's knife in hand
8. Lived with a packed suitcase—not an emergency backpack—always ready to leave my father
9. Left my father after every marital fight and moved back to her parents' home for days or weeks at a time
10. Left Dee and me to mother each other

5. 恩斷義絕

One day, after an Armageddon type of battle between my parents, I followed Mama from a distance and watched her leave the family bedroom with her suitcase. Abruptly, she turned around. Her weary glance lingered on me, her eyes pink-rimmed. She mouthed something. It was possible she asked me a question, but I couldn't hear her, so I shook my head. She should've known it meant "I don't know, I don't know, I don't know! Why do you and Father hate each other? Why do you tear our family apart? What do you want me to say? Tell me, tell me, tell me. I'll say anything you wish. Please stay so I have a mama!" But she gave me a sad look, shook her head with a sigh, waved a hand in the air, and left.

Wait, come back! What does that mean?

I wanted to scream. My insides churned in panic. A sour-bitter taste rushed to the back of my throat.

Whatever was decaying in my body, my spirit, and my mind would pass . . . without a sound . . .

Like Mama's sorrow and her shadow.

6. 衣冠禽獸

House rule #1: When the fishermen return from the sea, I must stay inside.

House rule #2: Never talk to them if they come to our window.

House rule #3: Never play with them.

Okay, but why was #3 a rule? I was only seven years old—why would I ever want to play with the neighborhood men anyway? Plus, I didn't need to leave home to see the happenings under the heavens. In the back of our house, a rickety, rusty iron ladder led to the concrete flat rooftop, where an unobstructed ocean view unfurled. My gaze contained an eternity of blue wonders, the majestic skies touching the magnificent waters.

Where the river met the ocean, a row of run-down shacks crowded the banks. Beaded curtains draped over the doors. Women with painted faces in gossamer clothes squatted outside, smoking cigarettes, calling out to men passing by.

Brawny husbands gambled in the alley, scooped beer from a plastic kiddie pool, and stained their tank tops with spilled alcohol. Skinned a cobra, drank its blood, and then brutally beat their wives like clockwork. Bawling women bolted down the alley, fleeing from flying blows, begging for mercy.

It was called *The Life of a Slum Wife*. My mama had been down that path. Her scream for help was the post-dinner entertainment bell, summoning neighbors young and old. Some of them stood, some sprawled in folding chairs. All of them watched, laughed, and cheered. None of them chose to see—really see—her suffering. Possibly it was called *The Life of a Slum Scum*.

Shaggy fishermen came back from the sea, giving neighborhood girls candies and shoving them into their shanties. What wonderful men! Hospitable, generous, and warm. What reasons did my father have to squirm?

The girls in the alley said I was missing out on the fun. The fishermen gave them Monopoly coins for playing the game of "Doctor." Afterward, they all went to the night market for steamed meat buns.

Okay, whatever! I just didn't see how a game involving medicine and shots could be any fun.

7. 撥雲見日

Hualien, Taiwan—December 4, 1986

No matter how narrow our alley was, it offered enough space to serve two-way traffic. In and out, left and right. Downtrodden wives ran for their lives. Rushing past them, hope arrived. When I answered the door that night, I was shocked to find two Caucasian young men standing outside, in a torrential downpour, next to their bikes. In my thirteen years of life, I had never seen anyone as tall as them, their faces above the awning. Adult ankle-length raincoats reached only their calves.

"Nihao, nihao. Is Mr. Hong here?" one of them asked in Chinese with some tonal errors.

I stared and stepped aside. As soon as they entered, I dashed toward the back of the house, waving my arms in the air and hollering, "Americans, Americans, Americans!"

My father appeared to be just as surprised, but he didn't look alarmed. Turns out that a year earlier, he had met a set of missionaries from The Church of Jesus Christ of Latter-day Saints in a city park seven hours away but had since forgotten about it.

My father proclaimed to be a Buddhist, although one could hardly describe him as spiritual. If he had ever prayed, he never taught me how to speak with God. Even so, he understood politeness, courtesy, and manners. That night, when he gestured for the missionaries to sit in our living room, my sister Dee and I didn't wait for his instructions. We knew to honor the houseguests by serving what little we had—boiled water and cheap candies.

The missionaries had a message to share with us: God is our Father in Heaven who loves each of us and answers our prayers. Families can be together forever in never-ending joy.

I didn't know what I didn't know. For one, I never knew peace and love until the missionaries brought them to us. For our weekly visits, they braved the bone-chilling wintry rains and biked miles to the dark slum, always carrying something. One of them hauled a projector and a case of slides to share a movie with my family, while the other balanced in one hand the banana bread he had baked in a rice cooker. They carried a distinctive kind of warmth with them, as if the sun was behind them wherever they went. And whenever they left our house, the light left with them.

Every Thursday night, I sat by the living room window, watching for the missionaries' elongated shadows to appear in the alley, listening for the squealing brakes of their bikes in front of our house.

In southeast Asia, on a tiny tropical island, in an impoverished village, in a dilapidated house, I waited for the sun.

8. 氣宇軒昂

About my father:

1. In his prime, a handsome devil
2. In his twenties, a Taiwanese frogman
3. An Asian Michael Phelps, with an elite swimmer's six-pack abs
4. An open-water swimmer
5. In mid-life, a semipro soccer, tennis, and ping-pong player
6. Still sober after drinking a dozen bottles of beer

7. Sought out intimate relationships with rich women, married or not

8. Couldn't have any sons, with the woman he married or any other one

9. Made it his life's calling to constantly tell me he hated daughters

10. Couldn't find the decency to tell me himself that he had divorced my mama

9. 晴天霹靂

Hualien, Taiwan—January 1987

When Dee and I got to the living room, our father had left the house, leaving the missionaries alone. Their shoulders were slumped, their gazes downcast, their faces like two photographs that had been left out in the great typhoon.

"What will you teach us today?" I asked.

I didn't understand why that simple question triggered an emotional avalanche, but both the missionaries burst out crying. Tall as oak trees, these young men sobbed like little boys with dangling snot. "Your parents are . . . divorced," one of them finally said between teary hiccups.

Um—okay? That was a long time coming. Tell me something new . . .

"Your father has asked us to leave and never come back," the other missionary explained.

I froze in stunned silence and rage. The gospel message was the source of my great joy, hope, peace, and all things nice. What had I ever done to my father that he would take that away from me?

But the missionaries weren't the only ones who would never come back. In the divorce, my father had sole custody, and my mother had no visitation rights. She was finally officially released from the slum life, trudging down the alley with her suitcase one last time. Only the lucky ones got to do that.

My father repeatedly threatened Dee and me that he would "break our dog legs" if we ever dared to contact Mama or visit her side of the family in the farming village two miles away. A few months after the divorce, he married the mistress he had been seeing for five years.

I wished he had broken my legs instead.

10. 蛇蠍心腸

Hualien, Taiwan—October 1988

I had no idea how my father came to the conclusion that his new wife—not my mama—deserved to live in a better place than the slum, but he moved us to a two-story house in an aborigine community. I also had no idea how he came to be at peace with the fact that since the arrival of his new wife, Dee's and my only daily meal was school lunch. It was slightly inconvenient that I happened to be a growing teenager with a full-time growling stomach. I could easily love anyone who fed me.

One night, while I was walking toward the upstairs bathroom, the stepmother abruptly emerged from her bedroom, reeking of body odor and alcohol. Never in a million years had I expected to catch her half-dressed, but there she was—a highly disturbing sight.

"What do you want?" she screeched, dashing toward the bathroom.

Wouldn't you like to know? Claw out my eyeballs, of course!

"Go away, you creep!" she yelled and slammed the door.

I stomped back to the study, gathered my homework, and stormed downstairs. Within earshot were the sounds of rushing water and her roaring laughter over the phone. Apparently, while drawing a bath, she was talking to someone who . . . actually liked her? I imagined that in her drunken state, she mistook the hairdryer for the phone and pulled it into the bath. *Oops, the cord is immersed in water. Who's laughing now?*

Soon after, I started doing my homework, and my father joined me in the living room, watching TV and drinking beer. Moments later, thunderous water rumbled down the stairs. It sounded like ten thousand horses carrying a ferocious cavalry, roaring and charging toward us. My father and I exchanged an astonished glance before he sprinted upstairs, fighting against a Niagara Falls in his own house. I quickly swept my homework into my book bag and slung it over my shoulder. If I lost my hard work in the stepmother's flash flood, I wouldn't know how to live with my own wrath.

Out in our small courtyard, in the abandoned koi pond that now collected junk, I found a shovel and used it to push the river out of the gate, into the gutter, in the drenching rain. Moments later, the step-mother's earth-shattering yell came from the living room. "It's your dog of a daughter!"

Before I realized what she was talking about, my father had come out to the courtyard like an executioner and dragged me back to the house.

"I was getting the water out—" I didn't need to explain myself. Anyone could see I was helping.

"Of course," the stepmother scoffed, her spittle flying, water drip-ping down her face from her matted hair. "It's your flood!"

"*Your* flood!" I shot back. "I was doing homework. My baba was here with me—"

"You were with her?" she cut me off, jabbing my father in the stomach. Strangely, that prompted my father to shoot me a sniper's glare.

"You know what?" The woman wiped the water off her face with her hand. "I'm bored. I want to watch you beat her."

What in the world?

I called to my father, "Baba, you were here! You know I didn't leave the bathwater running! You know right from wrong."

"Kazuo, are you letting your dog talk like this? Beat her!"

How dare she keep calling me a dog!

A sudden searing sensation scorched my cheek. It felt like my flesh was being torn apart.

Before I could react, the woman yelled, "You call that beating? I thought you were a frogman!"

Instantly a violent blow made contact with my head. The force was so strong that my eyes teared up. Through my blurry vision, I saw stars. Through my ringing ears, I heard a sneer.

"That was just a scratch, Kazuo!"

She wants me dead! That thought caused my throat to tighten up; I gasped. My trembling legs—weak from terror and rage—lifted me out of the house, with the surging bathwater, into the dark night, into the deluge of rain.

The woman sent out another deafening command for my father to "fix me," so he chased me down the alley the way he had done to Mama before, except he didn't have a butcher's knife in hand now. Was it different though? A hatred for the daughter of the ex-wife he also hated.

The end of the alley was a right-angle turn leading to the street. Row houses ended at the point of the angle and gave way to a rice field along the bend. I would've run along the alley into the street, but at this moment, as prey, survival mode prompted me to jump into the rice field instead.

Splash!

Gelid water stung me, bit my fingers, penetrated my flesh, and pierced my bones. Glacial water engulfed my bitter fifteen-year-old soul. Water, water everywhere, up and down, front and back, left and right, a unifying force of flood. I used to think that when the world crumpled, home was the shelter, refuge, and haven of troubled souls. Now I understood that my home was where the world crumpled.

When I was four years old, my father once told me our family name means *flood*; the Chinese character for it had *water* as the radical and *unity* as the component. *Water and unity*—us. Had he truly believed that? If so, why was I here, soaking in rain, tears, and plant water, hiding from him, contemplating ending my misery by my own hands?

I wasn't as scared of my father's violence as I was afraid of my upcoming thoughts—frightened of what actions they would lead me to. But no sooner had I envisioned how to exit this wretched life than I felt something stir within me. In this moment of helplessness, hopelessness, and despair, I looked back to my short life for a moment of true happiness. I couldn't find a single one—except on those wintry dark nights when the missionaries brought the sun to us and introduced us to the Son of God.

Their words percolated in my mind. God loves me—they had said so. I saw no reason why they would make that up. Heavenly Father's universe of love more than made up for my earthly father's bonfire of hate. I might be trembling in a field of icy water, but I was looking at a sea of infinite stars.

And just like that, I knew how to end my misery.

11. 重見光明

Hualien, Taiwan—1989

One Sunday morning, Dee and I biked to the local church meetinghouse, looking for the missionaries who had visited my family before. By then, those American young men had honorably finished their missions and returned home to the United States. Just when I thought the sun had left with them indefinitely, a set of sister missionaries welcomed us and introduced us to the Church members.

The sun had always been there. When I was ready, I saw it.

The Son of God had always been there. When the stepmother gave me hell, I turned to The Church of Jesus Christ of Latter-day Saints for heaven.

I found it.

* * *

Being baptized and confirmed as a member of The Church of Jesus Christ of Latter-day Saints didn't miraculously improve my family life. The stepmother and I still weren't friends. There still was no breakfast or dinner at home. But Church members were more than friends to me. They invited me to their houses for homemade meals. What they didn't tell me was that I would witness the teachings of the gospel of Jesus Christ applied unpretentiously in ordinary people's lives.

Watching my parents' violent relationship deteriorate, I didn't know there was any other way to be a married couple—until I saw parents in the Church gathering their children for weekly family nights, studying the scriptures, praying, singing, playing games, and enjoying treats together. I joined them on their family walks and observed the husband and wife hold hands, chat, and grin with beaming joy when their children shared fun facts they'd learned in Sunday School. It moved me to quiet weeping to see the teachings of the gospel of Jesus Christ enter their eyes, ears, and minds and settle in their hearts. They never once told me they were emulating the example of the Lord to live and love, but that is what I saw them doing. I never once told them my dream of a peaceful, happy family, but that is what they showed me—that it was, in fact, possible.

The Church's youth advisors took me to the deep mountains to build cardboard shelters for the aborigines. We went to a nursing home and cleaned their bathrooms. On Saturday afternoons, we frequented an institution for disabled girls and orphans, doing art projects, reading, singing, and laughing. I didn't know I was capable of loving those children who never once fed me. Over and over again, Church members invited me to spiritual and emotional feasts by taking me to service projects. How foolish had I been to think I was famished only physically?

* * *

Going home was for the blessed souls.

After doing much good, Church members went back to their loving homes. They deserved that blessing.

Reporting my whereabouts to my parents wasn't something they taught me to do, if they taught me anything at all. When my mama moved out and the stepmother moved in, I didn't see a rational reason why I should start keeping that strange woman informed either. After school, I stayed on campus and played volleyball. When the last teacher told me to go home so he could lock the gates, I roamed the streets until dark.

That was before I found a home in the Church. Now, after school, I sat by the door of the church meetinghouse and waited for someone to show up. On my lucky days, missionaries came for their appointments with the people who wanted to learn about the gospel. I asked to sit through the discussions with them, even though I wasn't fluent in the language of deep doctrine.

Sometimes the choir members came and I asked to practice with them, even though my singing voice was a frog's croaking.

Sometimes the janitor came and I asked to clean with her. "You shouldn't be here," she said. "You're the college type. You should be home studying for exams." Then she'd hand me a mop, point to the faucet, and say, "Make yourself at home!"

12. 重生父母

God works in mysterious ways. What does that look like in my insignificant life?

Let's say that a pathetic, filthy slum girl, such as myself, was transported to a parabolic sphere far, far away and wandered into an affluent kingdom, knocking on every door and asking, "Do you need a little child to love?" Then the Almighty God, who lived in the most glorious and magnificent mansion, asked his beloved messengers, Mr. and Mrs. Bushman, to take me in.

A year after my baptism, the Bushmans—a couple of senior missionaries from Utah—were assigned to serve in my hometown. Brother Bushman was a retired construction company owner in his seventies. Sister Bushman was a former schoolteacher and a stay-at-home mother in her sixties. Like all missionaries, the Bushmans' choice to volunteer required them to fund themselves for their eighteen-month service. Before arriving in Taiwan, they'd spent two months learning Chinese at the Missionary Training Center in Utah.

There was an unspeakable power—humility and gratitude, actually—in knowing I was deeply loved when I entered the Bushmans' apartment in Hualien.

Going home was for the blessed souls. I had finally become one.

Sitting at the Bushmans' dining table of glowing candles and fresh flowers and feasting on a hot, homemade meal were other children who also wandered up and down the street after school, roaming in and out of dark alleys like I had. We used to exist in the cracks between buildings, behind doghouse-sized shrines, neglected and forgotten.

No more.

You wouldn't find me there.

I had gone home.

To my Mom and Dad Bushman.

13. 斷絕關係

Taiwan—Chinese New Year's Eve, 1994

My father was alone. Prefect!

"Baba," I called to him after taking a nervous gulp. For months, I had imagined this moment. Several times, I had rehearsed what to say. But now I felt like a little mouse approaching my lion of a father. Luckily, I only had to do it once. I cleared my throat. "Baba, I want to, uh . . . go . . . serve a mission. For the Church."

A glassy film glazed over his eyes. His cheek muscles contracted. "You WHAT? Are you retarded?"

His reaction was understandable. I'd expected it.

Three years earlier, I had passed the National University Entrance Exam and been admitted into a prestigious university in Taipei. Only about 20 percent of the high school graduates on the island were accepted into colleges, and to give up the hard-earned educational opportunity for a self-funded service mission could indeed sound unreasonable.

Quickly, I assured him I would finish my degree after my mission, as if I alone had the authority to make it happen the way I wanted. Of course, that assurance wasn't good enough for my father. He paced the living room, red-faced, veins bulging on his forehead.

"Disgrace! People will hear what an idiot you are, and I'll lose face because of it!" he yelled.

"Lose face? Really? I'm going to proselytize, not to prostitute—"

Abruptly, he shoved me out to the porch. "Go! Go serve your stupid god and don't ever come back! I don't want to see you!" He slammed the door in my face. I supposed that saved his face. It's better to have a daughter who was dead to him than a daughter who disgraced him.

If he disowned me, that meant I became fatherless. Was I still a child? Did I still belong to a family? Who was I, then, having my father lost to me? And his father, his father's father, and all the fathers before him—were they all lost to me? How could this be?

When I was born, I entered the world as one soul. But I bleed the blood of countless ancestors—from the Eurasian Stepped, Daur, Mongolia, Tibet, and beyond. I carry their genes, their hair, their eyes, their nose, their lips, their chin. I'm all of them—thousands of years of human spirits in me. I stand as eternity. So what did the disownment even mean?

The lashing rain dimmed the amber glow of the streetlamps. I pulled up my jacket collar, but it did nothing to keep the sideways rain from getting in under my shirt. This night, Chinese New Year's Eve, the streets were empty. Most people had returned home to celebrate over the reunion dinner. Through their windows, I glanced at the togetherness of other families, parents giving children red envelopes stuffed with gift money—the kind of warmth and happiness that came once a year with this festivity.

I was alone on the street, shivering in the cold, going up and down the sidewalks searching for forgotten coins in payphone change slots. If my father had seen me right now, he probably would have said this was my punishment for not living up to the virtue conditioning and the cultural expectation for Chinese women and girls to abide by the Three Obediences: obey father, obey husband, and obey sons in widowhood.

For years, I had obeyed my father—to please him and make him proud. But all was wasted effort. No matter what I did, I couldn't be the child of his preferred gender. The problem was . . . I had no problem being a girl, now crossing over into the identity of a woman with the beliefs of her own choosing.

I believe in God, the Eternal Father, and in His Son, Jesus Christ, and in the Holy Ghost.

I believe the gospel changes lives for the better. For one, it helps me see the purpose and meaning of my mortal experience. It helps me understand the great worth of my soul. I cannot unbelieve what I believe.

It would be the new year in a couple of hours. The Year of the Rooster would cross over into the Year of the Dog. At the age of twenty-one, I had celebrated quite a few Chinese New Years in the past, almost completing the cycle of the twelve zodiac animals twice. So how was this one different from the others?

How?

I was alone.

Homeless.

Penniless.

If I walked alone, should I still walk?

Yes.

I knew how to be alone.

I knew how to move in the dark.

I kept walking.

14. 棄妻傳奇

Texas—About a Week Before Thanksgiving, 1996

I leaned against the exterior wall of my apartment and slowly lowered myself to the ground until my bottom hit the concrete corridor with a loud thud. The chills of the November night were gnawing on my cheeks, ears, and fingers while my mind continuously replayed what had just happened. It could be categorized as part psychological thriller, part mystery, but altogether a shocking betrayal. I closed my eyes and retraced my steps:

The first time I met Cameron in Taipei four years earlier, I knew he would someday be my husband. It was unexplainable how that knowledge came to me. I was young at the time, a university freshman, but not so young that I didn't know what was impossible. Cameron and I were from different worlds. He grew up in Texas; I in Taiwan. He spoke scattered Chinese; I, pathetic English. He could be described as good-looking; I . . . no comment. The early 1990s Western-boy-meets-Eastern-girl story hardly went without sacrifices of some sort.

Cameron returned home to the United States a year after we'd met. With financial support from Mom and Dad Bushman, I was able to answer the call to go on a full-time mission in Taichung, Taiwan. After my service, Cameron helped me apply to the same university he was attending in Texas. I didn't tell him about the hunch I had at our first meeting, but when he put a ring on my finger, naturally, I thought, *Of course.* On the tenth day of my arrival in America, we got married in Dallas. His parents were our only guests and witnesses.

Cameron and I fought away most of our newlywed days. I was lost. I couldn't fully understand people. The English they spoke was unfamiliar and confusing. I was lonely. I didn't bring Taiwan with me—no family or friends to speak Chinese with or to share our collective love for Chinese food. I had Cameron, but he had others.

So we fought. Mostly because I was frustrated and hurt. It felt like I suffered from both migraine headaches and menstrual cramps every day. And how many crappy days like that could Cameron tolerate?

About four hundred and eighty.

Sixteen months into our marriage, a week before Thanksgiving, on this night, I came home to our apartment and was shocked to discover that during my two-hour absence, Cameron's folks had helped him move everything out, discontinued all the utilities, ended the apartment lease, withdrawn all the money in our bank account, placed a restraining order on me, and served me divorce papers.

I was back on the street. Back to darkness. Back to the cold. Back to being the little filthy slum girl wandering in a wealthy kingdom, begging.

I got on my knees, praying to Heavenly Father. *Please help, help, help!*

I got on my feet—because my rebirth parents responded to the call from God to take me in. "Here we are. Hang on, hang on, hang on . . ."

15. 高深莫測

The decade of my twenties saw a radical transformation:

1. Became a university dropout
2. Became homeless
3. Became a missionary
4. Became an international student at a university in the United States
5. Became an immigrant wife
6. Became a discarded starter wife
7. Became homeless again
8. Became motherless
9. Became an immigrant wife again
10. Became a mother of three

16. 水火同源三百年

Utah—2006 to 2009

Every night after I tucked my kids in bed at 8 p.m., I had about two to three hours to myself. Instead of participating in any "girls' night out" type of activities, I rearranged the furniture at home. One night, I asked my husband Drake to help me move the couch from the basement to the second floor. He had questions:

"Didn't we just move it from the second floor to the basement the other day?" (Yes, we had.)

"Why don't you try doing something different?" (Like what?)

"Oh, I don't know . . . blogging?"

"Flogging?" I gasped.

I'd never heard of blogging, but the next day I didn't rearrange the furniture. Or the day after that. During school hours, I volunteered in my boys' classes. At night, I researched and worked on a blog.

* * *

Growing up among white children, my sons were somewhat conscious about the Chinese part of their identity. The culture was strange to them. In school, when they opened their lunch boxes that contained bone-in chicken curry and rice, their classmates pinched their noses and gagged. So my kids asked for peanut butter and jelly sandwiches. Their friends said I talked funny; they mock-mimicked my accent. So my boys asked me to do only quiet jobs for their teachers—organizing the classroom library, grading homework, and laminating posters.

I'd survived a tumultuous slum childhood to get here—to have a peaceful, happy family of my dreams where my genes and DNA carriers could live in a blissful home. My children are an extension of me. If they were embarrassed by how different I was—if they couldn't embrace the Chinese aspect of their identity—how could they accept the entirety of themselves?

It was my parental obligation to share my culture with them, so I wrote about it in my blog, under the conviction that I was passing down my legacy. I don't know why I thought they would read it someday; after all, I wrote in Chinese. Turns out that before my sons had a chance to find out about the existence of my blog, I abandoned it and worked on a memoir instead. Much to my surprise, when I turned one of my old blog posts into an essay, it won the National Championship (Grand Prize) in the 2009 Life Story Writing Contest in Taiwan.

On Labor Day weekend, while I was giving the three-minute winner's acceptance speech in Taipei, the future moved through the present. My mind's eye was opened, and I saw an older version of me delivering another winner's acceptance speech (in English!) somewhere in the United States. In that moment, I was determined to take a daring move on my memoir project—to write it in English.

Some of my ancestors built the Great Wall of China to keep out their enemies. Some of my ancestors were the reason why the Great Wall of China was built. Their conflict lives within me. I war against myself.

"You can't do it. You have a reading disorder."

"You can't do it. English is ridiculously hard."

"You can't do it. The publishing industry is brutally competitive."

"But yes, yes, yes, I can! My love for my sons is greater than my weaknesses, shortcomings, and imperfections."

It was fall. I was tired of being small.

17. 笙磬同音

Columbia, Maryland—November 2023

Drake and I are like whipped cream dissolving in hot chocolate, our cultures swirling around each other.

He traveled hundreds of miles with me across the nation to the award ceremony that celebrated my literary work. This moment was when his American upbringing and my Chinese conditioning became the same narrative. He leaned against the doorframe, pointed the phone camera at me, and glowed with pride. I bowed to him and then started my acceptance speech. "I come from a bowing culture . . ."

Chinese culture taught me to express gratitude by bowing—bow to the trees for the shade, bow to the fields for the harvest, and bow to the rivers for the drinking water. The effect of the bowing culture manifests in everyday life too. As I bend over to make my bed in the morning, I express my gratitude for the comfort, warmth, and rest it provides.

Before the missionaries taught me the gospel, I didn't know who to thank for the gift of life. I imagined genealogy was like drive-through-window kindness, where a complete stranger pays for the order of the driver behind her. The giver will never see the face of the person who comes after her. She will never know their name or hear the word of thanks from the individual who comes after her. But she gives anyway.

In that case, I'm a receiving driver. My foremothers—the women who traditionally had no voice or choice in the culture—chose to carry, labor, and deliver children. No childbirth is without risks or price. Even though their mortal experience would never overlap with mine, even though in the flesh they would never see my face or know my name, generation after generation, the women in my family made the parental sacrifice so that I could have a place to stand in the world today.

I carry them now—in my blood, in my hair, in my skin. With gratitude, I bow.

To my parents.

To my rebirth parents.

To Drake.

To our children.

The Chinese say, "A dragon begets a dragon, a phoenix births a phoenix, and the child of a mouse is good at digging holes." As a child of a frogman, I can't swim—I remain anchored on land. But as a child of God, I remain firmly grounded in the gospel of Jesus Christ and create my own path. In the spirit of the words of Rumi the poet, "There are hundreds of ways to kneel and kiss the ground." I bow to God in the way I'm grateful for the ocean.

4

KIMBERLY DOWDELL
The Down Syndrome Advocate

I FELL IN LOVE WITH MY HUSBAND SWINGING

"You're Mormon, right?" a girl asked one day as we waited in line for lunch.

I nodded cautiously.

"Don't you guys, like, dig up dead bodies and baptize them?" She cocked her head to the side, sending her ponytail swinging, and smirked.

My stomach did a flip.

I had just moved to California from Utah a couple of weeks earlier, right in the middle of the school year. Everything felt so different—the palm trees, the old, drab house we now lived in that desperately needed some help, and of course, the kids at my new middle school. I was thirteen, awkward, and just trying to fly under the radar.

"What?" I blinked. Back in Utah, I'd grown up around people who shared my faith, but now I was in a place where people didn't even understand what being "Mormon" meant. And I had no idea what to say.

She shrugged like it was no big deal. "Yeah, I heard you do weird stuff like that."

I could only stare. "Um, no. That's . . . not even close," I replied.

But it didn't matter. By then, she had already turned to her friends, laughing about it. I wanted to crawl into a hole and disappear. From that point on, I wasn't sure if I wanted anyone to know about my faith. If I couldn't explain, what would be the point? Fitting in felt impossible.

But even as I stood there, wanting to blend into the background, I felt this strange sense of bravery rise in me. *You're not going to back down on who you are.* I was determined to stand by what I believed, even if it meant standing out.

The rest of the day passed in a blur. The faces around me still weren't familiar, and the hallways felt like a never-ending maze. I was starting to believe this place would never feel like home. But then I saw him.

Across the quad, in the middle of a sea of kids, stood a boy wearing a blue BYU sweatshirt. My heart just about skipped a beat. It felt like a wink from God—a small piece of home in this big, strange place. He was showing me He was aware of me and letting me know that everything was going to be okay.

BYU—Brigham Young University—is a big deal if you're a member of The Church of Jesus Christ of Latter-day Saints. It's a big deal to many nonmembers as well, placing in the top twenty-five schools in the "Best Colleges in America" rankings, along with Princeton, MIT, Yale, Stanford, and Harvard. Seeing that sweatshirt in the middle of Southern California felt like spotting a familiar face in a crowd of strangers. Suddenly I didn't feel so alone; middle school got easier. Before I knew it, time had passed, and almost in a blink, middle school was behind me.

It was September 1992, and I was just trying to survive freshman year. But at least I had one thing to look forward to—seminary.

Seminary is an early-morning religious study class for teenagers who are members of the Church. And when you live outside of Utah, like I did now, that meant dragging yourself out of bed at 5:30 a.m. to be there by 6 a.m. Pretty brutal for a fourteen-year-old, but honestly, it was worth it.

Seminary was like my escape. For one hour, I could focus on something uplifting, surrounded by other teens who believed the same things I did.

High school? That was a whole different story. You're surrounded by all kinds of people, choosing all kinds of paths—some good, some . . . well, not so good. It was easy to feel like you could get pulled in any direction. But seminary? That kept me on the path I wanted to follow. It reminded me of the life I was trying to live—a Christ-centered one. It was the bright spot in my day, keeping me grounded and helping me stick to what mattered most to me.

Excited for my first day, despite the early hour, I walked into the classroom, trying not to trip over my own feet, when suddenly I saw him—again. It was the boy in the blue BYU sweatshirt I'd seen over a year ago—he happened to be wearing it again today. He strolled in, looking half-asleep, and sat right behind me. I later learned his name was Devon.

"Hey, you went to Tuffree, right?" he asked.

I turned around and smiled. "Yeah, I thought I recognized you."

That's how it started. Devon and I didn't talk much at first, but since he sat behind me, he'd sometimes do little things like play with my hair. At first I ignored it. My hair was long and maybe he was just bored. But one day, he tugged gently on the ends and leaned forward, whispering, "You've got split ends."

I turned around, shocked, my brows pinching in. "What?"

He grinned. "Yeah, you need to get those trimmed."

I wasn't sure whether to laugh or punch him—he was pretty cute, so I was leaning toward the former. "Thanks for the beauty tip, but I think I'll pass."

He chuckled, and for the first time, I realized he was just trying to flirt—in the most awkward, teenage-boy way possible.

As the months went on, Devon and I became good friends. I found my footing at school too, partly because I made the cheerleading squad. It gave me a sense of belonging, but it wasn't always easy. Many of the girls on the squad didn't share my values. A lot of them were already experimenting with things like drinking, while I stood on the sidelines, sticking to what I'd been taught.

One day after practice, one of the girls threw her arm around my shoulder and grinned. "Hey, are you coming to the party this weekend?"

I shook my head. "I don't think so—it's not really my scene."

She rolled her eyes. "You're so innocent. Don't you ever want to just, I don't know . . . live a little?"

I smiled, but it didn't reach my eyes. "I'm living just fine."

It wasn't easy being the odd one out. Sometimes it made me feel naïve and maybe even a little inexperienced. But deep down, I knew I was making the right choice. In terms of dating, I wanted to date someone who shared my values, and that realization only got stronger as I watched some of my friends get swept up in things I wasn't comfortable with.

And then, as fate would have it, Devon showed up in my history class junior year. We ended up sitting next to each other, and our friendship grew even closer.

One day, I worked up the nerve to invite him to a church youth activity. I'd always wanted to ask him, but it took a bit of courage to actually do it. *Be brave,* I told myself, and I finally just asked him.

Swing dancing had become *the* thing in the mid-90s, and all of us at church wanted to learn the moves. Youth dances were huge events for teens like us—a chance to meet other Latter-day Saint youth from all over Southern California.

"Want to come with me?" I asked him, trying to sound casual but probably failing miserably.

He raised an eyebrow, giving me that teasing look like he might actually say no.

For a second, I almost believed it and my stomach turned flip-flops. Devon was always such a tease, and I could tell he was enjoying making me squirm.

"Swing dancing? Absolutely!" There was mischief in his blue eyes.

"Really?" I asked, practically bouncing in my seat.

"Yeah, I'm in!" He said it like I'd just invited him on the adventure of a lifetime.

That night, Devon pulled into my driveway for the swing dance practice. I couldn't help but smile when I saw his car—a red 1988 Honda Prelude, with its sleek lines and that "I'm cool but don't need to brag about it" vibe. Butterflies fluttered around my stomach.

I opened the passenger door and slid in, noticing the light scent of cologne lingering in the air. It was subtle but nice, and I liked it.

It felt like he had taken just enough care but not so much that it was obvious.

"Hey!" I greeted him with a broad smile, trying not to overthink how excited I was. "Ready to learn how to dance?" I teased, fastening my seatbelt.

"Hey," he replied, a little shy but smiling back. He glanced over at me as we pulled away. "Sure, as long as you don't mind dancing with two left feet."

I laughed. Devon had spent most of his life on the baseball field, and his athletic build showed it. But dancing? That was uncharted territory for him.

I had grown up surrounded by music, and moving to the rhythm was second nature to me, so the idea of teaching him made me beam. This was going to be so much fun!

The drive was easy, light, and exciting. We talked about school, music, and whatever random things popped into our heads—no awkward pauses, no trying too hard. By the time we pulled into the church parking lot, I was feeling a lot less nervous.

Inside, couples had already arrived, some practicing their moves while others laughed and chatted. The youth leader in charge, a guy named Brother Cheng, welcomed us with a big smile as we introduced ourselves.

"Glad to see you both here!" He shook Devon's hand and gave me a nod. "Swing dancing's all the rage right now, huh? Seriously, it's so much fun. You're gonna love it!"

We glanced around the crowded gym where everyone seemed to be doing their own thing—teaching each other steps, messing up, laughing, and trying again. It was a little awkward at first. Devon and I exchanged a look—brows raised, mouths forming an "eek" shape. *What have we gotten ourselves into?*

Already smoother than he realized, he took my hand in a confident grip and led me to the dance floor. I might have swooned if I hadn't told myself to hold it together.

We tried a few steps to "In the Mood." "I have no idea what I'm doing," Devon admitted with a chuckle.

"Me neither," I laughed. "I feel like we both have two left feet."

We stumbled through the first few moves, stepping on each other's toes more than once. But when we made mistakes, we couldn't help but laugh. The awkwardness melted away with each little misstep, and soon enough, we were spinning and twirling—well, sort of.

We managed a half-decent spin, and I said, "I think we're getting the hang of it."

"Yeah, maybe by next year we'll look like we know what we're doing," Devon teased, flashing that crooked grin that made my heart skip. Plus, did he say "next year"? Was he planning on dancing with me for that long? I sure hoped so.

By the end of the night, we were both exhausted but had the best time. On the drive home, the conversation was just as light and easy as before, but there was a new underlying excitement. We agreed to meet up again for practice the next week. I couldn't wait.

The following Saturday night was the big dance. I wore a blue floral dress with a fitted bodice and a flowing skirt that twirled just right with every spin. The gym was decorated with streamers and lights, and you could feel the excitement in the air. As soon as the first notes of "Sing, Sing, Sing" started playing, the room seemed to pulse with energy. The drums pounded, the brass came in bold and strong—it was the kind of music that made you want to move, like something exciting was just around the corner.

I stood there, scanning the sea of people, trying to play it cool as I looked for Devon. Then I spotted him moving through the crowd, heading straight toward me. He looked effortlessly sharp in a crisp white shirt, classic tie, and dark suspenders that gave him a touch of vintage charm.

My heart did that ridiculous fluttery thing as he got closer, the music building with every step. He wasn't in a hurry, teasing as always, and I watched him, nervous and excited all at once, wondering if he was really going to ask me to dance. When he finally got to me, he flashed that smile of his and held out his hand.

"Wanna dance?" he asked, grinning like he knew I'd say yes. He was right—there was no way I'd say no.

"Of course." I tried not to sound too excited, but I was *definitely* excited.

When we hit the dance floor, something clicked. There we were, doing these swing moves we'd practiced, surrounded by other couples, but at that moment, it felt like it was just the two of us. The music, the spinning, the thrill of dancing together—it was exhilarating. I couldn't stop smiling.

This friendship was turning into something more, and I couldn't deny it.

Devon and I started spending more time together outside of school and church activities. We'd talk for hours—about life, about faith, about our future dreams. He shared my values, my beliefs, and most importantly, my faith. It was like I had found someone who understood the deepest parts of me.

One night, while we were practicing swing dancing again at church, a boy from the group—one of the regulars also trying to master the steps—walked up to us with a sly grin.

By now, we all knew each other pretty well. Week after week, we'd been showing up, and people had started to notice. It was like everyone else could see what was happening between Devon and me long before we were willing to admit it ourselves.

"Are you guys, like . . .?" He raised his eyebrows, waiting for us to confirm what everyone was already thinking—that we were definitely more than just friends.

Devon and I exchanged a glance and played dumb. "Like what?" we both said, trying to keep straight faces.

The guy rolled his eyes. "Oh, you know. Like a couple."

We laughed, brushing it off.

"Nah, we're just dancing," Devon said, but there was this unspoken feeling between us that maybe we *weren't* just dancing.

Not long after that, Devon finally asked me. We were sitting in his car after a swing practice, enjoying the cool evening air. There was a quiet moment, and then he turned to me like he'd been thinking about it for a while.

"So . . ." he began, looking a little nervous. "Do you maybe . . . want to be my girlfriend?"

My heart raced, but I kept it cool. "I thought you'd never ask."

As our time in high school passed, everything seemed to fall into place. Devon wasn't just my boyfriend—he was my best friend. Everything about high school was better because of him.

We would spend hours talking about our future, dreaming of the life we would build together. It was almost impossible to imagine my world without him in it, and the thought of being apart for two years while he served a mission for the Church seemed unbearable. But deep down, I believed we could conquer anything. Together, we were invincible.

One night, after a long day of school and cheer practice, we sat in his car listening to the hum of the engine as the cool night air filtered in through the cracked windows. The stars above felt so close, like we could reach out and touch them.

"You ever think about the future?" I turned to him.

He glanced at me, his expression soft but certain. "All the time."

"Do you think . . . do you think we can handle whatever comes our way?" I wasn't really doubting us—it was more like I just needed to hear it out loud.

He smiled, that easy grin that always made me feel like everything would be okay. "Absolutely. We can do anything."

At that moment, I believed him with my whole heart. We felt unstoppable. Life was just beginning, and no matter what challenges or hardships were waiting for us down the road, I was convinced we could handle it all. I had no idea how much we'd be tested, but I trusted in us—in our shared faith, our connection, and our strength together. Devon had a way of making everything seem possible.

* * *

High school had just ended, and we were lucky enough to graduate together. Tossing our caps into the air felt like the perfect way to close that chapter of our lives. We were full of excitement, ready to take on whatever came next.

But there was one moment that stood out—something I could never forget. It was right before Devon left for his mission, after he'd received his patriarchal blessing—a special message of guidance from God, given by priesthood holders, for his life.

We were sitting on his family room couch, the soft hum of the television in the background. Devon had a thoughtful look on his face, his eyes distant like he was still processing everything from his blessing.

He looked over at me, his voice low and serious, and said, "There's something I need to tell you. It's not in my blessing, but I had a really strong impression—that someday, I might have a child born with special needs."

I stared at him, trying to keep my expression neutral, but inside, I felt my heart skip a beat. A child with special needs? My mind raced, trying to absorb what he was saying.

I managed to nod, offering what I hoped was a supportive smile. "Oh, wow! That's . . . that's really something."

He nodded, staring at his hands, and I could tell it weighed heavily on him.

All I could think was, *Well, then I guess you're not marrying me*—because nowhere in my patriarchal blessing did it say anything like that. And that thought hurt—that he might end up with someone else. I never said those words out loud, of course, but I wondered what that meant for us.

We kept talking, sharing our hopes for the future, all while I tried to convince myself that everything would work out the way it was meant to. But a part of me couldn't shake the unease—the question that lingered in the back of my mind: *What if this changes everything?*

* * *

I was heading to Ricks College, and two months later, Devon would be leaving to serve a two-year mission in the Philippines. We both knew what that meant—two years of being apart. And while we had talked about it so many times, the reality of it finally hit.

"You're going to do amazing things at school," Devon said, his voice steady but soft as we stood in my driveway the night before I left. The sun was setting, casting long shadows across the pavement.

I smiled, trying to push back the lump forming in my throat. "And you're going to make one fantastic missionary."

He pulled me in for a hug, holding me close. "We'll get through this," he whispered into my hair. "We've talked about the future for so long . . . and this is just part of it."

I nodded, not trusting myself to speak. Part of me was excited for the next chapter of life, but another part of me felt like I was leaving a piece of my heart behind.

Devon and I were both off in different directions, each of us taking on new challenges, learning, and growing in ways we hadn't expected. We were doing things that pushed us out of our comfort zones, being brave in our own ways. It's funny how life works like that—how God can lead us on paths we didn't even see coming, quietly shaping us into who He knows we can become. And when we let Him work through us—trusting His timing—He can take even the hardest moments and turn them into something beautiful.

College was a whirlwind, and through it all, I grew more confident in who I was, standing on my own. But even as I made memories that would last a lifetime, I couldn't shake the excitement of what was waiting for me after graduation: coming home to Devon.

When Devon finally came home from his mission, I was nervous, unsure of what it would be like after all this time apart.

I didn't have to wonder for long. Devon pulled into my driveway, and as I ran up to greet him, there he was with the happiest expression I'd ever seen lighting up his face. All my doubts vanished.

"Hey, stranger," he said, and before I could even respond, he pulled me into a big hug, his arms wrapping around me so tight that it felt like no time had passed.

I laughed against his shoulder. "It's been a while."

"Yeah." He pulled back just enough to look at me. "I told you I'd see you at the finish line."

And just like that, we fell back into place—the same conversations, the same dreams we'd shared before, only now they felt more real. Those dreams weren't distant anymore; they were right in front of us.

We knew what we wanted. We'd spent enough time apart to be sure of it. And before long, the conversations about marriage weren't just distant ideas—they were real plans for our future together.

* * *

January 15, 2000. That day is etched in my memory like a perfect snapshot. But the night before? Let's just say it wasn't picture-perfect.

It was around 8 p.m. when Devon called.

"Hey, babe, I need you to stay calm," he said.

My throat constricted and my stomach dropped. The words "stay calm" were not words I wanted to hear the night before my wedding. I was in my room, making sure everything was set for our big day tomorrow and my honeymoon bag was packed, when my mom handed me the phone.

I sat down on my bed, heart already racing.

"What's going on?" I braced myself for whatever was coming next.

"I . . . forgot to pick up my tux."

I gasped. "What? Devon, we're getting married tomorrow!" Tears started to well up as I felt the impending doom.

"I know! I'm already on the freeway, driving to the Brea Mall right now. I need you to call the mall for me and check when they close—I didn't even think to get the number before I left."

I grabbed the phone book and frantically searched for the number, trying to stay calm. I called, found out they were closing in twenty minutes, and called Devon back.

"They close in twenty minutes." My voice shook.

"Okay, I'm speeding down the 57! I'll call you when I get there."

I closed my eyes, imagining the worst—a wedding with no groom's tux—while Devon was out there speeding like a man on a mission. I took deep breaths. *It's going to be fine. Everything is going to be fine.*

Finally my phone rang. I scrambled to answer it, nearly dropping it in my haste. "Please tell me you have good news!"

"I got it!" Devon exclaimed, relief flooding his voice. "I had to sweet-talk the lady at the store into staying open a few extra minutes, but she let me in. It's a little short in the arms, but it'll do!"

I sniffled. "You're lucky I love you."

"You won't even notice the sleeves," he joked. "You'll be too busy staring into my eyes."

The next day, the Los Angeles Temple stood tall against the bright blue sky as we arrived for our temple sealing. I was nervous, but the moment I saw Devon, my nerves melted away. There he was, walking toward me, tux and all—though I'll admit, those sleeves were definitely a little short!

"You're right," I said with a smirk. "That tux is a little . . . snug."

He shrugged, giving me that playful smile I knew so well. "Hey, it's not about the tux. It's about the bride."

I laughed. "Good save."

Before we walked inside for the marriage ceremony, Devon took my hand and leaned in, his voice soft. "You ready for forever?"

I smiled back at him, feeling the significance of the moment. "I've been ready for this my whole life."

* * *

After the ceremony, we stepped out into the sunshine, hand in hand, as husband and wife. The moment felt surreal. Our families rushed toward us, laughter and joy filling the air. My dad clapped Devon on the back. "Well, you didn't mess it up, son. Good job!"

Devon chuckled. "Thanks—I think."

And my grandma, who always had a quick remark, looked at me and said, "You look stunning, sweetheart. And Devon, that tux! Very . . ."—she quirked a brow—". . . modern."

Devon chuckled sheepishly. "It's a new style, Grandma."

At the reception, the night was full of music, dancing, and so much love. Twinkling lights were strung to the ceiling above, casting a soft, magical glow over everything. But the real highlight? That came when Sister McFerson—one of the first people from church to introduce herself when we moved to California—walked up to me with a knowing smile. "I knew it," she said, pulling me into a hug. "I always had a feeling about you two. I remember chaperoning those youth dances and watching you two swinging together."

As Devon and I danced, I was soaking in the moment, thinking about how everything had led us here. All those years of staying true to my values, holding on to the hope that I'd find someone who shared my faith and dreams—it was one of those moments where you just know that God is in the details, quietly guiding you all along.

Devon, ever the playful one, suddenly decided to show off. With a grin, he twirled me around, throwing in some of those old swing dance moves we learned together all those years ago. I laughed as he dipped me dramatically. The twinkling lights above made it feel like we were back at one of those youth dances. It was sweet, a little cheesy, and absolutely perfect.

He smiled down at me. "I still can't believe the girl I teased about split ends—the girl I had a major crush on in high school—is now the one I get to spend eternity with."

I laughed, my heart full. "Dreams do come true, don't they?"

He nodded, pulling me closer. "You're my forever."

And just like that, in that moment, I knew exactly where we were meant to be—together, part of a plan much bigger than us. And God had been in the details all along.

Getting My Groove Back

The door to the garage slammed shut, and I jolted awake on the couch. I sat up, rubbed the crick in my neck, and glanced around. The sink overflowed with dishes, toys were scattered like confetti across the living room, and me? I was probably the biggest mess of all. I glanced down at my T-shirt and saw peanut butter smeared across the front. A chunk of my hair escaped from my messy-bun-in-theory, making it a messy-bun-in-practice. The clock on the wall was a blurry haze until I squinted hard enough to read it. It was 10:33. Great.

Devon walked into the room, taking in the scene. He was late again—no surprise there. And he looked good, sharp in his suit and tie, with his blond hair neatly combed to the sides. A full day of work and he was still put together.

His eyes scanned the room and then landed on me. He offered a slightly bashful look, one that told me he knew exactly what kind of day I'd had: the kind where I spent every ounce of energy getting the kids to bed and had absolutely none left to clean or even change out of my food-splattered pajamas.

He set his bag down and came over to the couch. With a groan, I flopped back into the cushions, covering my face with my arm like I was waving a white flag. *I give up! Surrender. Whatever. Just make it stop.*

The couch dipped as he sat next to me. He gently pulled my arm away and looked at me with that soft, knowing smile—the one that had pulled me through so many tough days. "Kim," he said quietly, "I think you need something just for you."

We'd been married seven years, living in sunny San Diego with our three kids—one girl, Taylor, and two boys, Luke and Blake. Devon worked hard to support us, and I stayed home with the kids, which I loved, but some days, well . . . some days I didn't know who I was anymore beyond being "Mom."

I turned to him, not sure whether to laugh or cry. "Like what?" I asked, almost daring him to give me an answer that made sense.

He smiled again, his blue eyes filled with warmth. "I don't know— maybe a hobby? Something that makes you feel like yourself again."

I knew he was right, but I didn't have the faintest idea what that could be.

A few days later, I sat in the church foyer on Sunday, rocking my tired baby in my arms, while another mom sat next to me doing the same.

We shared a laugh about the challenges of motherhood when she suddenly lit up. "Hey, Kim! You should come to my new Pilates class! You'll love it!"

I stared at her, stunned. It was like Heavenly Father had sent her directly to me. How did she know? *I* hadn't even known.

"Really?" I tried to sound casual. "Maybe I will."

"You'll love it!" she insisted. "Just show up. I'll save you a spot."

That first class was tough, but I felt alive in a way I hadn't in a long time—this really was what I'd been needing. After a few weeks, I felt stronger, both physically and mentally.

Sometime later, after weeks of class, I sat at the kitchen table and glanced over at Devon who was gently rocking Blake in his arms.

"Hey, you know what Becky told me today?" I said, trying to sound casual but feeling the excitement build. "She thinks I'd make a great Pilates instructor."

Devon looked up, his easy smile spreading across his face. "Wow, that's awesome. What do you think?"

I hesitated for just a second and then nodded. "I'm interested. I think I want to go for it."

His eyes lit up, and he didn't miss a beat. "I think you should! It'll give me more time with the kids. You should totally do it!"

His words wrapped around me like a warm hug, filling me with the confidence I needed. "Thanks." I smiled. "I'm really going to do it."

And so I did. That one small conversation turned into something bigger than I ever imagined. It wasn't just about Pilates—it was about rediscovering a part of myself I didn't even realize I'd lost.

Soon after getting certified, I was offered to teach a class once a week. I remember walking into the studio for the first time, the sunlight spilling through the windows, warming the golden-colored wooden floors. The air smelled like fresh mats, and the room was filled with the quiet buzz of people stretching.

I never pictured myself balancing work and motherhood—it always seemed overwhelming. But this hobby-turned-career? Heavenly Father knew I needed it even when I didn't. Looking back, I can see how He guided me through small nudges, leading to this pivotal moment. Stepping out of my comfort zone took quiet bravery, but God knew those hidden parts of me—the strengths I was only beginning to discover. By listening to those gentle impressions, I found a purpose that gave me the strength I hadn't known I'd need—but He did. He always did.

* * *

Not long after, on January 15, 2007, we were preparing to celebrate our anniversary. Devon took the day off so we could make the most of it. We had everything planned—first, a trip to the Wild Animal Park with the kids, then dropping them off with a friend so we could enjoy a romantic dinner in La Jolla. No sippy cups, and no Cheerios in the car seats. I was ready.

The weather was perfect—the kind of San Diego day when the sun shines just right and the clouds look like they're straight out of a painting.

We walked through the park, stopping to look at the giraffes as they wrestled with a salt lick in front of us. The kids giggled and tugged on our hands, pulling us close.

Devon's phone buzzed, and he pulled it from his pocket. "It's my boss," he said, sounding worried. "I need to hop on a quick call—emergency company meeting."

I shrugged. "No big deal," I joked. "Just don't miss the giraffes."

He gave me a forced smile as he walked off, sending my stomach tumbling.

Fifteen minutes later, Devon came back. His crestfallen expression said it all. I left the older kids with the giraffes and met him halfway with the stroller between us.

"What happened?" I asked, but I already knew it wasn't good.

He hesitated for a moment. "They laid me off," he said, voice flat. "Four thousand of us. They'll send the details tonight."

I stood there, trying to process it. *Laid off? What? Today?*

Our anniversary, a day meant for celebration, turned into one of uncertainty—a day we'd never forget for all the wrong reasons.

In my typical fashion, I blurted out, "Well, at least you don't have to miss the giraffes!"

Devon stared at me like I'd lost it. We moved to a nearby bench where we could watch our kids and talk without worrying them. We sat in silence for a moment, both of us feeling the blow. How were we going to get through this?

Finally, I spoke up. "Maybe this is the push we needed. You've been wanting to go back to school, and Cedar City keeps coming up. Maybe this is part of the plan."

Devon took a deep breath. "Yeah, maybe you're right. We've been praying about it, and it's felt right. Maybe it's time to trust that."

We sat there, the uncertainty still lingering, but in the middle of it all, there was a glimmer of hope. Moving for Devon to go back to school wasn't exactly what we had planned, but for the first time since getting the news, it felt like we could breathe again. We didn't have all the answers, but we knew we'd face this new chapter together, with faith leading the way.

Devon and I shared a smile, a quiet confidence settling between us. God was in the details, and as long as we trusted that, we'd be brave enough to face whatever came next.

* * *

As Devon climbed into the truck three months later, I slid into the passenger seat, trying to push aside the overwhelming sense of defeat. The rumble of the truck's engine starting up felt weirdly symbolic— like the soundtrack to our life falling apart. I was still processing the fact that we were driving away from the house we'd poured so much into.

Devon glanced over, giving me a sheepish grin. "Hey, you want to hear something weird?"

I shot him a look that said "Now is not the time for weird."

He just grinned wider. "Well, too bad. I called about student loans, and they marked us down as . . . homeless."

I blinked. "Wait, what?"

"Yep. No job, no home—we're 'homeless' according to the government."

"Homeless?" I repeated, trying to process it. It didn't seem real. We had family, friends, a community that would never let us end up on the streets. But there it was.

I stared out at the setting sun, everything feeling so different from just a few months before. The house, the job, the security—it was all gone.

When we finally pulled into Cedar City, Devon's parents were waiting in the driveway, arms open wide. The kids ran to hug their grandparents. It was a relief to be there, but as I looked around at our new surroundings, it all felt so unfamiliar.

Later that night, sitting on the porch with Devon, looking up at the stars in the quiet night, I let out a sigh. "Do you think we'll ever have again what we had in San Diego?"

He wrapped his arm around me, pulling me close. "Maybe not in the same way," he said softly. "But we'll build new roots. We always do. And hey, we've got each other, right?"

I leaned into him, feeling a flicker of peace. He was right. We had each other, and that was more than enough to face whatever came next.

Shortly after we settled into Cedar City, Devon jumped right into school, and boy, did he have his work cut out for him! Taking on a heavy course load was no joke, especially with three little ones running around.

One evening, after the kids finally settled down, he plopped into a chair, rubbing his temples like he was trying to massage away all the stress. "Twenty-one units . . . What was I thinking?"

I looked over at him. "I know it's a lot, but you can do it! You always finish what you set your mind to."

Devon leaned back, studying me with a thoughtful look. "You should think about teaching Pilates again. You loved it, and it really helped you cope with all the craziness."

"You're right," I said. "I've been missing it like crazy!"

A few days later, I took the plunge and contacted the local gym. Walking in felt like stepping into a new adventure; I was filled with excitement and a sprinkle of nerves. Could I recreate the magic I had in San Diego?

The owner was a friendly guy with an infectious passion for fitness. "So you've taught group fitness before?" He glanced over my resume like it was a treasure map.

"Yep," I nodded, feeling a mix of pride and anticipation. "I taught for a year before moving here. It's more than just exercise for me—it's about community and connection."

He smiled, and I could tell he got it. "That's what it's all about, isn't it? The friendships we build. You'll fit right in. By the way, have you heard of Zumba?"

I raised an eyebrow, intrigued. "Zumba? Isn't that the dance thing?"

"Exactly! It's a dance-based fitness craze that everyone loves. We're thinking of adding it to our lineup. Want to get certified?"

Suddenly, the idea lit up in my mind like a disco ball. Dance had always been a part of my life—cheerleading in high school, swinging with Devon—and now I could combine that with fitness? "You know what? That sounds like a blast! I'm totally in."

He beamed. "Awesome! I'll send you the details about the certification. I have a feeling you're going to rock this."

I left the gym that day with a giddy excitement bubbling inside me. Teaching fitness again? And Zumba on top of that? Yes, please!

The day of my Zumba certification was a whirlwind of nerves and excitement. As I walked into the gym, I felt like I'd just stepped into a party—the kind where everyone knows the moves except me.

The front row was lined with people sporting the brightest neon clothes (think pinks, greens, and yellows), and their arms were adorned with colorful bracelets jingling as they moved. They had so much confidence—the kind that comes from hours of practice—and I couldn't help but feel like a fish out of water.

The moment the music began pumping through the speakers, it was like walking into a nightclub, but instead of a bar, there were mats and mirrors. The instructor led us in a master class, and the energy in the room was electric.

I turned to the woman next to me, her bright pink top shining like a beacon.

She smiled, her enthusiasm infectious. "You're gonna love it. I've been doing Zumba for a year now, and I can't wait to get certified. It's such a blast!"

As the instructor guided us through the moves, I felt a mix of anticipation and nervousness. I was determined to keep up, even as I stumbled through the choreography. Everyone around me seemed so fluid, while I felt like a puppy trying to imitate the big dogs.

As the music pulsed louder, and my body began to move in time with the beat, the nerves slowly melted away. By the time the training wrapped up, something had clicked. It felt like I'd found the missing piece to a puzzle I didn't even know I was trying to solve. There was this spark—like a part of me I hadn't seen in years had suddenly come back to life.

All those years of dancing and cheering as a teenager—I'd forgotten just how much joy it had brought me. Zumba wasn't just a workout; it felt like rediscovering a piece of myself that had been buried beneath the demands of life and motherhood. By the end of the day, it was like I'd revived a side of me that used to light up a room, and I couldn't help but think that maybe this was exactly what I'd needed all along.

When it was finally time to teach my first class back in Cedar City, I could hardly believe my eyes. The gym marquee announced the start of Zumba, and I expected maybe seven or ten people, just like any other class in our small town. Instead, I walked into a room packed with over sixty people!

My heart raced. *This is unreal!* I thought as I faced the crowd, my stomach doing flips.

As the music started, the energy was contagious. "Let's go, everyone!" My nervousness melted away as we moved together. The room exploded with laughter and cheers, and I couldn't help but smile from ear to ear.

After class, people swarmed me, showering me with compliments. "That was amazing! I loved it! When's the next class?" one woman exclaimed.

"I was having a rough day, but this class completely turned it around!" another chimed in.

"I wish I could do this every day."

When I got home, Devon was waiting for me, a curious look on his face. "How'd it go?"

I practically danced into the room, my energy still buzzing. "It was incredible. You won't believe how many people showed up. I've never taught a class that big before, and they were all so into it—it felt like a party!"

His eyes lit up. "That's amazing! I knew you'd be great at it."

I felt like I was finally living my dream—combining my love of dance and fitness with the community I adored. It was a kind of joy I had never expected, and it felt just right.

A year had zipped by, and sometimes it felt like we were pedaling uphill with no finish line in sight. Yet as we settled into this new chapter, I couldn't help but smile. The kids had found great friends, our home was filled with laughter, and my new friends at the gym lifted my spirits. Life was hard but good!

Money was tight—something we hadn't experienced in San Diego—but we found happiness in the small moments: the kids giggling over breakfast cereal, and Devon's playful teasing that always made my heart flutter.

One night, it was just the two of us on a much-anticipated date night. As we cruised down the quiet streets, the soft hum of the car felt cozy. The glow from the dashboard lights cast a warm light on Devon's face, and we started reminiscing. If someone had told us a year ago where we'd be now, we wouldn't have believed it. And yet here we were—from homeless to surviving, maybe even thriving, despite all the bumps along the way. It's amazing how God leads us in these little ways, showing us again and again that He's in the details, guiding us every step of the way.

"We've really come a long way, haven't we?" Devon said.

As I listened to him, a thought surfaced that I couldn't ignore any longer. "You know, I still feel like something's missing," I said. "There's this feeling in my heart telling me our family isn't complete."

Devon turned to me, eyebrows raised in surprise. "Really?

"Really." I swallowed.

A smile covered his face. "I feel the same way."

The Beat Drops When You Least Expect It

I couldn't contain my excitement as I stared at the positive pregnancy test in my hands. I was practically bouncing off the walls! It was the last semester of school for Devon, and our little miracle would arrive that fall, just after graduation. The timing felt absolutely perfect. "Can you believe it?" I exclaimed, my heart racing. "We're going to have a baby!"

Devon wrapped his arms around me, his eyes shining with joy. "This is amazing! It's like everything is finally falling into place."

We had weathered so many trials and hardships together, but now we were finally looking ahead to brighter days—better days. As I continued to teach my classes, I felt energized and alive. Zumba had become my happy place—my little addiction.

One day, as I finished up a particularly exhilarating class, one of my friends came up to me, her eyes sparkling with excitement. "This baby is going to come out wearing a sombrero!"

I couldn't help but laugh and echo her sentiment. "Right? Somewhere deep down, I just have this strong feeling that this little one will come out dancing and loving music."

Devon's graduation day finally arrived, and even though it was the end of May, the weather was freezing. My breath puffed out in little clouds. But honestly, I barely noticed the cold. The excitement buzzing inside me kept me warm. I watched Devon as he stood in line with the other graduates, that familiar smile lighting up the whole field.

I leaned over and told the person next to me, "That's my guy!"

As he walked across the stage, my heart skipped a beat. I couldn't contain my excitement anymore. Standing on my tiptoes, I waved my hands in the air like a cheerleader. "You did it, babe!"

He looked out into the crowd, searching for me, and when he spotted me, that grin of his grew even wider. He gave me a little salute, like he was saying, *Yeah, I did.* I swear, his smile could've melted the ice on the ground.

I cupped my hands around my mouth and yelled again, "I'm so proud of you!"

He winked, his eyes twinkling as if he were saying, "Wait till you see me in that cap and gown later."

After the ceremony, I wrapped my arms around him. "Thank you for being such a hardworking man and sacrificing so much for our family. You've accomplished so much in just two years."

"I just kept my eyes on the prize." He chuckled, but I could see the emotion behind his eyes.

Shortly after graduation, we got the news we'd been praying for— Devon was offered a job in Salt Lake City, about four hours north. With him having been out of work for two years and me having a baby on the way, this was a huge relief; we desperately needed the job—and the insurance. Devon's training would take him to Chicago for eight weeks, so the plan was for me to stay in Cedar City until after the baby was born, then we'd all move to Salt Lake City once he finished.

I was thrilled for him, but when I learned his training would begin around my due date, a wave of anxiety hit me.

We sat in our living room as I took in the information. "Devon, what if you're not here for the baby's birth?" Concern crept into my voice as the pressure of it all began to settle on my shoulders.

He reached for my hand, giving it a reassuring squeeze. "Let's talk to Dr. Carter about options. There's got to be a way to make this work."

"Yeah, but what if we can't figure it out?" I bit my lip, the uneasiness building.

Later, we met with Dr Carter. He welcomed us with his usual calm demeanor. "Let's see what we can do." He flipped through his notes. "If we schedule an induction, we can choose a date that works with Devon's schedule."

"Really?" A flicker of hope lit up inside me.

Devon nodded, looking more relaxed. "Yeah, they promised to fly me home every couple of weeks. We could time it perfectly."

Looking at his notes, Dr Carter smiled. "I can induce you a week early on October 10th."

I exhaled, sitting a little straighter in my chair. "That helps," I said and ran my fingers over the cool surface of the exam table.

Devon stood beside me, leaning casually against the wall. "We've got this." His steady and reassuring voice helped to make me feel lighter.

Later that evening, as I stood by the kitchen sink, rinsing out a mug from earlier, my mind wandered back to the appointment. I felt better knowing there was a plan, but there was something else lingering in the back of my mind—something my sister Robyn had mentioned. Her husband Joe had been debating running the St. George marathon in early October, and she had said they might come down.

I dried my hands on a towel and grabbed the phone, dialing her number. "Hey, Robyn. I was just thinking . . . is Joe still planning to run the marathon?"

"Oh, yeah!" She laughed on the other end of the line. "Even if he doesn't run, I'll still be there. If you go into labor early, you won't be alone, I promise."

I leaned against the counter, letting her words sink in. "Thanks. I don't really think I'll go into labor early, but knowing you'll be there helps."

"Well, duh! I'll bring pom-poms to cheer Joe on—if he runs—and I'll save some to cheer you on during labor. You've got this!" she said, her voice full of her usual energy.

I chuckled, picturing her doing a cheerleader jump. "I think I'm gonna need those pom-poms."

As I hung up the phone, I sat down on the couch, the house quiet now that the kids were in bed. With Robyn on board, it felt like a little piece of the puzzle had clicked into place. I stared at the phone for a minute longer, grateful for the backup.

* * *

As the early morning light peeked through the curtains, Devon zipped up his suitcase. I sat on the edge of the bed, my hands resting on my lap, watching him move about. It all felt a bit surreal. In just a couple of weeks, our lives were going to change in a big way.

Devon looked at me and leaned down. His lips met mine in a soft, lingering kiss that both comforted me and sent tingles down my spine.

He pulled back and smiled. "We've got this." His voice was steady and sure.

With that, he was gone, and the quiet of the morning settled in around me.

A week later, on October 3, 2010, I woke to the sound of my children laughing and playing with their cousins in the living room. Sunlight peeked through the curtains, casting a soft glow over the room, and for a moment, everything felt peaceful.

I stretched under the covers, feeling the warmth of the morning. But then, a light contraction rolled through my body, one twinge of pain followed by another. I winced, then sighed, and placed my hand on my belly. But this wasn't my first rodeo, and I figured it was nothing to worry about.

The day felt so full of life and noise—like a perfect Sunday morning. I shook off the lingering discomfort, refusing to let it ruin the day.

As the afternoon crept by, the contractions hadn't really gone away, but I was determined to ignore them. I had dinner to make. I was slicing up potatoes for the roast when another strong contraction made me pause. I gripped the edge of the counter, my breath catching for a moment.

"You sure you're okay?" Robyn asked, giving me a look that said she wasn't buying my cool act.

"I'm fine," I replied, waving her off. "Just some practice contractions. It's nothing serious." I forced a smile, trying to convince both of us that I wasn't in labor. Not yet.

She raised an eyebrow. "You sure?"

I nodded, trying to focus on setting the table as if everything was perfectly normal. "Yeah, totally. I've done this before, remember? Besides, I can't have this baby until Devon gets here next week."

But as I dished up food for the kids, another long, strong tightening at the top of my uterus rolled down, cramping my stomach and lower back with mind-numbing force. I stopped mid-scoop, closing my eyes and willing it to pass. My heart raced, not just from the contractions but from the thought of doing this without Devon. I was supposed to hold off. We had a plan.

Still, I couldn't ignore reality any longer. The contractions were getting stronger and more frequent. As much as I wanted to hit the pause button and wait for Devon to get home, I had this sinking feeling that the baby had other plans.

"I think it's time," I told Robyn, frustration bubbling up in my voice. Devon should've been here, but instead, I was trying to hold it together with each passing contraction.

Robyn, calm as ever, grabbed the keys. "Let's go."

By the time we piled into the car, the sky was a beautiful mix of pinks and oranges, but I couldn't appreciate any of it. "Left at the light," I instructed, gripping the door handle as another contraction hit hard. "I'm so mad at Devon for missing this."

Robyn glanced over, her eyes filled with both nervousness and reassurance. "You're doing great. We'll be there soon."

With each turn, the pain intensified, and all I could think about was how this wasn't the plan.

"I'm never letting Devon forget this," I said through gritted teeth as Robyn made a wrong turn and I tried to guide her back. "Of all the times not to be here . . ."

Robyn gave me a half smile. "He owes you one for sure."

But somewhere in the middle of the chaos, as much as I wanted Devon with me, I realized that this moment—this challenge—was mine to face. There was no turning back now—no rewinding the clock.

As my pain increased, I felt it again: that flicker of bravery rising up, reminding me that I could do this. I had to.

We pulled up to the hospital, the glowing lights above the entrance casting long beams onto the pavement. The warmth of the evening clung to the air, but with each step, it felt harder to move. I stumbled out of the car, barely able to walk, clinging to the door for support as another contraction hit hard, doubling me over.

With a deep breath, I finally forced myself forward, somehow making it inside.

We approached the front desk and I blurted out, "I think . . . I'm in labor."

The receptionist, calm as ever, nodded and quickly called for a wheelchair. Within moments, a nurse appeared, wheeling me into a room as my body trembled from wave after wave of new pressure. They hooked me up to all the monitors, my heart still racing, the steady beeps of the machines a cruel reminder of how real this was.

I lay back on the bed, still trying to wrap my head around it all. *This can't be happening. Please let this be false labor.*

But when the nurse checked me, her words sent a shock through my body. "You're dilated to five centimeters."

"What?" I gasped, tears flowing freely now. *How can I be in labor with my husband 1,500 miles away?* A mix of fear and anger coursed through me.

The air felt sterile and cold, a sharp contrast to the warmth and comfort I had imagined with Devon by my side. *If only he were here to hold my hand.* I gripped the edge of the thin blanket that barely covered me.

I dialed Devon, keeping him on speakerphone as I fought to stay calm. "We're having a baby tonight," I said, my voice shaky.

"Wait, what?" The surprise in his voice was clear, even on the other end of the line on the other side of the country. "Are you serious?"

My voice broke, and I wiped at the tears that had started to fall. "I'm at the hospital, and the nurse says I'm dilated!"

Full of empathy, he said, "I'm so sorry! I wish I could be there to hold your hand and do this together."

"They're giving me an epidural," I managed to say through gritted teeth before handing the phone over to Robyn. Devon stayed on speakerphone, listening to every word.

The epidural offered some relief, but the room still felt too empty without him there. That's when Robyn, ever the cheerleader, came to my side, her smile so wide you'd think we were at a pep rally. She gave my hand a little squeeze, and I couldn't help but crack a smile, despite the pain.

"You've got this!" Her voice bubbled with enthusiasm like she was rallying the crowd at a football game.

I let out a breathy laugh. "You're so ridiculous," I muttered, but her bright spirit was exactly what I needed at that moment.

The nurse instructed me to start pushing, and with each push, Robyn's encouragement never wavered, her voice full of enthusiasm. "You're almost there!" she yelled, as if we were on the field and I was about to score the winning touchdown.

After a couple of strong pushes, our baby boy finally made his entrance into the world. It was the most painful delivery I'd ever experienced—so intense I thought I might pass out—but then there he was, just five pounds and thirteen ounces. So tiny. The room seemed to hold its breath as the nurses whisked him to the warming table.

As I lay there, catching my breath, my eyes followed him. His skin was dark purple, not the healthy pink I had hoped to see.

At that moment, it felt like time stood still.

Why isn't he crying? Panic clutched my heart, the joyful moment quickly turning to fear. I held my breath, waiting for any sign that he was okay.

"Is he okay?" My voice trembled.

The nurses spoke in hushed tones, their expressions grave. I felt a dark cloud of dread settle over me. Then I heard my OB ask, "Is there a heart murmur?"

"No," the nurses replied.

Oh, good. No heart murmur, I thought, but I couldn't shake the gnawing fear in my stomach. Why was I still so scared?

The nurses moved quickly, pumping amniotic fluid from his stomach and trying to get his body temperature up. I watched them closely, my heart racing, but then I noticed something shift. The tension in their faces began to soften, and their movements became less hurried and more controlled.

Slowly, the tightness in my chest began to ease. His skin, which had been so pale and purple, was now turning a soft, healthy pink. I could see the gentle rise and fall of his back as he started breathing more easily.

I took a deep breath, mirroring the steady rhythm of his tiny breaths. The room, once filled with worry, was now quieter, calmer.

Finally, one of the nurses smiled down at me. "He's doing just fine," she said softly. Then, as if this was the moment we'd all been waiting for, she gently placed him on my chest.

The warmth of his tiny body against mine melted away the fear and anxiety I'd been carrying for what felt like forever. I gazed down at his soft blond hair, his round cheeks, and those perfect little fingers. My heart swelled with a love I hadn't known was possible.

The nurse lingered beside me for a moment and asked, "Does he have a name?"

I looked at him lovingly, feeling the overwhelming connection between us. "His name is Jack," I whispered, a smile tugging at the corners of my mouth. We'd decided some time ago.

The nurse smiled and gently stepped away, leaving me to soak in this perfect moment. But as I continued to gaze at him, something felt a little . . . different. I couldn't quite explain it, and I didn't have a word for what I was noticing, so I brushed it off, figuring it was just the haze of being a new mom.

I lifted the phone to my ear, trying to keep my voice steady. "Everything seems okay," I told Devon, hoping the words would reassure us both.

Devon, calm and steady as ever, seemed to believe it too. Throughout the entire delivery, he stayed on speakerphone, listening to every moment. "I'll be there as soon as I can," he promised before we hung up.

Just as I began to relax, the door creaked open and in strolled the pediatrician, surprisingly upbeat for the hour. It was almost midnight. *Do pediatricians always make rounds this late?*

He whistled softly, and his shoes squeaked on the linoleum floor. I couldn't help but be caught off guard by his mood.

"We hear he looks like Blake." He sounded a little too casual. His forced smile didn't quite reach his eyes, and something about the way he avoided my gaze set off an alarm in my head.

My heart sank.

He cleared his throat and shuffled his feet a bit, glancing at his clipboard before looking back up. "I don't know if you overheard the nurses," he began, scratching his chin awkwardly, "but . . . we think he has Down syndrome."

The words hit me like a ton of bricks. My chest tightened, and the room started to spin. I stared at the doctor, frozen, completely unsure of how to respond. Maybe I looked scared. Maybe I looked confused. Either way, he seemed to sense the depth of my silence.

He backpedaled quickly, his voice now filled with hesitation. "Oh, I really shouldn't have said anything. Forget I mentioned it! He probably doesn't. I just . . . I wish I hadn't said anything."

And just like that, he turned on his heel and made a quick exit, the clomps of his footsteps fading down the hall, leaving me in silence and a whirlwind of emotions. I sat there, numb, unable to move or process what had just happened.

How could someone drop news like that and leave? I wanted to chase after him and give him a piece of my mind, but I couldn't, even if I wanted to—I was still numb from the epidural.

I looked up at Robyn, my throat tightening and the tears already welling up in my eyes.

She met my gaze, her hand gripping mine. "It doesn't matter," she said, her voice steady and sure. At that moment, I knew—this was exactly why she needed to be here: to say those words that only she could. It was as if God had orchestrated every detail, making sure she was by my side to remind me of what truly mattered. Her words were exactly what I needed to hear.

I pulled myself together just enough to call Devon, but when his voice came through the phone, I realized I didn't have much to say. My voice trembled and I said, "They think he has Down syndrome . . ."

There was a pause on the other end, and I could almost feel his heart sinking across the miles. "Why do they think that?"

His concern wrapped around me, but I still felt lost. "I don't know." Tears fell down my cheeks. "I just don't know . . ."

After we hung up, the room felt heavier. Robyn sat quietly next to me, neither of us saying a word as our minds raced.

Soon after, my brother-in-law, Curtis, and Devon's dad arrived to give Jack a priesthood blessing. As they laid their hands gently on his head and began to pray, a calmness washed over the room like a soft blanket of peace. Their presence, and the blessing, reminded me that we weren't alone in this. God was aware of us—He always had been.

Curtis smiled at me afterward, his eyes twinkling. "You know," he said, "this kid was born without the misery gene."

Through my tears, I chuckled. It was a tiny flicker of hope in the middle of the storm. Maybe Jack would face life's challenges with joy, and for a moment, I believed that too.

We cried on and off through the night. The room was quiet.

The next morning, we asked our family to pray that Jack didn't have Down syndrome. It seemed like the right thing to pray for—a "normal" life for our son.

But my brother, with his gentle wisdom, said something that stuck with me. "I don't know if we should pray for that. We don't know what blessings might come if he does have it."

His words lingered in my heart, and slowly they added to the glimmer of hope that already existed.

Later that day, the doctor and nurse came in, their demeanor calm but a little more serious. She gently checked Jack's vitals.

The doctor's voice was gentle as he said, "I'm so sorry. The test came back positive for trisomy 21." He paused and then added, "Let me show you some of the physical features we noticed at birth."

Carefully, the doctor lifted Jack's tiny hand, pointing out a single crease running straight across his palm. "This is called a simian crease," he explained gently. "It's one of the markers we often see in babies with Down syndrome, along with his almond-shaped eyes and lower muscle tone." He paused, offering a reassuring smile. "I've also checked his heart, and there's good news—about fifty percent of children with Down syndrome have heart problems, but Jack's heart is strong, with no murmurs. He's off to a good start."

I stared at Jack's little hand, trying to absorb what he was saying. The crease, the shape of his eyes, the softness of his body—it was all right there in front of me, and yet part of me still wanted to deny it.

"I know it's a lot to take in," the nurse continued, her voice soothing. "But it's important to remember that Jack is just like any other baby. He'll need a little extra care, but he's strong. And so are you."

I nodded, feeling the lump in my throat grow. Jack stirred in my arms, his tiny face so peaceful despite everything. Looking at him, I still couldn't wrap my mind around it—how something so perfect, so beautiful, could feel so overwhelming.

As I held him close, I couldn't help but remember that thing Devon had told me years ago before he went on his mission, when he'd just gotten his patriarchal blessing. "It's not in my blessing, but I had a really strong impression—that someday, I might have a child born with special needs."

I didn't think much of it at the time. I mean, how could I? But at this moment, it hit me like a ton of bricks. *God knew. He always knew.*

Then I thought about my patriarchal blessing. It talked about living a life of service and love. I remember thinking, *Well, duh. Isn't that what moms do?* But now, looking down at Jack, I realized it was more than I had imagined. This was what my blessing had meant all along. It wasn't just about being a mom; it was about embracing a path that was bigger than me—one that would challenge and change me in ways I hadn't even begun to understand.

The next morning, while I was still trying to process everything, Devon was halfway across the country, in Chicago, arriving at work. He had barely slept and couldn't focus on anything else. As he walked into his office, standing in front of his brand-new boss, the words tumbled out before he could stop them. "My wife had the baby. They think he has Down syndrome."

His boss didn't hesitate. "Go home," she said, her voice firm but understanding. "We'll figure things out here. Go be with your family."

When he finally walked through the hospital door, it felt like time stopped.

I looked up from my bed, and the sight of him standing there, his eyes filled with both exhaustion and relief, made the floodgates open. The tears I had been holding in all day came rushing out.

He dropped his bags and crossed the room in just a few strides, pulling me into his arms as he sat down on the bed next to me. "I'm here," he whispered, pressing his forehead against mine, his voice thick with emotion. "I'm so sorry I wasn't here sooner."

I shook my head, tears still streaming down my face. "You're here now," I said, my voice barely above a breath. "That's all that matters."

For a while, we just sat there, the two of us, holding each other and our new little bundle. Devon gently kissed the top of Jack's head as we took turns admiring him, counting his tiny fingers and toes. Jack was so small, so fragile, but he had this undeniable strength about him. We both saw it.

Devon gently stroked Jack's cheek. "He came to the right family. We're going to love him so much." There was such certainty in his voice.

Taylor, Luke, and Blake were more excited than ever to meet their new little brother. The moment we arrived home from the hospital, they swarmed around us, eager to smother Jack with love, cuddles, and kisses.

Taylor, our oldest, bent down with a proud grin, her hair brushing his cheeks, making him squirm. "He's so tiny, Mom!"

Luke stared wide-eyed. "Can he play cars with me when he's bigger?"

Blake leaned in close, touching Jack's cheek with his chubby hand, and declared, "I'm gonna teach him how to be a Transformer like me!"

Devon watched the scene unfold with that familiar, dashing smile, then scooped each of the kids up into his big daddy bear hug. "I love you guys so much," he said, his voice full of warmth.

The kids giggled and wriggled in his embrace, their laughter filling the room. But behind his smile, I could see the burden he carried, knowing he had to leave for Chicago again so soon. He only had a couple of days with us in Cedar City before heading back to finish his training.

Jack hadn't been eating well in the hospital, which had concerned the nurses, but they discharged us anyway. We were eager to get home, to settle in, and I convinced myself things would improve once we were home.

Something in the pit of my stomach wouldn't settle. I'd sit on the couch, cradling Jack, trying to get him to latch and eat, but he struggled. The house was too quiet, and every little sound from Jack made me feel like the walls were closing in.

Later, as Devon packed his bag to head back to Chicago, the thought of him leaving again made my chest ache with sadness. He kissed me gently, then leaned down to kiss Jack's tiny forehead, his hand lingering on his little head as if he didn't want to let go. Devon then gave Taylor, Luke, and Blake a big hug, a squeeze, and a reminder to be good while he was away.

"I love you guys so much." His voice was full of emotion. "Take care of Mom, okay?"

They nodded, hugging him back, unaware of how hard it was for him to go.

With one last look at all of us, Devon walked to the door. "I'll be back before you know it." His gaze lingered as if he didn't want to leave.

I kept my gaze on him as he stepped out, the door closing behind him, and was already counting down the days until he'd be home again.

The following Friday, we sat in the pediatrician's office, the scale telling us what my heart already knew—Jack wasn't gaining weight. Just two weeks after his birth, he was down a pound, weighing four pounds, thirteen ounces. That might not sound like much, but when you're a newborn that tiny, it's the equivalent of an adult losing a sixth of their body weight in just a couple of days.

As I glanced down at Jack, bundled up in his little blanket, I felt a wave of fear wash over me.

The pediatrician, however, didn't share my concern. "It's normal for newborns," he said, his tone casual as he typed notes into the computer. "Babies lose weight in the first few days. Just fortify his breast milk with formula. He'll bounce back."

But I wasn't entirely convinced. How could he not see what I was seeing? Jack wasn't just losing a little weight—he was slipping away right in front of me. Every feeding felt like an uphill battle, and I could see the effort it took for him to even try. Still, I reminded myself that doctors are trained to know what to do. I trusted him—he had years of experience, and surely he'd know if something was seriously wrong.

So we left the office with no real answers, only a gnawing sense of dread that I couldn't shake. Despite what the doctor said, deep down I knew my gut was telling me something was wrong.

By Sunday night, exactly two weeks after Jack's birth, my fear had only grown. His feedings hadn't improved; he couldn't keep anything down, and he was becoming lethargic. I was exhausted from trying to feed him around the clock, and every failed attempt felt like another piece of hope slipping away.

That night, after another unsuccessful feeding, I called the pediatrician again, desperate for someone to listen. "Something's wrong." My voice shook with fear and frustration.

The doctor, still calm and unconcerned, brushed me off. "If it'll make you feel better, take him to the ER."

That was all I needed to hear.

My mom was already on her feet before I could even process what was happening. "We're going," she said firmly, grabbing her coat with determined urgency. There was no hesitation, no second-guessing. We both knew this wasn't just a case of new-mom jitters—Jack needed help, and he needed it now.

Helen, Devon's mom, stayed behind to take care of the kids, who were completely oblivious to the seriousness of the situation. All they knew was that they had a cute, brand-new baby brother. Before I walked out the door, I bent down to give each of them a quick hug and kiss goodbye.

"Listen to Grandma," I said gently, brushing the hair out of Taylor's face. "And make sure you go to bed when she says, okay?"

They nodded, distracted by their play. Taylor was busy with her dolls, Luke was still glued to the TV, and Blake was stomping around the living room, pretending to be a Transformer, his little voice making robot sounds as he crashed his toys together.

The house hummed with the sound of their innocent joy, a stark contrast to the storm of emotions swirling inside me. As I bundled Jack into his car seat, my hands shook. My mom gave me a reassuring nod, her calm presence keeping me grounded as we hurried out the door and headed to the emergency room.

On our way to the hospital, the same one where I had delivered just two weeks earlier, the drive felt like it stretched on forever. My mom and I sat in silence, both too stressed to speak. The darkness outside seemed to press in, mirroring the tension I felt inside. Every bump in the road made my worry worse, and I gripped the edge of my seat, trying to stay calm.

I could hear my mom exhaling quietly next to me, her hands gripping the steering wheel tightly. The streetlights passed in a blur, casting brief, flickering shadows across our faces. I stared out the window, watching them flash by one after the other until my vision blurred with the tears I was struggling to hold back.

When we finally pulled up to the hospital, the bright lights of the ER felt jarring against the dark sky. The doors slid open, and a rush of cold air hit my face as we walked in. The scent of disinfectant filled the room, sterile and sharp. The quiet hum of machines in the distance made the whole place feel even more impersonal. A nurse greeted us at the front desk, her calm demeanor almost unsettling against the whirlwind of panic swirling inside me.

Her voice was soft and steady as she asked, "How can we help you?"

But all I could think about was Jack—small, fragile, and in need of something, though I wasn't sure what. Helplessness gnawed at me, and I could barely breathe as they led us back to one of the small, sterile rooms. The fluorescent lights above buzzed softly, making the room feel even colder.

A nurse greeted us as we entered. She glanced at Jack, her expression indifferent. "He doesn't look dehydrated," she said as if she were commenting on the weather. "But we'll run some tests to be sure."

Her calm response didn't match the tension building inside me.

I stood there, holding Jack close, trying to keep my voice steady as I answered her questions. But inside I was screaming. How could they not see what I saw? How could they not feel the urgency I felt in my bones?

My mom placed a hand on my shoulder, her presence a quiet reminder that I wasn't alone. "Don't worry. They're going to get him the help he needs," she said, her voice filled with determination.

And with that, we were admitted and taken to a room where they hooked Jack up to monitors and started running tests. I sat beside him, watching his tiny chest rise and fall, praying with everything I had that they'd figure out what was wrong—and that it wasn't too late.

That night, things took a turn for the worse. Jack's oxygen levels dropped, and the nurse quickly put him on oxygen.

"Has anyone mentioned seeing a specialist?" she asked, her voice gentle, but the question hit me like a punch to the gut.

I shook my head, a lump forming in my throat. "No . . . should they have?"

She didn't say anything more—just adjusted the oxygen to make sure Jack was stable.

I watched my baby fight through the night, eating very little and vomiting even more. The hours dragged on, and they were heavy with exhaustion and fear.

But the next morning, something shifted. As they wheeled us down for an upper GI test, I felt a flicker of hope. The hallways were bright, and for the first time in days, it felt like maybe things would finally start to change for the better. I fed Jack a bottle of contrast, hoping for good news, but as soon as the liquid hit his stomach, he vomited—this time, a sickly green.

The nurse assisting looked startled. The radiologist, however, nodded as if everything suddenly made sense. "Yep, it's definitely pyloric stenosis."

Not long after, a transport tech showed up. "We're transferring him to Salt Lake City for surgery."

I looked at my mom, trying to keep it together. She met my gaze, voice steady. "I'll go home, pack you a bag, and meet you there."

Before I knew it, we were in the ambulance headed four hours north. The drive felt endless and was filled with uncertainty.

The song "Temporary Home" by Carrie Underwood came on the radio, and the lyrics seemed to echo my thoughts. *This is just a stop,* I told myself. *Jack's going to be okay.*

We finally pulled up to the hospital, and as they gently carried Jack inside, I followed close behind, praying we were finally going to get some answers.

I had never seen a more beautiful sight than Primary Children's Hospital, known for its world-class care and compassionate staff. It was a place where miracles seemed to happen every day, and in that moment, I knew we were exactly where we were supposed to be.

The nurse immediately looked Jack over. She gently rubbed his head and frowned. "This baby is severely dehydrated," she said, noticing his sunken fontanel and how weak he seemed. Finally, someone saw what I did.

I felt my stomach tighten as I watched her work. "What's going on with him?"

She didn't say much—just continued her evaluation and made some notes before stepping out to get more supplies.

Seeing Jack with all the tubes was hard, but there was a small sense of relief knowing we were finally on the right path.

Later that afternoon, the surgeon came in. He stood beside Jack's crib and said, "Tell me what you've been told."

I went over everything.

The surgeon shook his head, his expression serious. "It's not pyloric stenosis. The problem is that his stomach isn't attached to his intestines, so he hasn't been able to digest anything for two weeks. He's been starving."

I gasped, my hand flying to my mouth as his words sank in. "Two weeks?" I echoed, my voice trembling. "He's been starving for two weeks?"

The shock hit me like a wave.

The surgeon nodded. "Yes. We need to get him hydrated before we can do the surgery, but we're confident he'll be fine."

I felt a wave of exhaustion mixed with relief. "How long will we be here?" I asked. "My husband's in Chicago, and I have three other kids at home."

"Plan for at least six weeks," he said.

After he left, I called Devon and filled him in.

"I know," I said, trying to keep my voice steady. "But we'll get through this."

After hanging up, I looked at Jack and finally let the tears fall. We were finally in the right place, but the road ahead still felt long.

* * *

It was late afternoon, and the Wasatch Mountains framed the window like a painting, their peaks glowing in the fading sunlight. The room was quiet except for the rhythmic beeping of machines and the soft murmur of nurses as they finished settling Jack into his bed. I stood beside him, brushing my fingers over his tiny hand, and a calmness washed over me as if invisible hands were holding us both. It was more than just the peace of the room.

My mom stood beside me, her hand resting on my shoulder. She'd arrived a few hours before. "You're not doing this alone. Angels are here, lifting you up."

I nodded, tears welling in my eyes, but my heart felt lighter. "I can feel them—like we're being carried through this."

It wasn't just the heavenly angels I sensed; our earthly angels were there too. Friends and family came in waves over the next few days, each bringing their love, their prayers, and their tears. They held Jack, kissed his forehead, and offered words of comfort. Each visit was a reminder that we weren't walking this path by ourselves.

Soon it was surgery day.

The nurse wheeled Jack's bed down the hall, and I kissed his tiny forehead. "You've got this, buddy." I tried to keep the tears back.

In the waiting room, the hours crawled by. The phone rang with updates—he was doing well, and everything was going as planned— but I couldn't relax. Not until it was over.

Finally, the surgeon came out, calm and collected, and sat beside us. He pulled out a sheet of paper and began sketching a quick diagram, showing how they had fixed Jack. "It all went smoothly." He gave us a reassuring smile. "He did great."

I felt a huge wave of relief. "Thank you." I tried not to cry.

"He's a brave one," the surgeon said with a smile.

As I watched Jack rest, something stirred inside me—something I hadn't fully realized before. I never knew I was capable of so much strength. But this is what faith does. It increases our understanding of God and His plan for us. It gives us a sense of hope during trying times and lifts us. When we don't feel we have the strength to carry on by ourselves, He carries us.

And when we look for Him, we will see Him. Even in the tiniest of details in our lives. I could see His hand in all of this—in Jack's strength, in the timing of the nurses, in the comforting presence of my family. He was there.

I looked down at Jack, feeling that flicker of bravery rise in me again. I squeezed his tiny hand and offered a silent prayer of thanks. Jack was brave, and I knew I would be too. Whatever came next, we'd face it together, knowing we weren't alone.

* * *

Recovery was long, and one night, everything came crashing down. Six weeks after the surgery, I was alone in Jack's room, sitting in that lumpy chair and staring at him, when I finally broke.

The tears came suddenly, without warning, and once they started, they wouldn't stop. I burst into sobs, my whole body trembling from everything I'd been carrying. I cried harder than I had in years, gasping for breath between the sobs that shook me to my core.

The nurse came in with her usual updates, but I shook my head. "I'm having a moment," I murmured, my voice so weak it hardly sounded like mine. She nodded and quietly stepped out of the room.

That was the day I finally let it all out—the hopelessness, the frustration, the fear. I sobbed until I thought I couldn't cry anymore, my chest heaving from the effort. The exhaustion, the constant worry—it all poured out, wave after wave, and I didn't know if I could stop it.

I cried until I had no tears left, my body slumped in the chair. And then, just when I thought I couldn't take any more, the door creaked open. The surgeon stepped in, his face serious but calm.

He sat beside me, his presence instantly calming. Though he was just a doctor, there was something different about him—he was an older man who radiated compassion.

His eyes, filled with sincere concern and love, made me feel as though I wasn't just another patient. Looking back, it reminds me of the Savior coming to His disciples during the fourth watch—when all hope seemed lost, He came to rescue them. And in that moment, it felt like this surgeon was doing the same for me. His calming presence, full of compassion and peace, was exactly what I needed.

"I've been waiting for this." His voice was calm and steady.

"Waiting for what?" I asked, wiping at my tear-streaked face.

"For you to break down," he said gently, a smile on his face. "It's okay. You've been carrying so much. But let me do the worrying now. Jack's going to be fine."

Something in his words struck me deeply. It wasn't just about Jack's surgery—it was about letting go of the burden I'd been holding on to so tightly. I wasn't alone.

"I prayed before the surgery," he continued, his voice steady with conviction. "And I know everything is going to be okay."

Hearing those words from him—a man of faith—brought a wave of reassurance. It wasn't just the skill of his hands but the faith behind them that gave me hope.

I blinked, the tears threatening to blur my vision, but instead of letting them fall, I leaped from my chair across from his and gave him a big hug. "Thank you," I said.

The next day, when I called the kids, a small sense of relief settled over me. We giggled and talked, and I even sang Blake his favorite Transformers song. For the first time in a while, things felt a little lighter. We weren't out of the woods yet, but we were closer.

This journey had been one of bravery—not just for Jack, but for all of us. There were times I doubted how we'd make it, but God was always there, in the smallest details, giving us glimmers of hope—in Devon's reassuring voice, the surgeon's steady hands, and the peace that reminded me we weren't alone. We had faced each step with courage, and with His guidance, we'd keep moving forward.

A Dance to Remember

We were home. After eight long weeks in the hospital that felt like forever, we were finally under one roof again. Devon had finished his training, and we'd made the move to Salt Lake City from Cedar City. The drive had been exhausting, but the relief of being together as a family made it all worthwhile.

Jack was out of the hospital, and Taylor, Luke, and Blake were buzzing with excitement, ready to smother their baby brother with love.

Taylor, ever the little caretaker, was the first to hold Jack and gently whisper soft words as she rocked him.

Luke sat next to them, telling Jack the silliest stories, watching closely for that sweet smile they all loved.

Blake, who just weeks ago had been the baby of the family, now looked like a giant next to his new little brother, his eyes wide with wonder. The three of them fussed over Jack as if he were the greatest thing they'd ever seen.

The house felt cozy as the kids played nearby, their laughter bouncing off the walls. Jack rested in my arms, his tiny chest rising and falling with each peaceful breath. I should've felt complete and relieved now that we were all together under one roof. But there was still a sense of unease I couldn't shake, like a shadow lingering in the corners of my mind, reminding me that even at this moment—when everything should've felt perfect—something was still off.

Devon, noticing my silence, sat down beside me. He didn't say anything at first—just reached over and gently brushed a strand of hair from my face. "You look like you're carrying the world on your shoulders," he said softly, his hand warm on my shoulder. "What's really going on?"

The tenderness in his voice broke through the wall I'd been building, and I felt my eyes sting. I took a shaky breath, finally letting the words tumble out. "I know," I began, my voice trembling. "But it feels like I should have it all figured out by now. Jack's going to need so much, and I don't know if I'm enough for him."

Devon wrapped his arm around me, pulling me closer. I sank further into the couch, the reality of it all pressing in. His blue eyes, full of love and concern, searched mine, and as always, he seemed to know exactly what to say when I felt overwhelmed.

"You are enough." His words were steady as he squeezed my hand. "You don't have to have all the answers today. We'll figure it out together, day by day. That's all we can do."

I wiped my eyes, but the frustration and tears wouldn't stop. "I keep thinking about all the things I have to learn—therapy, specialists, treatments. It just feels like a lot. I don't even know where to start."

"You don't have to do it all at once." Devon brushed my hair away from my eyes and looked deeply into them. "We're going to take it one step at a time. Nobody expects you to know everything right now."

I nodded, trying to let his words sink in. "I just want to be the mom he needs."

"You already are," he said, his voice firm yet full of love. "And whatever comes next, we'll face it together."

* * *

The days passed, but a lingering cloud of depression hung over me. One evening, after putting Jack to bed, I slumped onto the couch next to Devon and sighed. "I wish I could just see into the future. If I could have one little glimpse of what Jack's life is going to be like, then I'd know everything will be okay."

Devon thought for a moment, then he smiled and said, "Let's see if we can find that glimpse."

We sat together, scrolling through YouTube, when we stumbled on a video of a teenager with Down syndrome. The title caught our attention: "A Day in the Life of a Senior with Down Syndrome."

We clicked on it, and what we saw filled us with wonder. The boy made his own breakfast, rode his bike to the YMCA, and went about his day with confidence and joy.

We watched in amazement. When the video ended, Devon turned to me. "That's it," he said. "That's the glimpse you needed."

I nodded, tears welling up in my eyes. It was exactly what I had been longing for—hope for Jack's future. Watching that boy live his life brought a sense of peace I hadn't felt in weeks. It was as if God had created that video just for me to see a glimpse of the possibilities ahead. Maybe everything really would be okay.

A few days later, as we sat together at the kitchen table, Devon glanced at me, tapping his lips with the tip of his index finger. "You know, God usually works through people and experiences to help us. Maybe teaching Zumba again could be His way of helping you through this."

I blinked, surprised. "Zumba? Now?"

"I think you need something that brings you joy—something for you," he said, repeating the words he had used in times past.

I hadn't thought about it in months. Teaching had been my outlet, but with everything going on, I'd let it go. "I don't know how—"

"You light up when you teach," he gently cut me off, not wanting me to finish my self-defeating thoughts. "I really think this is what you need to feel like yourself again."

A small smile tugged at my lips. "I think you're right."

Finding a new gym felt overwhelming, but Devon wasn't one to let anything slow him down. Always the supportive and encouraging one, he'd been quietly following his own promptings on how to help me out of the slump I'd been in for weeks.

One evening, as I stirred a pot of spaghetti, the smell of garlic filling the kitchen, Devon walked in, his face lit up with a grin. "I found a gym that's looking for a Zumba instructor!" he announced, almost bouncing with excitement. "I gave them your name, and they want you to come in for an interview."

I blinked, staring at him for a second. "You did what?"

"You've got this!" He beamed, undeterred. "I just know it's exactly what you need. And I'll help with the kids, the dishes, whatever it takes. You've got to give it a shot."

Gratitude swelled in my chest. Devon always knew just how to nudge me in the right direction.

I froze mid-stir, excitement and nervousness bubbling up inside me. "Are you serious?"

Enthusiastically, he said, "Yes! They're going to love you."

The following week, I stepped into the gym, nerves fluttering inside me. But the moment the music started, it was as if the old me came rushing back. The bass thumped, my body moved, and all the worries I'd been carrying seemed to melt away. It was as if the dark cloud that had hung over my head for so long finally dissipated. By the end of class, I felt lighter and freer, like I'd once again rediscovered a piece of myself that had been lost.

When I walked through the door that evening, Devon was waiting. "How was it?"

I grinned. "Amazing! I didn't realize how much I needed this."

As my classes grew in popularity, the recognition started pouring in. The pinnacle of it all was when I was featured in *Zumba* magazine. It was the highest honor I could've imagined. Seeing my name in print was surreal, but even more humbling was the fact that this wasn't just about me—it was about the community we had built together in those classes.

People weren't just coming for the workout anymore; they were coming for the connection, the friendships, and the support system we'd built together. And it wasn't just my students who were feeling it—I was too.

Brittany, the group fitness assistant, told the reporter, "Kim's classes easily bring in fifty people each week, which is incredible. But it's more than that. Her energy is contagious—you just want to be around her."

And it was true. There was an energy in the room—an unspoken bond between all of us. Zumba wasn't just exercise anymore; it was therapy, it was community, it was healing.

"I've been teaching fitness for a while," I'd shared with the journalist, "but I've never seen anything like what's happened with Zumba. People come up to me and say, 'I was going through a divorce,' or 'I lost my mom,' or 'I was having a really hard time,' and they tell me how much the class has helped them. It's the most rewarding feeling."

Kristen, one of my longtime students and a dear friend, summed it up perfectly: "Kim's class isn't like anything else. You walk in feeling stressed or heavy, but by the time you leave, it's like you've found your strength again."

And it wasn't just the students. *I* was finding strength too. Teaching Zumba had become a part of my life in ways I never anticipated. Every time I walked into that room, I knew it was exactly where I was supposed to be. God had led me here—He knew what I needed, just as He knew what my students needed.

"I wouldn't go to anyone else's class," Leesa told the reporter. "Kim is the best out there, hands down."

It was humbling to be recognized as one of the top recognized Zumba instructors. We weren't just dancing. We were living proof that God was in the details, guiding us through the tough times and bringing us to places we never thought we'd be.

* * *

As Jack grew, his joy for life was contagious. His personality was larger than life, and people were drawn to him. Everywhere we went, people would ask, "Where's Jack?"

One afternoon, Jack sat at the kitchen table, grinning from ear to ear. "Jack, where's your favorite place to go?" I asked.

Without missing a beat, he nodded, flashing an irresistible grin just like his dad's. "The fast car! I go with Luke!"

Luke had been begging for a car for years, and when he unwrapped that 1993 Nissan 300zx on Christmas morning, it was like watching a dream come true.

But for Jack, it was more than just a car—it became an adventure. From the moment he saw it, he called it "the fast car."

And that car became Luke and Jack's thing. Every time Luke started the engine, Jack's excitement would bubble over. They'd roll down the windows, laughing all the way to 7-Eleven for a Slurpee, Jack belting out his favorite songs as if he were putting on a concert for Luke.

It wasn't just a car ride. It was everything Jack loved rolled into one moment: music, laughter, and the pure joy of being with his brother.

As I watched them drive off one afternoon, Jack shouting "See ya, suckers!" out the window, I thought, *I want to be more like him.*

Jack doesn't hold back his joy or dim his light. He's himself, and it's something I admire deeply.

Every time I see him, I'm reminded to let go of my fears and just be myself—because that's what Jack does. His carefree spirit carries into every moment with Luke. They'd take off in the fast car, returning with matching Slurpee mustaches, teasing each other the whole way. Those moments healed us all. Jack had a way of making life lighter, funnier, and better.

As time passed and the older kids moved out, it got harder for Jack. His sister, Taylor, had been the first to leave for college, and though he missed her, it was when Luke left for BYU that it really hit him hard.

On a beautiful fall afternoon, we were out on the back patio. Jack stood by the hoop, tossing basketballs while his iPad blasted his favorite song, "Born to Be Brave," for all the neighbors to hear.

Listening to the song and watching him play, I realized just how fitting that song was for him: "Born to Be Brave." Jack didn't just sing it—he *lived* it. Through all the challenges, through everything life had thrown his way, he faced it with more bravery than anyone I knew. And here he was, still teaching me what it meant to be brave, even when life felt uncertain and even when things weren't how we planned.

Jack tossed another basketball and out of nowhere said, "I miss Luke."

I walked over to him, wrapped my arms around him, and pulled him close.

"I know, buddy. He'll be home to visit soon."

Jack loves his people fiercely, and change is hard for him. One way we coped was by documenting the moments when his siblings returned home. Jack loves to rewatch these videos, and it's fun to share them with family and friends on social media.

We started a little tradition of capturing Jack's reactions whenever his siblings came home. It became something special for all of us.

Then one day, out of nowhere, Luke decided to surprise him.

It was late in the evening, cold and dark, but I heard his car pulling up in front of the house. The roar of the engine couldn't be missed, and it only meant one thing—Luke was home.

I quickly grabbed my phone, knowing exactly what was about to happen.

Jack stood on the front porch, wearing his pajamas, and despite the cold, he couldn't be bothered to put on a coat. His breath fogged up in the chilly air, but the excitement in his eyes made him forget about the temperature.

I pointed the camera toward Jack just as he realized who was pulling up.

"Lukey-boo!" Jack shouted, his smile as big as ever. But instead of running to him, he waited patiently on the porch, watching as Luke unloaded his things from the car.

When Luke finally made his way up the steps, Jack greeted him with his trademark grin.

"You home now . . . you done with college?" Jack's voice filled with joy.

Luke smiled, pulling Jack in for the biggest hug. "Not yet, buddy!"

That video went viral—3 million views!

My shock grew as the numbers continued to grow over the following days and weeks. It was like the world had suddenly discovered the magic Jack brought into our lives. But this wasn't just about one moment—it was an opportunity to bring awareness to the Down syndrome community. So I took it and ran with it.

I discovered I had a knack for creating videos—sharing our family, our faith, and our lives with Jack. Whether Jack was hopping on the bus with his bright smile or we were dancing around the living room, people connected with it. It felt natural, like God had placed this opportunity in my lap.

One evening, Devon and I sat on our couch, scrolling through the comments.

"Listen to this," Devon said. "'I was having a bad day, and this video turned it around.'"

I smiled. "And here's another: 'This is so heartwarming and wholesome.'"

"It's amazing, isn't it?" Devon said, shaking his head. "You're reaching millions with Jack's joy."

I nodded. "People are connecting with our family in ways I never imagined."

The videos weren't just about Jack anymore. I even shared my love for dance, doing routines with my sister or with Jack, and people loved it. Every post felt like a new way to show the world the joy in our home.

"You've created something special," Devon said. "Not everyone can say they've made viral video after viral video."

The opportunities were beyond anything I had imagined—interviews with WFLA, KSL, *Newsweek*, and *People* magazine. Even Chris Pratt shared one of our videos! I was invited to speak at conferences, collaborate on books, and appear on podcasts. It was like stepping into a whole new chapter.

"I never thought our story would reach so many people." I shook my head.

"And you're showing them that life with faith and love can make all the difference," Devon added.

People noticed the light in our home as we shared how our faith carried us through tough moments. The messages from people reconnecting with their own beliefs or finding hope through our story were incredible.

"It feels like this was meant to be," I said.

* * *

Two years later, with 350 million views across my social media platforms, I sat waiting to speak at the Utah Down Syndrome Foundation conference. My thoughts drifted back to those first few days in the hospital—how scared I had been and how uncertain everything felt. Devon had been there, steady as always, knowing exactly what to say, even when I felt completely lost. And now here I was, in a room full of new parents, each holding their own babies, who were feeling the same mix of love and fear I had once known so well.

As I looked around the room, it reminded me of another moment years ago, standing in the lunch line at thirteen years old, when someone questioned my faith. I remembered how small I had felt, wondering if I had the courage to be different. Back then, I had no idea where life would take me or how that quiet bravery would shape my future. But just like that day, I learned that bravery isn't always loud. It's often subtle but no less powerful. And in that moment, I realized how much God had prepared me, even from that young age, for what was happening now.

It was humbling to reflect on how far we'd come—how one viral video had led to something so much bigger, touching the lives of millions, bringing awareness, hope, and faith to others in ways I'd never imagined.

But something had changed in me over those years. I had grown. The fear that had once gripped me had been replaced with a deep sense of faith and purpose. And as I stood up to speak, I realized that it wasn't just Jack's story that had brought me here. It was my story too.

Jack's light was undeniable, yes. His joy, his love, and his ability to connect with people had touched millions. But none of this would have happened if I hadn't found the courage to share our lives with the world. I decided to show up on social media every day, to give our followers an honest look into what it was like raising a child with Down syndrome. It was my creativity, my talents, and, yes, my faith that made it all possible.

As I spoke to the room full of parents, I could see their eyes—some were filled with tears, others with hope—and I knew I had something valuable to offer them. I had been in their shoes, wondering how I would balance it all. I had questioned whether I could be a good mom and a faithful wife and still find time for myself and for my career. But the answer had always been clear—God was in the details. He had been there every step of the way, guiding me, strengthening me, and showing me that I didn't have to do it alone.

Faith has always been the cornerstone of our lives. It's the reason Devon and I have weathered every storm together, from the early days of marriage to the challenges of raising a child with special needs. But faith isn't just about surviving the hard times—it's about thriving. It's about using the gifts God has given me, both as a mother and as a professional, knowing that I could do both.

I spoke to the audience about the power of prayer and how it had carried me through the darkest moments. "There were nights when I didn't know how I was going to get through it," I told them, my voice steady, "but I knelt and prayed. And every time, I was reminded that I wasn't alone. God was there, and He still is."

After my speech, parents came up to me, one by one, with their babies in their arms, thanking me for giving them hope. I held their little ones, feeling the same mix of emotions I had felt when Jack was born. But this time, there was no fear—just peace.

Devon was waiting for me after the talk, his eyes full of pride. "You did great." He wrapped his arms around me.

I smiled, feeling the warmth of his support just as I always had. "Thanks. I just . . . I can't believe how far we've come."

"None of this would have happened without you." His tone was soft but full of conviction. "You're the one who had the courage to share our lives—to show people what it's like to raise a family with faith. You're the one who made this all possible."

I looked at him, my heart full. "We did it together," I said, resting my head against his shoulder.

And it was true. We had built this life together—through prayer, through love, through the everyday moments of raising a family and trusting in God's plan. I had learned that I could be a faithful member of the Church and still pursue my dreams, still have a career, and still be the mom and wife my family needed.

As we drove home that evening, I glanced in the rearview mirror, watching Jack's reflection as he sang along to his favorite songs. His laughter filled the car, and I smiled, knowing that the journey wasn't over. There would be more challenges and more moments of doubt. But there would also be joy. And as long as we had each other—and our faith—we would be just fine.

Because that's what life is really about. It's about showing up every day, trusting that God is in the details, and knowing that no matter what comes next, we were all born to be brave.

5

GANEL-LYN CONDIE
The Mental Health Educator

WALKING WITH JESUS

"You should die."

"Go back to the mental hospital where you belong."

"Who's your drug dealer?"

Hard to believe these comments all started with a simple dance.

It wasn't a big deal. Or so I thought.

On a normal afternoon in early spring of 2024, I was listening to my current favorite praise music, "Walk with Jesus" by the band Consumed by Fire. I'm not a professional dancer—but oh, you should have seen me that day. "Walk with Jesus" is one of those tunes that just consumes your thoughts and *makes* you dance. And not just dance, but clap and sing along too, because you're *consumed by the fire* of music and spirit.

That's exactly what I was doing, regardless of my dance skills. And I was filled with inexpressible joy.

Before I knew it, I decided that I needed to share that joy—not just with my little dog, Ruby Jane, but with the world.

There I was, dressed in a basic beige tracksuit. And just like that, I pressed "record" on my phone. I then proceeded to dance, moon walk, and sing my way through the first verse of the song. As I did, I felt authentic love for Jesus Christ. I was energized by the pure happiness I felt.

Some people would have tried three or four versions, or even more, all in a quest for the perfect video. Not me. I watched that first version once, then I posted it on Instagram Reels. After all, I like showing up as the real me. Over the past decade, I have valued and learned the power of imperfectly and authentically sharing myself through writing books, hosting podcasts, speaking, and doing media. Sharing the real me is sometimes high-risk but with high reward when you connect with that one viewer or reader. And of course, with the good always comes a handful of hate.

But little did I know what would happen this time.

I never could have predicted it. In fact, I never would have believed it. Neither would you.

A few days after I posted my little "dancing with Jesus" video, the feedback came pouring in. It wouldn't be too dramatic to say it was an explosion. And I wouldn't be exaggerating to say it was pretty hateful.

No. It was horrific.

"Middle-aged Christians are what's wrong with the world."

"I hate you. I hate Jesus."

"You should kill yourself."

Comments about mental health and killing myself wounded me especially deep because my much-loved younger sister Meggan had, indeed, died by suicide eleven years earlier.

Those kinds of comments were horrifying enough. But then the cruelty leaped from me to the Savior. You read that right: I was being inundated with hateful comments, reshares, and DMs about God and people of faith in general. I was reading purely evil attacks on everything from Jesus and Christmas to middle-aged women and my faith.

And attacks, too many to count, directed at me.

I was stunned. All it took was me, a nondescript tracksuit, and an amateur recording on my cell phone to summon up a deluge of the vilest comments imaginable.

I'm not talking just a few repulsive comments. They came pouring in by the *hundreds of thousands.* I'd never in eleven years tried to turn off, block, or delete comments, but I did then—though that didn't slow them down.

Online abusers found other ways to spew their vitriol. I was continually told to die, that I was on crack, that I was delusional, and that Jesus wasn't real.

Maybe at this point in my career, I should have had pretty thick skin—should've been able to just shake off the crazy criticism. And I tried to at some level. But underneath it all, I was scratching my head in shock.

I wondered, with all the really interesting—and often inane—content found online, why was my little Jesus video inciting so much negativity? Why was this dumb little slapdash video reaching millions of people? *Millions of people.* Millions of enraged, furious, livid people who didn't hold back with their contemptible comments. And there seemed to be only a handful of supporters.

Of all the positive content I had produced—books, interviews, videos, and otherwise—how had *this* garnered so much attention?

Some content creators tried to reassure me that this kind of viral interest, even when it's negative, is ultimately good for a platform. But it didn't feel good. Sometimes it felt scary, constantly confusing, and persistently mysterious. It was bullying at a viral level. I started to question whether the good I was trying to share in the world even helped. Maybe the bad had finally won out?

I have tried to show up authentically and share vulnerably over the years. I'm sometimes the only "Mormon" that people follow on social media, so talking openly about my specific beliefs and practices has been of great value to me.

I post on hard days, good days, and everything in between. I don't have a problem looking foolish, showing up without make-up, and being real—or dancing around in a beige tracksuit. I have shared my journey of infertility, job loss, mothering, lupus struggles, and grief, opening up about private and personal parts of my life. I have posted and written extensively about the juncture of faith and mental health. It's about inspiring just one desperate person to hold on to hope. No one has forced me to show up in the world this way. I believe that one of the main reasons I'm on the earth is to write books, speak, and share my perspectives. It feels like my mission, and it gives me purpose.

It's my "why."

One day, my husband came home from work and found me sitting in my home office. My heart raced as I scrolled through more viral hate and cruel direct messages. I barely noticed him come in.

With a perplexed expression, he asked, "What's wrong? You look pale."

Continuing to scroll, I just kept saying, "I don't understand why. Why is this making everyone *so* angry?"

I kept asking why. I felt like I was in *The Truman Show* where everyone seemed to know something I didn't know. My husband has always been supportive of my work, but he doesn't fully understand the space of content creation, social media, and trolls.

He sat on my desk and took my hand, and that small touch finally pulled my gaze from my phone. "I'm sorry this is happening to you."

I put my head down, tears filling my eyes. He squeezed my hand, giving me the comfort that only the touch from my best friend could offer—without any words. I knew he had my back, and that meant the world to me.

"I'll be okay," I sniffled.

He grabbed a tissue from the bathroom and handed it to me. "I know you will," he said, giving me space but staying close by. When I'm upset, I sometimes don't want to be touched but also don't want to be left totally alone.

Rob wrestled with what to say. "I know you're wondering if what you've done and shared and posted has made an impact," he said. "I know you're questioning if your efforts have made a difference. Just know that *I* know that they have."

After this conversation, my mind wandered. The intersection of faith, mental health, and real-life challenges is the space I love talking and teaching about, but maybe it wasn't enough. Questions weighed on my heart. *Maybe what I've tried to share over the years hasn't helped anyone after all. Maybe people would rather see voyeuristic and salacious content than things that are hopeful and helpful. Maybe it's finally time to leave social media.*

As I pondered deleting my accounts, I prayed. I sought God with all the fervor of my battered heart and my weary soul. I journaled, fasted, and decided to get to the temple earlier that week than

I normally went. For members of the Church, the temple is a sacred place where we go to worship and be closer to God, and I needed that comfort now.

While in the Mt. Timpanogos temple dressing room, another patron recognized me.

She put a hand on my arm. "Thank you for what you've been putting out in the world over the years. Your books and Instagram posts—especially where you've talked about mental health and losing your sister and raising kids with lupus—have made a huge impact on me."

My heart filled with joy, and I knew my prayers had been answered. That little conversation seemed to be the reminder I needed. For the hundreds and thousands of haters, there were everyday people trying just like I was—men and women wrestling with their faith, families, and friendships. For me, this sister represented *the* one I had always tried to keep showing up for. And in the dressing room that day, I felt God reminding me that I was indeed showing up for the one, just like He did.

So after praying and pondering, attending the temple, and talking to other content creators, I decided to keep trying to have complex and sometimes messy conversations on social platforms.

Instead of hiding from all the vicious comments, I messaged a group of other Latter-day Saint Christian content creators about the situation. I decided that instead of hiding and deleting the original dance video, what if I hooked arms with others and did even more?

So I posted a simple question on the group chat: "Does anyone want to join me in doing another 'Walk with Jesus' video?"

The response was amazing.

"I know the hate is loud, but the good you're doing matters."

"The way you've shown up authentically has helped me decide and design what kind of content creator I want to be."

"I want to walk with Jesus with you. Ignore the haters. Haters hate, but the love is real."

Two more "Walk with Jesus" videos came from that group. Even some brave non-influencers sent me clips of their "Walk with Jesus" dances and left me supportive messages.

"So sorry you're getting beat up in the world. Keep going!"

"What you have shared over the years has helped me feel seen and not so alone."

"Thank you for always being brave in talking about the hard things and sharing your faith, even though our faith is different from each other."

You can't imagine how this support and the kind messages buoyed me up.

And then something astonishing happened. Consumed by Fire, the band that produced the original "Walk with Jesus" song, messaged me their support, reshared my first controversial video, and started following me. They reshared my Jesus video, asking for their fans to send me some love because I was getting so much hate for dancing to their song. It was no longer an insignificant little video of a "Mormon" mom in a tracksuit. By August 2024, the number of views of the reels had reached more than 1.2 million.

The consistent calls for my death and destruction have been exhausting at times. There have been days when I have felt sad for the state of the world. But I have also learned a lot and met some kind-hearted people along my journey.

One day, I was shopping at a garden store. I was looking for summer flower seeds for my garden when a lovely woman came up to me and asked, "Aren't you the 'Walking with Jesus' lady?"

I was a bit surprised but nodded, not knowing what might come next. Then she said, "I just wanted to thank you for the good you share in the world."

I hugged her as my nerves neutralized.

We talked about the confusing world of social media and influencers. "For all the loud hate online," she said, "there are millions of quiet supporters that never comment or DM but appreciate what you share and who you are. You talk about and post about the hard stuff and do it in a way that helps us not feel so alone."

It was a reminder that there really are everyday people who don't spend their lives on social media but who *do* care. These are the people I post for. They are the ones who are just showing up for their families and friends and trying to take care of their mental health and live their faith.

Once again, I felt like God was putting kind strangers in my path so I could see the good behind the screen. With all the vitriol aimed at me, there have been some virtuous victories too.

GROWING UP DIFFERENT

"My dad doesn't live with us," I announced during my Primary class at church. ("Primary" is like Sunday school for kids between ages 3 and 11, and I was five.)

We sat in a semicircle for a lesson on families. Our teacher asked a question about what dads do at home and their roles in a family. My remark was an innocent response to a complicated situation. My parents had divorced, and my mom was balancing work and life as a single mom. In our faith at that time, having parents separated was rare.

Everyone turned to face me.

"Why doesn't he live with you?" Courtney asked, her long red braid swinging over the metal classroom chair.

"Did he die?" asked Brian, sitting on my other side.

"No, he's alive." I frowned. I wasn't sure how to answer their questions. I noticed the surprised look on my instructor's face. I responded with a shrug of my shoulders and a quiet, "He just doesn't live with us anymore."

"I don't understand." Lisa's eyes went abnormally wide.

"My mom and dad aren't married anymore," I said. "But we see him on the weekends!"

Our teacher clapped her hands together, trying to redirect the questions that were coming at me. "Okay, class! Tell me about your families."

My parents had been divorced for a couple of years, but it was a situation I was still trying to wrestle with and understand. After church, I shared with my mom that we had talked about families and dads in Primary.

Another time, I remember sitting with my little sister Meggan in sacrament meeting. Sister Shoemaker, the bishop's wife, turned around from the pew in front of us and said hello. "Your dress is so pretty," she told me with a bright smile. "I'm glad to see you and Meg at church today." I couldn't help but smile back.

Mom made sure we were at church every Sunday. Church provided us with community and support. And though I couldn't put words to it then, I felt it. Despite being different, I felt at home because I was part of a big ward family: people who cared about us (like Sister Shoemaker), noticed us, and showed up for us.

As a young girl, I loved church. Even though I only knew the basic doctrine of my faith, I felt it deeply. Once a month, our church holds what's called a "fast and testimony meeting" where any member is given the opportunity to get up and proclaim their faith over the pulpit.

One Sunday, when I was six years old, I sat listening to adults standing up, one after another, to share their feelings and faith. My heart was beating, and my face felt flush with a burning of the Spirit. It was as if the Lord pushed me to slide off the pew, onto the carpeted floor, and take that long walk up to stand at the pulpit. I knew that if I didn't stand and share, those feelings wouldn't calm.

My pulse was beating so hard that I could hear my heart like drums in my ears as I made my way to the front of the entire congregation to share the genuine feelings in my heart. With a smile, the bishop pulled out a little stool for me so I could step up and see over the podium.

I cleared my throat. "I want to bear my testimony. I know that Jesus Christ is the Son of God. And God loves me." Tears spilled down my cheeks as I tried to form childlike, coherent thoughts about complex feelings of belief, faith, and God. I don't remember the exact words I spoke, but I remember the strong feelings I wanted to share.

Sometimes the other kids would tease me for how often I'd get up to speak on fast and testimony Sundays—and for how easily I cried. But my young heart couldn't be silenced. The flip side of that was that many of their parents and other adults in the ward would thank me for my testimony.

Growing up as the "different" kid—with divorced parents and a tendency to cry easily—I found my safe haven in the Church. It's people and teachings gave me the connection and security I needed.

I didn't want cartoons. Instead I loved watching television where real people were the story lines. I also played with Barbies and made homemade furniture for my dolls because we couldn't afford the Barbie pink car and the dream house. I would take home the free bank registers and deposit slips from the bank and play banker with Meg, my little sister, who made a fantastic customer. I would put a chair in the middle of our bedroom and play "school" by reading Meg stories.

As much as I was her big sister, Meg was my comforter. I had a lot of nightmares growing up. When I would wake up screaming, Meg would gently say from her bed across the room, "You're okay. You're safe."

These gentle words, patiently repeated, were what allowed me to fall back to sleep.

Eventually, my mom met and married my stepfather, Jim. And my father met and married my stepmother, Cynthia.

When I turned eight years old, as is tradition in the Church, I was baptized in a font at the church building. Wearing an all-white jumpsuit, I walked into the lukewarm water. "Daddy Jim," my mom's new husband, baptized me. With love shining in his eyes, and his full head of naturally curly hair brushed neatly back for the occasion, he said the sacred words and then lowered me into the water. But my foot popped up.

"A toe came out of the water," Daddy Dan, my biological father, said from his spot standing as one of two required witnesses at the edge of the font.

Daddy Jim gave me a reassuring smile. "We need to do it again." I understood why—I had to be fully immersed for the baptism to count.

He repeated the words and lowered me in once more. And my toe came up again!

"Toe," Daddy Dan and the other witness said in unison.

I frowned, worried I was ruining the baptism by not being able to keep my foot down.

"It's okay," Daddy Jim said, comforting me, and we tried it one more time.

Thankfully, this time, my foot stayed down! I was finally baptized— an official member of The Church of Jesus Christ of Latter-day Saints.

I quickly went to the changing room where my mom waited with a towel and helped me change into my baptism dress. "I love you. I'm so proud of you," she said with a beaming smile on her face.

I went back out and sat on the front row waiting for the next step on this covenant path. There, Daddy Dan blessed me with the gift of the Holy Ghost by laying his big hands on my damp hair and saying a special prayer.

My mom led the music at the service, and we sang two of my favorite Primary songs, one about Jesus and one about Joseph Smith.

After the service, we drove to my grandparents' house. I felt so clean and fresh, like life was really beginning. I felt like I had a secret power now—to do life with God. I was walking with Jesus.

We got to my Nana and Papa's home, and as usual, my grandma had set a beautiful table and made a fancy dinner to celebrate my special day. After we ate, they gave me a carefully wrapped gift.

Opening the beautiful box, there was my first set of fancy scriptures—the King James Bible, the Book of Mormon, the Doctrine and Covenants, and the Pearl of Great Price, all bound together in leather. It was so beautiful!

In the front of my scriptures, my nana wrote in fancy scroll, "Understanding and reading the word of God will be a guide and a comfort throughout your life."

Little did I know how true that inscription would come to be. I didn't read them every day until I became an adult, but they were definitely a touchstone as I navigated childhood and the turbulent teenage years.

By the time I had turned ten, Daddy Jim and Mom had their first baby together. My sister Bonnie was born with two holes in her heart. After a year-and-a-half battle, many hospital stays, and multiple surgeries, she passed on.

My mom and Daddy Dan only had me and Meg before divorcing. We were so excited when Mom and Daddy Jim had four more children: three more girls—Bonnie, Amy, and Stacie—and my little brother Ben. Life was changing at home with my mom, but it was also changing at home with Daddy Dan and my stepmother Cynthia. They eventually had five children of their own: three girls—Carmel, Shevaun, and Kaitlyn—and two boys—Danny and Derek. I loved being a big sister to so many. I was always the first to volunteer to change diapers, do their hair, or help wherever I could as the second little momma.

When I was a preteen, our growing new family moved out of the Sacramento area to a rural community forty-five minutes north of the city. It was a big change. We had a small farm, including goats and sheep. I joined the 4-H, raised pigs, and tried to make new friends at a time when nothing seemed to fit quite right anymore, from my clothes to my own skin.

I started school at Foothill Intermediate School and was definitely the mysterious new "Mormon" girl. It was confusing. And it certainly didn't help that my name was different. (As an adult, I finally had the confidence to point out that it rhymes with "anal," but that wasn't a conversation I wanted to have with my new classmates and teachers. My stepdad would kindly say, "Ganel is angel with the G in the wrong place"—I liked that explanation the best.)

I didn't attend the community church that a lot of people went to. My mom made my shorts so that they were more modest. I don't remember being teased, but I was definitely aware that our family had less money and less name-brand clothes than the other kids at school had. And we didn't play with friends on Sundays—that was a rule because that was the day we worshipped in church and spent time together as a family.

Despite those differences, I grew to love my new small-town life. I wore purple Wrangler cords. I loved to go with my friends to the only burger stand in town for a pineapple milkshake and then hang out in the olive orchard talking about the school dance and which boys we thought were cute that week. Singing, roller-skating, and sleepovers filled my life with happy memories. I looked forward to the time I would turn fourteen and could participate in the school dances, an exciting rite of passage.

One of the blessings of that small northern California community was its diversity. I had Asian friends, Black friends, and friends of various religions—Catholic, Lutheran, Baptist, Jehovah's Witnesses, and more. There weren't very many "Mormons" in town. Most wards in the Church have between 250 and 600 members, while mine had less than 200. We were so small that we couldn't even be designated a ward and got the title of "branch" instead. The small size also meant that most people served and volunteered in multiple roles, but it also allowed our small faith village to bond and more fully rely on each other.

There was both a thriving Baptist church and Community Christian church in town. It was common at lunch to hear about what others had learned at church on Sunday or what their beliefs were. Talking about their doctrine often led to questions about mine.

Was I allowed to dance? Yes.

Could I wear makeup? Yes, but not until I was twelve—a family rule, not a Church one.

Did we celebrate holidays? Absolutely!

For many of my friends and community members, I became their walking "Mormon" encyclopedia. Most of the time, I found it easy to answer their questions and laugh off the awkward ones (like if we had horns—I've seriously been asked that multiple times throughout my life!).

I tried my best to answer questions and clarify misconceptions with my teenage understanding.

"Do you know the Osmonds?" I wish!

"Are you a polygamist?" Nope.

Others were a little more serious, like "Are you a Christian?" Yes!

Or "Do you worship Joseph Smith?" No, but we do respect him as a prophet of God, just like Noah, Elijah, Moses, and all the prophets in the Bible.

I did my best to answer not only with accuracy but with patience and empathy. When my friends asked me a question about what my church was like, I would try to ask them about theirs. This way, I hoped we were building community through curiosity and not with criticism.

During this time, the local community church started showing an anti-Mormon movie about what we do in our temples. A friend, Carrie,[1] who I'd always loved for how kind she was to everyone, was attending that community church, saw the movie, and started asking me about what happens in the temple. I can't remember all the questions she asked me, but it was a conversation that left me feeling uncomfortable and icky. I don't think she realized that I was swimming in deep waters. I wasn't old enough to go to the temple, so I didn't

---

1. The names of my friends and classmates have been changed throughout my narrative.

have context for what she was saying and couldn't accurately answer her pointed questions.

That said, our small branch of less than 200 people tried to be a positive part of the community by volunteering for the cemetery clean-up projects, road improvement assignments, and clothing drives for needy families, among other things. Doing my best at school, in student council meetings, and on the playground seemed to help people separate the myth from the "Mormon."

One day at lunch, my usually quiet friend, Katie, who was a practicing Lutheran, slapped a book down on the cafeteria table with a loud thump.

I hadn't seen her coming, nor had any of our other friends at the table, and we all jumped. As soon as we saw who it was, we giggled a nervous laugh, but my laughter stopped almost immediately as her gaze found mine with an unfamiliar seriousness. This wasn't my normally sweet friend before me. Something felt tense.

"Look what I have," she said. "This book lists cults, and you'll never believe what churches are mentioned here. Yours!"

My happy mood vanished, and my stomach plummeted. I knew what she was going to say before she even said it.

She eagerly showed us all her great discoveries. There were many religions, considered "cults," scattered through its pages. In the table of contents were chapters about Mormons and Catholics and Jehovah's Witnesses.

There at our full lunch table, my dear Catholic friend, Samantha, and I were face-to-face with many of our friends and a book that labeled us as cult followers. Our other classmates were watching to see how we'd respond to this accusation.

In shock, we both set down our half-eaten pizza slices and unopened chocolate milk cartons. My stomach churned. And it was a bummer too because pizza day was my favorite.

The air was thick with awkward silence. We tried to distract and redirect the discussion with a few simple facts.

Looking at Samantha, Katie said, "You worship Mother Mary." She then turned her gaze to me. "And you worship Joseph Smith."

"We don't," Samantha and I said in unison. We then both tried to explain as our other friends got quieter and quieter and the air got thicker and thicker around us until we both felt we could barely breathe.

Katie continued to insist with her accusations, so Samantha and I talked about our faith in God and our love of Christ. I wanted so badly to show her that what she was saying wasn't true, but she wasn't listening.

Katie glanced around our friends at the table, almost as if she were looking for them to join her claim. "According to this book, and what my parents have said, you are cult members," she said. "Don't you worship Joseph Smith?"

I didn't understand her. In our short conversation, I'd already professed my belief in Jesus Christ several times, and yet she was still making this untrue statement: "You're not Christian." And her parents had given her more than just a book to prove her point—they had given her some talking points.

We then told her that we worshipped the same God she did, even if we did it in a little different way or embraced a few cultural variations from her particular sect. The conversation ended there. We threw away our unfinished lunch, went back to class, and waited for the school day to come to an end so we could finally go home.

As I rode the bus home that afternoon, a lump caught in my throat. So big, I couldn't speak. I could barely lift my eyes to look at anyone. Samantha was on her own bus crying, just like me.

Both our families helped us make sense of what had happened. Mom sat with me, gently answering my questions and giving me better ways to explain my faith to others. Samantha's mother did the same for her. What could have driven us apart, instead, drew us closer. We'd weathered our first real junior high storm together and it changed us both. I knew that despite our different churches, Samantha had my back. We became each other's faith-keepers, protecting our right to believe differently even as I became more cautious talking about my beliefs.

I don't think we ever managed to change Katie's opinion. I don't remember us ever talking about religion in the same way again. We stayed friends but stayed away from discussions about church and cults.

Because of Katie, I changed. For the first time, I saw my faith through someone else's eyes, and the image didn't match what I knew to be true.

I never wanted any person of faith to feel attacked because of my questions or judgment. I decided then to show reverence for those who worship differently than I do—a holy envy. I want every person I encounter, regardless of religious faith or tradition, to know that they are safe with me.

Looking to the Temple

As a scared eighteen-year-old girl, I got into my family's old station wagon with my siblings and all my belongings, and we started the long trip from California to Rexburg, Idaho. I was enrolled in Ricks College. After I had gotten settled, I remember my little brother Ben being so small and so confused about why I wasn't getting back in the car with Meg, Amy, Stacie, and him. Meg hugged me tight, knowing we could still stay connected with collect calls.

Moving into my college townhome, I anxiously met my five new roommates. They were from all over the country: New Mexico, Arizona, California, Iowa, and Montana. Our bishopric matched girls' apartments with guys' apartments for "family home evening" groups (or FHE groups) that would get together for fun and spiritual activities each week. Our FHE brothers included a football player, his brother, and a shy, newly returned missionary just back from Portugal.

Our first get-together with boys included the M&M game where the color of candy you grab determines what questions you answer about yourself (a classic get-to-know-you game). Most of the guys talked about sports. I shared how I love to clean (just needed to shake things up). And then we made smoothies.

Rob Condie organized the FHE night. He was so kind and a bit quiet. Rob struggled, like many people do, to say my name correctly.

Over the next few weeks and months, Rob started spending a lot of time over at our apartment. His roommates were a bit wild—sneaking girls into their rooms at night and partying a bit—so he avoided being at his apartment and would hang out with us instead.

Rob was who we asked for priesthood blessings—heavenly blessing provided in much the same way as I received the gift of the Holy Ghost. He would place his hands on our heads, and with the priesthood power, he would say a prayer and ask for blessings on our behalf. He also helped us get groceries, helped with homework, and was a calming force.

Mom came to visit for Mother's Week, and I think she may have fallen in love with Rob when we heard him sing with his barbershop group. She offered to pay him to date me. Of course, I didn't want that—he was just my friend and he was already dating my roommate, Annie. Then again, Annie also had a boyfriend serving as a missionary for the Church in a foreign country. He was only nine months into his two-year mission, and she had a promise ring from him. It was a little reality TV–ish.

Over that first year of college, I went to therapy to process some trauma and anxiety. Even though I wasn't sure what all my issues were, I knew I needed to sort out the big worries I was having about family members back at home—like Meg, who struggled with depression and anxiety and was suicidal—and also the anxiety I was experiencing being away from home and in college.

I started out as a news broadcasting major and then decided the newsroom was too cutthroat for my heart. I shifted to majoring in psychology. I had grown up in a home with mental health needs constantly shouting for attention. Throughout college I went to therapy, and I wasn't the only one.

Meg suffered from a learning disability, mental health issues, and the effects of trauma. But she was also a great basketball player and great to go on a road trip with. During my freshman year of college, Meg's mental health needs peaked. She was hospitalized for depression and suicidal ideation.

This played a part in my desire to go into psychology. I wanted to understand how my brain worked, how others' brains worked, how to fix family dynamics, and how to help people heal.

Soon I realized that if I continued on the path of becoming a therapist, I would end up talking my clients' ears off. A good therapist is a good listener, and oh, how I wanted to talk with people to help them feel better, be happy, and buoy up!

I loved organizing and reading, so I considered library science for a minute. But then I realized I'd get kicked out of the library for talking too much. Oh, how I loved discussing what I learned from the books I'd read!

Many of my elementary school report cards said "Good student—talks too much."

Was there a career for me where "talks too much" would be a good thing?

My walk with Jesus included serving in my first Church calling as a Relief Society teacher and learning to love reading the scriptures because of my Book of Mormon class. I also learned to live with five very different and lovely roommates.

During my second year at Ricks College, I moved back into the same complex, living with two of my previous roomies, Annie and Karen. Only now Annie and Rob were on again and off again. Not that it mattered—I had my own soap opera happening and was on again and off again with my high school boyfriend too.

Still, Rob and I had grown a deep friendship and trust—a bond that morphed into something more than just friends while I didn't even notice it happening. Over time, he became so easy to confide in. I felt I could be myself around him.

During one of his "off" times with Annie, I had a conversation with him about an icky situation with another guy I had gone on a date with recently, I realized I wanted the best for Rob and wanted him to see the best in me. This was definitely a sign we were more than just friends. The realization struck me.

"Do you want to kiss me?" I asked Rob nervously. We hadn't even been on a first date.

"Yes, please." I'll never forget the way he slowly leaned in, anxious at first, before gently pressing his lips against mine. Everything about it just felt right. It felt like coming home.

We shared with our family and roommates the change in our relationship status. That news led to me moving out and into another apartment because things got awkward with Annie.

Rob and I started making plans. We fasted and prayed and separately got the confirmation that we wanted an eternal relationship.

Funny how we tried to map out our life and timeline. I wonder if God chuckled when He saw what we thought life would look like.

We got engaged and started planning the wedding. We scheduled our sealing—the marriage ceremony performed in the temple—for June 1st at the Portland Oregon Temple. There were also two receptions on the books—one in Florence, Oregon, where Rob grew up, and then a few weeks later in Marysville, California, where I had graduated high school.

In preparation for the big day, my grandparents, Nana and Papa, offered to pay for my wedding dress, temple clothing, and garments. My grandma was a power shopper. Her taste in clothing and shoes, jewelry, and home furnishings was impeccable. So when Nana invited me to go on a special shopping trip to ZCMI to get lingerie, I was so excited.

Nana and I were really close. We often got mistaken as mother and daughter, which always made us smile because she was my grandma by marriage and not by blood. (She was my grandpa's third wife and not my mom's mom.) I loved shopping, decorating, and going out to eat with her.

We walked into the fancy ZCMI luxury department store and headed to the women's section. We found the silky and satin nightgowns, and soon I spotted a pretty little pink spaghetti-strap nightie. Taking it off the rack, I asked Nana, "What do you think of this one?"

She looked up and examined the nightgown. "Well," she said, "you can't wear that with your garments."

I hadn't gone through the temple yet. (When members over the age of eighteen feel they are ready, they may choose to go to the temple to make covenants and receive their garments.) I was definitely ready for this commitment to the Lord, but her response startled me.

Growing up, I was very used to seeing my parents and grandparents walking around in their garments around the house, and it felt really normal. (Fabrics and lengths vary, but the basic men's style looks like white bike shorts and a Hanes T-shirt, and the women's garments can be described as white knee-length Spanx with a camisole top.) However, it had always been my understanding that you didn't wear them for certain activities.

"What do you mean?" I asked. After all, I'd be wearing this cute spaghetti-strap nightie on my honeymoon with Rob.

My eyebrows shot up to my permed bob. Was I supposed to wear my garments when I had sex?

Seeing the expression on my face, my grandma furrowed her brow. With a comforting hand on my arm and a nervous glance around to see who was listening, she steered me aside. We talked a little bit about how Nana thought you wore garments. And the conversation did *not* reassure me or settle my concerns.

We finished shopping, picking a silky robe so that the subject of garments, sex, and lingerie could be dropped. As soon as we were home, I quickly ran to call my mom.

"Momma, do I have to wear my garments when Rob and I have sex? Nana kept saying we couldn't get certain pajamas because my garments would show."

"Don't worry," she reassured me. "That's a generational thing." Mom went on to explain that it was an older generation and cultural approach to living your covenants. That was definitely not how it was done now—thankfully.

My mom chuckled a little and reassured me that I didn't have to keep my garments on when I showered, exercised, or was intimate. I took a deep breath of relief. She counseled me to just drop it and not discuss it further with Nana.

A week before getting married in the Portland Temple, I went through the Oakland California Temple to receive my endowment. It was amazing and overwhelming. I learned so much, and my sweet nana kept whispering to me in the session, "Stop trying to memorize everything. You get to keep coming back and learning over time."

I loved feeling the power of priesthood blessings and covenants with me day and night. Being in the temple didn't feel like being anywhere else on the planet, and wearing my garments was very much like taking a piece of the temple with me. For this California girl who had grown up with modest homemade shorts, not a lot of my wardrobe had to be altered for me to wear garments.

Rob had been endowed before going on his mission, so he was used to wearing garments. I was still figuring things out a week later when Rob and I were married in the temple. We were married for time and all eternity, through priesthood power reserved for use in the temple for ceremonies as important as marriage, among other things.

Being newly married was a journey of discovery. Rob and I came from very different families. We were really open and sometimes intense in our communication. Rob had grown up in a home where they tended to talk less about things.

Together we were trying to find a happy medium. Living together meant getting to practice patience and understanding concerning our differences in habits, humor, and how to solve problems.

We moved to Arizona to work, figure out marriage, and finish our degrees. After completing my generals at Glendale Community College, decisions needed to happen. Rob had settled on accounting, but I wasn't so sure of what I wanted. Oprah? The Today Show? Therapist? Or teaching?

"ASU West has an amazing teaching program. It's brand new up on the West Campus. I think you should check it out," my sister-in-law Jen shared with me the day after her graduation.

I was accepted and two years later graduated *summa cum laude* from Arizona State University with a bachelors in education on May 12, 1995.

One day when I was driving home from work at the YMCA, I got a sunburn in the car and ended up running a fever. My feet swelled so big that I couldn't put my shoes on. It was miserable, and I couldn't understand what could possibly be happening. So I made a doctor's appointment, and Rob and I showed up on time.

The doctor ran some labs. He walked into the exam room and solemnly shared, "Your symptoms and labs directly correlate to a diagnosis of lupus. I'm so sorry."

Rob and I stared at one another. We really had no idea what this meant for our future.

"What does that mean?" I asked in a near whisper.

The doctor explained. "Lupus is a chronic autoimmune disease that causes the body's immune system to attack healthy tissues and organs. This attack can cause inflammation and permanent tissue damage." Rob's dad was fighting for his life with a multiple sclerosis battle, so we understood a little the enormity of an autoimmune disease diagnosis.

"What does that mean for us?" Rob asked for further clarification.

The doctor sighed. "You're looking at headaches, mouth ulcers, hair loss, weight loss, swollen glands, depression and anxiety, chest and stomach pain, and heart problems, among other symptoms . . ."

My stomach churned and I sucked in a breath. Rob dropped his arm around me and squeezed, lightly offering that quiet support that would help carry me through our lives, through all sorts of trials.

Over the next year, we researched what this meant for our future.

The lupus progressed quickly and moved into a dangerous place—my heart. I was then put on a weekly chemotherapy drug to try and control the inflammation in my heart. The medical journals said I had ten years to live, and the doctors told us that having children was highly unlikely—and dangerous.

We joined a support group for lupus sufferers and their partners. But we only went a few times because it was obvious at the meetings that I was dealing with the most severe case in the group. I was the walking worst-case scenario that everyone else looked at and thought, "At least I'm not that bad."

We pressed on because that's what we do.

Finishing our degrees, helping Rob pass the CPA exam and start his first job as an accountant, and moving from Arizona to San Diego, California—one of the most beautiful areas of the world ever—was an adventure.

I started working as a long-term substitute teacher and also volunteered every week in the San Diego Temple as a temple worker. I would take naps on my temple shift so I could make it through because my body was still recovering from a year of chemotherapy treatments. I relied on the promised blessings in the temple ordinances guaranteeing health, strength, and family. I grabbed onto them and claimed them as my own, even while the visible evidence said otherwise.

After being in San Diego for a few years, we found a specialist to start a conversation with about potentially trying to get pregnant and starting our family. God led us to the doctor who had written the section on lupus and pregnancy for the main medical textbooks. What a blessing to be with the specialist we needed. But even after the green light came for us to really try, we faced heartbreak.

Every time my period was a few days late, we hoped. I eagerly invested in pregnancy tests that always came back negative. I'd stare at the white spot and pray for a pink line—or two lines depending on the test. It was negative, every time.

I went to baby showers, for friends, truly happy for them, repeating the words of a blessing I'd been given: "I will be a mother of children. I will be a mother of children." I was tired of praying and trying for something so good but feeling like it would never happen for us. I congratulated new moms, second time moms, and in a few cases third time moms while waiting for those promises to be kept.

Eventually, hopelessness enveloped us. I was tired of praying and trying for something so good, but feeling like it would never happen for us.

Sometime later, after a trip to Mexico with some friends, I felt tired and nauseous. I chalked it up to the street tacos.

Early one morning, I tiptoed into the bathroom after getting back from our vacation. I didn't want to wake anyone up, but my period still hadn't started. It was time to take another test. This time, it was different. *It was positive!*

I fell onto the bathroom floor crying with joy. My weeping awakened our friends in the guest room. They thought it was a sign that we weren't pregnant. I went in and told Rob the good news. We cried and hugged in disbelief. It felt like the biggest gift ever.

We tapped on our friends' door.

Bleary-eyed, they opened up. "We're so sorry you aren't pregnant."

"No, we are! We're going to have a baby!"

Jaren and Julie cried with us, hugging us in congratulations.

On December 6, 1997, in the middle of an El Niño storm, our son Cameron was delivered through an emergency C-section. Our little boy was not so little. He was born two weeks before the due date at a whopping ten pounds. He had a full head of dark hair and cried a deep, manly cry. I looked at him, and instantly all the heartache of chemotherapy, nausea, and infertility washed away.

"Cameron, it's mommy. I'm here. I love you." My baby boy calmed as soon as he heard me speak.

The words of Elder Holland, a Church leader, filled my soul: "Some blessings come soon, some come late, and some don't come until heaven; but for those who embrace the gospel of Jesus Christ, *they come.*"[2]

After ten years of wrestling with lupus, I did not die. Those promises in my patriarchal blessing and temple covenants were fulfilled when Cameron's best friend, our daughter Brooklyn, was born on January 14, 2004. I was now a mother of *children.*

For our thirtieth anniversary, Rob and I made a trip back to the Pacific Northwest to visit the Portland Temple. As we drove through the thick grove of trees and I saw the majestic white spires of the temple, I was overcome with a sense of the power of making and keeping covenants.

In that moment, it was as if God opened a video of the last three decades of my life—marriage, job loss, illness, grief, raising children, paying tithing, and creating a family—and I could sense and see how my temple covenants had kept me.

Rob noticed the tears filling my eyes. "Are you all right?"

"I don't have words for what I'm feeling. Thirty years . . . I can almost see all these millions of moments when the power of covenants healed and helped. Everything we have, everything that really matters—it's all here because of where our marriage started."

DREAMS REALLY DO COME TRUE

We moved to Provo, Utah, for Rob to get his master's degree from BYU. Life was busy and full. Rob worked long hours as a CPA. I served as Primary president (serving the children in the ward) and then as Relief Society president (serving the women in the ward). I loved being a full-time momma. But there were also other dreams on my list.

Parts of me, from long ago, felt called to share on the macro levels of the world, not just on the micro levels. Meanwhile, Meg had struggled, married, divorced, and moved back home with my parents. She was in and out of relationships and in and out of Church activity.

As the oldest child of ten children, from two different families, I was always doing things first—first to go to college, get married, and

---

2. Jeffrey R. Holland, "An High Priest of Good Things to Come," *Ensign*, Nov. 1999, 38; emphasis in original.

have children. I was figuring out a work-life balance, raising kids, and navigating the unexpected parts of life without someone ahead of me on the trail to show me the way.

One day, I was watching *Good Things Utah*, a local daily television show, and there was a segment about a new local women's magazine called *Wasatch Woman Magazine*. As the editor, Barbara Vineyard, talked about the "why" for the publication, something lit up inside me.

I thought, "*Wasatch Woman Magazine* isn't just a television segment—it should be its own show. And I should be its Oprah."

And of course, through it all, Rob was there to support and encourage me in my dreams. He constantly reminded me that I was a great mom and that it would not burden the family if I explored other interests outside of the home. But I was sensitive to my capacity while juggling lupus and motherhood. I wanted to do more, but I was worried about doing too much more and losing my balance. But this new magazine wouldn't leave me alone—it was one thing I couldn't get my mind off.

I found Barbara, reached out, and set up a meeting with her business partners. That conversation didn't lead to *Wasatch Woman Television*, but it did lead to regular television segments and me writing a regular column, becoming the magazine's public relations director, and eventually becoming the managing editor.

I interviewed Cokie Roberts, Michael Reagan, and Richard Paul Evans. But the most inspiring profiles were the everyday women of the Wasatch Front. These women were my neighbors and coworkers, CEOs, and community leaders. This was at the beginning of social media. We didn't have online groups and awareness of other people back then like we have with Instagram now. Instead, we were trying to create connection and community via a magazine. And we did it!

I'm so grateful for my time with the magazine. I made amazing connections—from the governor and Mrs. Huntsman to my forever best friend, Shawna Fillmore. Because of the magazine, I was able to have those *real* conversations with *real* people about *real* life.

I started appearing on television and learned about marketing and event planning—all while still being a stay-at-home mom to my two miracle children.

Writing profiles and columns and being editor in chief was just the beginning of a publishing career I hadn't foreseen, including working with amazing and well-known people in the government, business world, and community. Media One, the company that owned both major local newspapers at the time, eventually bought *Wasatch Woman* from Barb and hired me to be editor in chief. This was before remote work was normalized. Jed agreed to have me only come into the office once a week and manage the magazine from home so I could still be available for my kids.

This was revolutionary. No one else in the corporate office was working from home and coming into the office part-time. I was blazing a new trail of work-life balance.

After a few years with *Wasatch Woman Magazine*, I was sitting in an endowment session in the Bountiful Temple thinking about all my blessings.

As I listened to the teachings, I heard the Spirit whisper, "It's time to quit the magazine. And you need to tell your boss that Pam will be the new editor in chief." I didn't know Pam well—except that she periodically wrote a news column—but the Spirit had spoken to me in this way before, so I recognized it and knew I needed to listen.

Still, my first thought was "Now?" I had just gotten a promotion and been appointed to an important advisory board. But I had learned that God held my dreams for me. He had them protected. And if I trusted Him, they would all come true—but in *His* timing. Women have fought so hard to break glass ceilings and find a seat at the boardroom table that we feel like we have to have it all right now—everything at the same time. I wanted that too, but I promised myself I would never stop listening to the Lord and following His counsel.

I waited until my husband and I got back to the car to tearfully share the clear direction I had received. I knew it was going to be a deeper, longer conversation.

"Wow, that's a big change." He took my hand as he navigated the streets of Provo to our house. "I know you love the editor's position, and you've worked so hard on the magazine. But if that's what the Spirit told you, then that's what we need to do, right?"

I nodded.

We went home from the temple and had a conversation with our kids. We sat them down at the kitchen table so we could all look at one another.

"You're leaving your job?" little Brooklyn asked. Even at the age of four, she knew something big was happening.

"Sometimes when you get a yes from the Lord, it later changes into a no," I explained. "But that doesn't mean the original yes was wrong."

"But I thought you loved your job at the magazine. Don't you?" ten-year-old Cameron asked.

"I do," I said, trying to think of a way to explain this. "It's kind of like a mission. If someday you choose to serve missions, that mission will eventually come to an end, and it will be time for you to come home. This is like that. I feel like my mission with *Wasatch Woman Magazine* is at an end, and it's time for me to go in a different direction."

"And more importantly," Rob added, "it's what the Lord asked your mother to do."

"Even though I don't know what's around the corner, God does," I said. "So I'm trusting His prompting to leave the magazine."

The next day, I had a difficult conversation with Jed. I sat in the leather chair in front of his desk with my hands folded in front of me as I told him of my decision.

He breathed out and ran a hand through his hair, and then asked, "I know we could do more to support you. What do you need to stay?" Jed almost pleaded for me to make a different decision. After giving him as much of an explanation as I could, I finally decided to be vulnerable and tell him the real reason, knowing that he was also an active member of the Church and would likely understand.

With my throat constricting with emotion, I said, "When I was in the temple, it was clear that it's time for me to step aside."

Jed knew he couldn't talk me out of leaving after I shared that.

I wasn't sure why God was closing this door, but I knew I was going to keep walking with Him.

The next few years were heavy with homeschooling and healing parts of my heart. Then God started whispering something about writing a book. I didn't talk about it openly until the prompting wouldn't stop.

At a later date, I sat in the temple with my best friend, Shawna, and said, "I think I'm supposed to write a book. I know the title and the format." I went on to share the vision that had been shared with me.

Over the next few months and years, I compiled and edited stories about hard things—stories of mental health, financial stress, infertility, grief, and the deconstruction of faith. I found those everyday women of faith—"Mormon" women who were living hard things with God but weren't necessarily authors. Like Heather, who had lost her baby; and Alice Ann, a mother of ten who had eight of her children leave the faith; and Andrea, who had struggled with financial stress. Their amazing stories inspired me, and I worked to midwife their tales into the reality of a book.

Rob was too—he was my biggest cheerleader even though he didn't know anything about the world of publishing.

And my sister Meg? She was so excited about me publishing a book.

Meg was dealing with her own mental health struggles, and I would see her sometimes isolate herself from friends and family, but she knew that connection and faith were essential to happiness. This book was about normalizing the hard things we all face in life. And Meg wanted it published. She was strengthened by hearing stories of other women who struggled and hearing about how they managed. It was healing for both of us in a lot of ways.

With a finished manuscript, I submitted it to a publisher. Since I had never published a book, I didn't know how long and vulnerable of a process it is to become an author. After waiting for months, I got a rejection letter. I then resubmitted it to another publisher. Months passed.

Opening the mail, my heart fell because once again I read, "Thank you for your submission, but it's not a fit for us right now. Good luck in the future."

I almost gave up. Maybe God wanted me to write a book just for me to have the experience of compiling these sacred stories.

My husband's secretary, Cheri, was part of a writer's group. She offered to help me with edits and introduce me to an editor at a new publisher.

Six months passed.

Still, Rob, Meg, and many others never gave up on me or this project. They wouldn't let me give up hope.

On March 11, we had just finished celebrating my mom's birthday. My stepdad Jim took a call out in the garage, and I knew something wasn't right. I was turning off the lights and closing up the house for the night when I heard the garage door open.

Jim came into the kitchen, his face somber.

My heart sped up; my breathing became shallow. The room slowly started to grow quiet as a dark cloud descend, crushing any hope or joy with it. It was like a screaming buzz was building in my ears.

My brother Ben had called because he had stopped over at Oma and Opa's house to check on Meg. He found her dead.

My heart constricted. My breathing stopped while I cried out a hoarse scream. Meg had died days before by suicide.

I can barely remember anything that happened after that moment that night, but I do remember climbing the stairs to get to my daughter and running back down into the basement to check on Cameron. I couldn't breathe or talk, but I turned to Rob and asked him to call our friend Betsy. She was a friend who could comfort my kids while all hell was breaking loose.

Rob was steady as usual. I call him "the old oak tree." When the storms are swirling, I can always look to him for steadiness.

In the weeks and months after that horrific phone call—after planning her funeral and helping settle her affairs—the grief settled over my heart and home like a thick January fog. I kept trying to take care of my family, doing the laundry, washing dishes, feeding people, and going through the motions of managing a home, all while my worst nightmare had come true.

Meg had fought throughout her life with depression, anxiety, a learning disability, and the effects of abuse. I had watched her overcome much, but I had also watched her fall into the mental health pit many, many times. Even though I had always tried to be a strength for her, and help her find a lifeline to hold on to, she too had been a source of comfort for me. It had always been the two of us together visiting other family members, going on road trips with Nana and Papa, and during the scary nights filled with bad dreams, she was my comfort.

Now I woke up often with horrific nightmares fueled by grief and Meg's suicide. And she wasn't alive anymore to comfort me. To tell me I was okay. That we were safe.

I was plagued with "why." There is no simple answer to that question—not that I found. It's a decision someone makes, but it's a sliver of time that ripples for decades and even for generations.

Six weeks after Meg's passing, I got an important email. The last submission of my book had been accepted. The publisher wanted to publish *I Can Do Hard Things with God*, and they were also interested in working with me on future book projects.

At the time, I was swimming in a deep ocean of grief. But I knew Meg had a hand in this. She had been so excited about this project. She had always believed in me and the book. I knew she had done whatever she could do from the other side to push this project forward.

Now, all of a sudden, I understood the two previous rejections. I understood why the "what" was right but the "when" had to wait until 2014. There was a story missing from the manuscript, and that story was mine. My hard thing wasn't lupus, or how long it took to conceive, or even my times of unemployment. My hardest thing was losing my little sister, my cherished friend, one of my earthy sources of comfort. It was Meg dying by suicide. The book couldn't be published until this pivotal piece of the project had happened.

I rewrote the original submission to include a new first chapter: the story of my Meg.

It's been over a decade since losing Meg, but my sister's death changed my world forever.

I Can Do Hard Things with God was published. Two more books in the *With God* series came, and now I'm the author of sixteen published books. Meg was my biggest cheerleader in this life, always seeing the best in me and complimenting me when I doubted. And now she has become my mission companion working from the other side. My speaking career started before the first book was published, but because of my writing, the media and keynoting opportunities have also expanded.

I have had the great privilege over the past nine years as a regular monthly contributor, and periodic guest host, on *Good Things Utah*. The same daily TV show where I had watched Barb talk about her new women's magazine so many years ago is now the place I get to show up and have conversations about important topics like marriage, communication, interfaith, and *mental health*.

My first book was the first of its kind. It was a compilation of heartbreaking, vulnerable stories of "Mormon" women. I shared the messy and the meaningful parts of real people, real families, and real faith. There hadn't been a lot, if any, previously published stories and books of Latter-day Saints openly dealing with pornography addiction and suicide loss, bipolar disorder and children walking away from faith, among other daily struggles—while also fully living the gospel. To say the covenant path is smooth would be like saying you can drive a car without gas—it just doesn't work like that.

Walking with Jesus doesn't mean avoiding the bumpy pathways of mortality.

Because of that first book—and in many ways, because of Meg's death—I have had the opportunity to be the "Mormon" Oprah, and be Jane Pauly on local television, and teach on stages across the globe.

Dreams really do come true—even through the darkest and hardest trials of life.

I am so grateful for a husband who has counseled, cheered, encouraged, and enabled me to be a mom, wife, and more.

Rob believed in me when I sometimes doubted myself.

Rob's support of my career recently shone through in the planning of my book launch for *Words of Jesus*. Even though I had done other events in the past for my previous fourteen published books, I kept feeling like this specific project—about loving and understanding the beatitudes—deserved to be celebrated in a bigger way than previous launches had been.

I was worried about hosting a VIP event. I wondered if the effort, costs, and catering were worth it and the best use of our family's funds. But as Rob had done in the past, he kept gently pushing me and reassuring me that he supported my vision. And he believed in this special teal-covered book featuring a single-lined image of the Savior.

He met those words with action as he patiently talked through the menu, centerpieces, and invitations. Then, on an early August evening, at the stunning Willow Creek Country Club, Rob stood with my dear friend Becky and sang "I Need Thee Every Hour" to kick off my *Words of Jesus* event.

Our thirty-plus years together have given me much to think about, talk about, and more people to love than I can count. Through Christ, the tragedies of my life have been transformed into treasures. This is why I have, and do, and will keep dancing/walking with Jesus.

Awkwardly and always.

6

Caroline Melazzo
The Podcaster

Roots of Strength: A New Path

I always wanted a marriage like my parents. They met at a bank in São Paulo, Brazil when my mom was twenty-two years old. They knew right away that they wanted to be together, but my mom made it clear that the only way their relationship would work was if he understood and embraced her faith. She had been baptized at fourteen after the missionaries knocked on her door. My mother saw the gospel of Jesus Christ as the answer—a way to save her family from unnecessary hardships. When my mother heard about eternal families, she felt in her heart that this was what she wanted.

My father, Esmeraldo, was a fun-loving man whose joy was infectious. He often mentioned how when he first heard the Church's teachings, it was easy for him to believe. So when my mom introduced him to the missionaries, he was baptized within the same week. When he spoke about the gospel, it was clear that his words came from deep within his heart. I could see his passion for the gospel. Together, he and my mom built a life of service, including serving in the temple.

The temple has always been a source of strength for me and my family. My mom faced many trials, including difficulties getting pregnant. Through her struggles to get pregnant, she leaned on the blessing of the temple. In the temple, she was promised that she would have children, and she trusted in that promise. After five long years of trying, she finally got pregnant with me.

They said it was a miracle, one they had prayed for, and my parents couldn't have been more overjoyed. I was their miracle baby, born into a home that radiated faith and love, where hymns and classical music filled the air in celebration of my arrival. I always dreamed that one day I would have the chance to build a home just like the one I was raised in with a family of my own that would love as I had been loved, as I had seen my parents love each other.

My mother once reflected on a disagreement she had with my father and said, "You know, if I were to divorce your dad and marry someone else, I'd just face a whole new set of challenges. Every man has his own weaknesses and mistakes, and we'd still have to work together to fix those issues. So why wouldn't I choose to work things out with your dad, my eternal companion? We have something good here, and we can make it even better."

I wanted to be with someone who would laugh with me through the hard times I knew would come. I love when someone can make me laugh—laughter, to me, is one of the greatest joys of life. As Marjorie Hinckley once said, "The only way to get through life is to laugh your way through it. You either have to laugh or cry. I prefer to laugh. Crying gives me a headache."[3]

A Sacred Union: Building Our Forever

One day, as I was walking with my friend Patricia between our classes at university, she turned to me and said, "You should write to my cousin Daniel."

I frowned, not sure how I felt about setups. "Uh . . ."

Patricia nudged me with her elbow. "He's serving a mission and is one of the most spiritually strong people I've ever met. You'd love him."

After weeks of encouragement, I finally gave in and decided to start writing Elder Melazzo, as I called him. My first letter went something like this:

---

3. Marjorie Pay Hinckley, "At Home with the Hinckleys," *Ensign*, Oct. 2003, 24.

Dear Elder Melazzo,

My name is Caroline and I'm Patricia's friend. She speaks so highly of you. It's so amazing that you're serving a mission. I'm glad to make a new friend.

It was a simple, heartfelt note, but when he replied, his words struck me in an unexpected way.

Dear Caroline,

Thank you for your kind note! It's wonderful to hear from Patricia's friends. Serving a mission has been an incredible experience, and I'm grateful to connect with you.

We exchanged letters for six months; sometimes they would arrive every other week, while other times, depending on his transfers, I'd have to wait a whole month for a reply. But each time I received a letter, it felt like Christmas morning.

I remember the thrill of running to the mailbox, tearing open the envelope, and eagerly reading every word he wrote. Each letter was filled with stories of his experiences, insights about faith, and encouragement that brightened my days. His words carried a warmth that transcended the distance between us, and I often found myself rereading them, savoring the connection we shared. Those letters became a lifeline, reminding me that even though we were apart, our bond was strong and growing deeper with every exchange. I used to show the letters to my close friends, and they all got excited too.

One day, he sent me a small book by James E. Faust, and I was deeply moved by his thoughtfulness and spirituality. His words and actions filled me with anticipation about the possibility of meeting him in person. He wasn't just another pen pal; he was someone whose heart and faith I found myself drawn to.

Just a week after he returned from his mission, everything would change on the evening of a church dance when our paths would finally cross.

I had been looking forward to the dance for weeks, and that evening, I went to pick up Patricia. Elder Melazzo lived next door to her. In a letter he'd written to me, he asked if I wanted to meet him at the airport.

I declined, thinking, *That's too much. I'm not the kind of girl who rushes to the airport to meet someone I've never met in person.* Still, I couldn't help but wonder what it would be like to finally meet him after all those letters.

As I pulled up to Patricia's house to give her a ride to the dance, there he was, standing in her driveway. I instantly knew this wasn't just a coincidence. Of course, he knew I was going to be there. My heart skipped a beat as we made eye contact for the first time.

"Hi, it's nice to meet you." He smiled and extended his hand. "I'm Elder Melazzo."

Heart racing, I shook it. "Nice to meet you too," I managed to say, trying to keep my composure. He looked incredibly handsome—tall at 6'3", with light brown hair, fair skin, and a few remnants of adolescence on his face. I couldn't believe that after six months of letters, we were finally seeing one another in person!

He'd sent me a picture of himself while on his mission, standing in front of the Porto Alegre Temple, the area where he served. In the photo, he was pointing to the plaque mounted on the temple wall commemorating its dedication in 2000—a symbol of his commitment and dedication. I had thought he was cute in that moment, but standing face-to-face felt surreal. The image I had stared at so many times transformed into a living, breathing person right in front of me. I could now see the subtle details that made him even more appealing—the way his eyes crinkled at the corners when he smiled, and the warmth that radiated from him in person. This was no longer just a distant pen pal or a face in a photo; he was here, real and vibrant, and I felt a mixture of awe and joy at the reality of our meeting.

As I took him in, I couldn't help but think, *Wow, he* is *really cute.*

There was an awkward pause as we both smiled, sizing each other up. He was about to say something when I cut in. "I'm heading to the dance now."

He hesitated for a moment. "Oh, are you? Well, I guess I'll see you later then."

I nodded, still flustered. "Yeah, I'll see you later." And with that, Patricia and I headed to the dance, leaving him standing there.

The whole drive, I couldn't stop thinking about him. I was so in love, and yet meeting him in person felt overwhelming. When we arrived at the dance, which was being held at our stake center—a church building where we hold meetings for various local congregations—I tried to shake it off, chatting with my friends and pretending nothing unusual had just happened. But everyone knew. Even my mother was there, and she knew I had been writing to him.

Not long into the evening, a group of my friends rushed over, their eyes wide with excitement. "Caroline, he's here! He's here!"

I froze, my heart pounding in my chest. He's here? The realization sent a rush of adrenaline through me, mixing excitement with a hint of anxiety. I scanned the room, searching for him among the crowd of swirling lights and laughter.

I turned to my mom, who smiled knowingly. My parents loved to attend activities, especially dances. They often went as leaders alongside their friends, bringing a sense of community and joy to these gatherings. It was heartwarming to see my mom enjoying the evening, adding to the festive atmosphere, and making the moment even more special.

After I met him at Patricia's, Elder Melazzo had gone to be released from his mission by his local church leader and then came straight to the dance. He stood out in the crowd, easily a head above the rest—he was easy to spot back against the stage, especially given that his gaze was right on me. My heart leaped in my chest as he wandered over. The moment felt magical as we mingled with our friends, laughing and dancing together as a group.

Finally, he turned to me and extended his hand. "Caroline, would you like to dance?" he asked, a warm smile on his face.

"Yes, I'd love to!" I tried to keep my cool as he took my hand in his and pulled me onto the dance floor and into his arms.

As Daniel and I swayed to the music, I couldn't help but think that he seemed interested in me too. There was a connection—a spark that made the dance floor feel even more alive. After a few songs, our group of friends decided to head to the movies. To my surprise, Patricia wasn't his only cousin in our friend group, which made it even more fun.

As we started walking to the movie theater, he said, "Hey, Caroline, I have something for you."

Curious, I extended my hand, expecting a small gift or maybe a snack, but instead, he took my hand in his. At that moment, butterflies fluttered in my stomach.

"Wow, your hand is so nice," I blurted out.

He smiled, "I'm just trying to keep it cozy." His eyes sparkled with mischief, and I couldn't help but giggle.

When we arrived at the movies, we settled into our seats next to each other, still holding hands. I felt his fingers lightly tracing patterns on my palm, sending delightful shivers up my spine.

"Are you enjoying the movie?" he whispered, leaning closer.

"Yeah, it's great," I whispered back, my heart racing as I caught a whiff of his cologne.

Even though we didn't kiss or do anything more than hold hands, the chemistry between us was undeniable. The warmth of his hand enveloping mine felt like a promise of something beautiful. After the movie, as we walked back to our cars, I couldn't wipe the smile off my face.

That night, I returned home feeling giddy and elated. I couldn't stop replaying the evening in my mind. I had just experienced one of the best nights of my life, and I knew deep down that this was just the beginning of something special. As I lay in bed, I felt excited for the future, imagining all the possibilities that lie ahead. It was as if Heavenly Father's plan for me was aligning in a way that hinted at a beautiful journey unfolding—one I couldn't wait to explore.

* * *

The following week, I was filled with excitement for the upcoming singles youth camp, an event for single adults from various stakes (geographical areas comprising several wards). A bus was scheduled to pick up the youth from my stake, and I could hardly contain my anticipation, especially knowing that Daniel might be there.

On the day of the camp, my friends and I boarded the bus, our chatter filled with hopes of seeing him. We eagerly looked out the windows, scanning the scenery going by. As the bus pulled over to pick up more youth from our stake, my friend exclaimed, "Caroline, that's him! Daniel's over there!"

I leaned closer to the window, and to my surprise, there he was, dressed in a gaucho outfit that made him look both hilarious and charming. He wore a large hat and bombacho pants, traditional attire from the South. I laughed.

"Oh my gosh, that *cannot* be him!" I chuckled at his boldness. But it was indeed him, showcasing his unique personality and sense of humor. After serving his mission, he decided to embrace this cultural style, and it suited him in the most endearing way.

Once we were all settled on the bus, I found myself sitting next to him. Daniel had brought a small chess set.

He looked at me. "Hey, do you want to play?"

"Sure!" I nodded eagerly, excited to spend some one-on-one time with him. As we set up the board, the noise around us faded into the background. Each move became a playful challenge, filled with laughter and friendly banter. The game turned into a delightful distraction, and I found myself not only enjoying the chess but also cherishing the easy connection that Daniel and I were forming. As we played, we talked and laughed, sharing little stories about ourselves. It was easy and comfortable, and I enjoyed every moment.

When we finally arrived at the youth camp, I was blown away by the beautiful surroundings. The lush greenery and open space felt so peaceful. They organized us into groups for activities, and to my delight, we ended up in the same group. It felt like fate.

That first night, there was another dance. When we sat down next to each other after dancing for a while, I could feel the electricity between us. He took my hand gently, whispering sweet compliments that made my heart flutter. I felt a rush of affection, and in a moment of spontaneity, I leaned in and kissed him on the cheek. I flushed with both excitement and a hint of shyness. It was a natural expression of the connection we had built, and I hoped it conveyed the feelings blooming within me. As I pulled back, I caught a glimpse of surprise and delight in his eyes, solidifying the bond we were starting to create.

A smile spread across his face. "Wow, you're bold!" His tone was playful yet genuinely impressed.

That reaction made my heart race even faster, a mix of exhilaration and relief flooding through me. I had taken a leap, and it felt like it had landed perfectly. His warm laughter filled the space between us, and I couldn't help but smile back, feeling a rush of confidence.

A little later, he leaned in closer and kissed me, this time on the lips. It felt magical.

As the night went on, we talked about everything and nothing, our connection deepening with each passing moment. The music played softly in the background, but we barely noticed. At that moment, nothing else mattered.

Finally, as the stars twinkled above us, he looked into my eyes and asked, "So . . . would you like to start dating?"

Without hesitation, I replied, "Yes, of course! Yes!" My heart soared as we solidified our feelings for each other and started our incredible journey together.

Our dating journey unfolded across the backdrop of different cities, each visit filled with anticipation and excitement. Since neither Daniel nor I had our own cars at the time, we had to get creative. He would take the bus to come see me, while I drove my father's car to visit him. Despite the logistics, we took turns making the trips, and it always felt worth it. Those moments together were special; we cherished every second.

We filled our weekends with adventures, attending religious classes and single adult activities where we'd laugh and meet new friends. Movie nights became a favorite, whether at a theater or snuggled up on the couch at one of our homes. Sundays were particularly meaningful, as we often shared lunch with my family or his, exchanging stories and laughter over delicious food. Each experience drew us closer.

After a year and a half of dating, Daniel and I finally got married. He wanted to marry sooner, but I wanted to make sure we had enough time to truly know each other and not rush into anything. Our timing was just right.

Our wedding day was incredibly special.

We had three ceremonies, all in one day. It was so crazy—I don't know how I agreed to that! We chose to have all the ceremonies on the same day because we had booked our honeymoon to Rio de Janeiro for the very next morning. With an early flight ahead, we wanted to ensure that we could fully celebrate our marriage without the stress of juggling schedules. It was super busy for us, but as always, it all worked out in the end.

First, we went to the city hall for a simple marriage with a notary and a witness. In Brazil, the law requires couples to be married civilly before they can be married in the temple. We could have had the party and the notary together, but we wanted to be able to focus while at the temple, so we decided to have the party afterward. It felt surreal to finally be standing there together, but it was just the beginning. Immediately after, we headed to the temple, which was the highlight of the day.

The atmosphere was sacred, and I felt the Savior's love envelop me as soon as I stepped inside. The experience was so profound; I felt like I was literally in heaven as we listened to the beautiful words spoken by our sealer—the man performing the marriage ceremony. He reminded us that we were married for eternity, emphasizing that life would bring challenges and that we must always support one another. I recalled the analogy of the triangle: As we draw closer to God, we inevitably grow closer to one another. Strengthening our relationship with the Lord would deepen our bond as a couple, creating a strong foundation for our marriage that could withstand any challenge. This understanding filled me with hope.

I felt such overwhelming joy knowing that this was a commitment for forever. What made it even more special was that the sealer was the same priesthood holder who had given my mother a blessing before she became pregnant with me when my parents were struggling with pregnancy. He had also sealed Daniel's parents, which added an extra layer of significance to our ceremony. It felt like our families were intertwined in a beautiful way.

After the ceremony, we stepped outside the temple to take pictures. I was still in my white dress, feeling the joy of the moment, when a temple worker came up to me and asked, "Do you have a bouquet?"

"No," I replied.

"There's this bouquet of flowers right here. We don't know where it came from, but you can use it." She handed me a stunning bouquet of all-white flowers, and it felt like the perfect touch for our photos. This kind gesture was a beautiful reminder of the Savior's love for me, reinforcing the blessings of the day and making the moment even more special.

Later, we went back to prepare for our wedding party that evening. It was an absolute blast! My cousin had gifted us a beautiful venue downtown, and we invited around 300 guests. To my surprise, way more than that showed up to celebrate with us. The energy in the room was electric, and it was heartwarming to be surrounded by so much love and joy.

The day was everything I had dreamed of and more, filled with love, laughter, and memories that I would cherish forever.

Daniel and I danced together for the first time as husband and wife to the dulcet tones of "Endless Love" by Lionel Richie and Diana Ross, and I couldn't help but feel grateful for the journey that had brought us to this moment. It was the perfect beginning to our life together.

* * *

A year after our wedding, I felt a strong desire to become a mother, and I was blessed with my first child when I was just twenty-one years old. While marrying young brought me joy, becoming a mother presented its own challenges. My son needed casts starting just thirteen days after birth, and I won't lie—I was scared about what that might mean for his future.

The day I went for my twenty-week ultrasound (officially called a fetal anatomy scan), when the nurse applied the gel on my belly and began moving the ultrasound probe from side to side, her expression changed from calm to concerned. My heart sank.

"Is something wrong?" I asked.

She hesitated, her brow furrowing. "There's an issue with your baby's feet. I need to call your doctor to discuss this further." Her words sent a wave of anxiety through me. Why wouldn't she go into detail? My mind raced with questions. Was this something serious? A knot tightened in my stomach.

We couldn't speak with the doctor before I had to leave for work, so they said she would call. I went straight to work, overwhelmed with worry. I cried at my desk as I thought about what this might mean. When my doctor, Roberta, called later that day, she wanted to see me right away. I rushed over, my heart racing. Sitting in her office, I felt a mix of dread and hope.

"Roberta, what did the ultrasound show?" My voice trembled.

She looked me in the eyes and said gently, "Your son has congenital clubfoot." She went on to explain that this condition, known medically as congenital talipes equinovarus, occurs when a baby's foot or feet are twisted out of shape or position. "In clubfoot," she continued, "the affected foot typically appears to be turned inward and downward, resembling a golf club, which is where the name comes from." She assured me that while the exact cause is often unknown, it can occur in isolation or as part of a genetic syndrome. "The good news is that with early treatment, most children can grow up to lead normal, active lives."

The fear I felt lingered. "Is there anything else? Are there other issues?" I pressed, anxiety rising within me.

"Thankfully no," she assured me. "This will be a challenge for you as parents, but it won't be a burden for your child. He'll grow up and likely not even remember having this condition." Her calm demeanor and reassuring words brought me a sense of relief, but I continued to worry about what was to come. Yet through it all, I felt the Lord's hand guiding me.

It was no coincidence that while working at Mattel, the toy manufacturer, I had a coworker whose son faced the same condition as my baby. She recommended a doctor, and to my surprise, a manager at my workplace was friends with that very doctor.

Under the care of Dr. Monica Nogueira, my son transitioned from casts to special boots after three months. I felt immense gratitude for the divine connections that helped us navigate this challenging time.

We first visited Dr. Nogueira's clinic before my son was born, and it was an eye-opening experience. I had never seen so many children with club feet gathered in one place; it was a world I didn't even know existed. Families had traveled from Japan and other parts of Brazil just to see her, and in that moment, I realized how blessed we were to have found such an incredible doctor. Dr. Nogueira came to visit us in the hospital when my son was only thirteen days old, and that was a great blessing.

For the first three weeks, we went to her clinic every Tuesday and Friday to change my son's cast. It was winter, and our home didn't have a fireplace, so the cold was biting. The treatment spanned through July and August, the coldest months in São Paulo, but my family was always there to support me. While my husband had to work, my parents would take Miguel and me to the doctor's appointments. My mom regularly made lunch and dinner for our family of three, and my brother and sister were always loving and supportive through those cold months.

Dr. Nogueira advised me to use a hair dryer to make sure his casts dried properly and to keep his legs warm. The casts covered most of both legs, and my baby cried, realizing that his freedom to kick and move had been taken away.

At night, I would lay him down on the bed and gently dry his casts with the hair dryer, keeping it at a safe distance. Those first nights were tough—he didn't sleep at all. Bathing him was also really difficult. Daniel and I would take turns bathing him and wrapping plastic bags around his casts to try to keep them from getting wet.

Daniel made an effort to get up in the middle of the night to be with Miguel so I could get some sleep. Those three weeks were hard, but they brought us closer together as a family.

After three weeks, we returned to Dr. Nogueira's clinic for the next step in his treatment. She applied a local anesthetic cream and performed a small procedure to cut his tendons, allowing his feet to move up and down. This was part of the Ponseti method, which was difficult for me to watch, but I trusted the process.

Things became more challenging when my son had to wear orthopedic boots, which featured metal bars to keep his feet in place. They cut into his skin and caused bleeding. I had to use a special gel-like bandage that acted like a second skin to cushion his bones.

"Don't worry, it's not hurting him. He'll be fine," Dr. Nogueira reassured me, yet it was still painful to witness.

Later, back at home, Daniel watched as I carefully placed the silicone gel bandages on Miguel's ankles, trying to protect his tender skin. "Do you think this is too much?" Daniel asked, gnawing on his thumbnail as he watched.

I looked at Miguel's little face and sighed. "It's hard to watch, but it's going to be worth it. His feet are getting better, and this is the best technique. He'll be running around like any other kid one day."

After Daniel saw how to apply the bandages, he and I would take turns applying them to Miguel's feet.

Those three months of wearing the boots around the clock were hard work. Breastfeeding also presented challenges as he struggled to move his legs freely. Eventually, he wore the boots for fourteen hours each day, and he did that until he was two years old.

Some nights, the *thud, thud, thud* of boots echoing through the hallway found our ears as Miguel crawled as fast as ever across the tiled floor, making his way to our bedroom. He moved faster with those boots than I ever thought possible.

It was hard to watch my son struggle with those boots on his feet, but I could see him growing stronger because of them. I could see Daniel and I growing stronger as a couple as well. When we were married in the temple, we promised that we would be there for each other, as all couples promise when they say, "To have and to hold, to cherish, in sickness and in health." But in the temple, we also receive the promise that as we keep our vows, God will be there to help us and support us too.

Knowing that Daniel was as committed to me as I was to him, and that together we were committed to Miguel, created a level of security and connection that made me feel part of something bigger than just myself. At times, motherhood can feel overwhelming and bigger than any woman is able to manage, but having a partner to share the burden with makes such a difference. It made it so that I never felt alone. If I made a mistake, there was someone there to catch me, and if we struggled together, God was there to catch us.

Through the trials and joys of marriage, I learned that a strong foundation built on faith and shared values can sustain us. My husband and I continue to grow together, deepening our commitment to one another and to our family. Our journey serves as a reminder that love, patience, and faith are essential parts in the beautiful tapestry of marriage.

It was such a relief when that phase of treatment finally came to an end. What a victory it was for all of us!

A Journey of Teachings and Resilience

Motherhood has been an incredible journey—one filled with profound blessings, significant challenges, and many sacrifices. When I was pregnant with Miguel, I graduated with my degree in business and was working my way up the corporate ladder. When he was born, I was working in the joint position of assistant to the HR department and to the office of the CEO. I loved my job and was looking at the possibility of being promoted or transferred to a new department with increased pay and responsibilities.

Miguel brought immeasurable joy and light into our lives, and I loved the time I was able to spend with him during my maternity leave. With his sweet spirit and sociable nature, he connected effortlessly with everyone around him.

While I was still on maternity leave, I received a phone call from the HR department asking if I was interested in a position in the company's licensing department. They had a position that was opening up around the time I would be coming back, and they wanted to know if I wanted the position. I was ecstatic and accepted it on the spot. Besides it being the department I had hoped to be transferred to, it came with a pay raise that I knew would help cover Miguel's treatments. With a new job waiting for me, I felt more relaxed and was able to focus more on Miguel and on myself.

Daniel and I lived on the same street where my parents lived with my brother and sister, and we would go over to have dinner with my family regularly. It was special having daily contact with my parents and siblings. I will forever be grateful for the times after Miguel was born when we could all be together.

After dinner one night, my mom brought my sister, my brother, Daniel, and me into the living room. She told us she had gone to the doctor recently because she had been bleeding. The doctor had found a tumor in her intestine and diagnosed her with advanced cancer, the same cancer my grandmother had died from two years earlier. She needed to have surgery to remove thirty centimeters of her large intestine.

When my mom told us that news, I knew there would be a hard road ahead. I had seen how difficult it was for my grandmother to endure her cancer, and I knew that my mother would likely spend so much time in the hospital that it would become like a second home to her. I hoped she would get better and make a full recovery, but I didn't know if she would. What I did know was that whether she was alive on this earth or not, because of the covenants our family had made in the temple, our family would always be together. And it was that knowledge that made it bearable.

After my mom was diagnosed with cancer, I was incredibly sad and worried about her. One night when I was praying for her, I prayed that she would have the strength and energy that she needed. And I prayed that she would be able to have the help that she needed. As I was praying, I was overcome with the feeling that my mom needed *my* help. She had been there for me my whole life, and now it was my turn to be there for her when she needed me. I knew that this meant I would have to step away from work and turn down the new position I had accepted.

In 2010, President Dieter F. Uchtdorf, a leader in The Church of Jesus Christ of Latter-day Saints, shared this thought in general conference: "We would do well to slow down a little, proceed at the optimum speed for our circumstances, focus on the significant, lift up our eyes, and truly see the things that matter most."[4] This quote came to my mind, and everything became crystal clear. When weighing the needs of my mom against my job, there really wasn't any choice in the matter. Family is the thing that matters most.

While Miguel continued his treatments and my mom prepared to start her cancer treatments, I started to experience significant bleeding. I knew there had to be a problem with the contraception I was taking, so I scheduled an appointment with my doctor. When I arrived, she asked if I was pregnant, and I told her no. "My son is only nine months old. I'd like to wait a little bit before I get pregnant again." She asked me to take a test just to make sure, and when I got the test result back, it was positive. I was seventeen weeks pregnant. Terrified that the bleeding meant I had lost the baby, I rushed over to

---

4. Dieter F. Uchtdorf, "Of Things That Matter Most," *Ensign* or *Liahona*, Nov. 2010.

the ER, where they gave me an ultrasound. It was there that I heard Arthur's heartbeat for the first time.

Arthur's arrival felt like a precious gift, and by the time he turned one, he was already chatting away about everything. Life with two boys dramatically shifted our family dynamic, multiplying not just our joy but also the delightful chaos that came with it.

With Arthur now in our life, we transitioned into a family of four. Balancing the responsibilities of raising two energetic boys while staying committed to our church attendance and gospel-centered living became increasingly important. Sibling rivalry occasionally sparked, but my husband and I leaned on our faith and love for the Lord to navigate these challenges. We knew that our shared values would guide us through any storms we faced.

Three children felt like the right number for us; growing up with two siblings, I always imagined three would be ideal. When my third baby, Pedro, arrived, I felt blessed yet again. He was our New Year's baby. That night, after watching the beautiful fireworks display, I went to sleep, only to be awakened suddenly in the middle of the night.

As I stood to check on my boys, I felt my water break. A strange smell filled the air, and I quickly shook my husband awake, exclaiming, "My water broke. My water broke!"

"Wait, what?" He jolted awake, his eyes wide with urgency.

"I just called my doctor, and he didn't leave town for the holidays! We need to go to the hospital!"

"Let's go!" he replied, quickly grabbing a towel and handing it to me. He led me out to the car, got me situated, and then ran to the driver's side. "Just hold on tight!"

The hospital was close by, but it felt like a lifetime as we raced through the quiet streets. "You're doing great, Caroline." Daniel glanced over at me. "Just focus on your breathing."

Once we got settled into a room at the hospital, I turned to him, panic rising. "Daniel, my contractions." They were rolling through me so fast—too fast. "I'm in so much pain. Please, call for a nurse!"

"I'll find someone." He rushed off, leaving me gripping the edge of the bed, waves of pain crashing over me. Time felt distorted in those moments, seconds stretching into what felt like hours.

Fortunately, the anesthetist arrived soon after, bringing with him a flicker of hope.

"I'm here to help," he said. As he administered the epidural, I let out a breath I didn't know I was holding. "Just a little longer," he encouraged.

Almost immediately, the pain began to ease, and I could finally focus on the joy of welcoming our new baby.

A few hours later, with Daniel by my side, I welcomed Pedro into the world. As I held him in my arms, tears of joy filled my eyes. "He's perfect," I whispered.

Daniel squeezed my hand, his eyes shining with pride and happiness. "I knew you could do it," he said, leaning in to kiss my forehead. "Welcome to our family, little Pedro. You've completed us."

In that moment, our hearts swelled with love, knowing that our family of five was finally whole.

* * *

Just ten months after Pedro's birth, we faced another heavy trial. My father was diagnosed with hepatitis C, a consequence of a blood transfusion he had received forty years prior. While we awaited his liver transplant, my mother continued her courageous fight against cancer. By this point, she had been courageously battling cancer for five years. This was an especially trying time for all of us, and the weight of these challenges pressed heavily on my heart.

When my mother was pregnant with my sister, Jacqueline, I was almost four years old. At that time, my parents bought their second home. It wasn't perfect—there were rats in the house, and my father took it upon himself to handle the problem. He set out poison to get rid of them, but tragically, he didn't protect himself properly, and the poison entered his bloodstream, stopping his body from producing white blood cells.

One Sunday morning, as he was shaving before church, he cut himself and the bleeding wouldn't stop. Alarmed, he went to the hospital. It was a close call—he nearly died that day. My mother called a doctor from our ward, who rushed to the hospital. When the doctor arrived, he administered a priesthood blessing to my father—evoking the power of God—and then helped take care of his bleeding.

The priesthood blessing my father received was a miracle that day, keeping him alive. He required multiple blood transfusions to replenish his blood supply, but while those transfusions saved his life, there was an unexpected consequence: Some of the blood he received was contaminated, leading to his diagnosis of hepatitis C.

For years, the disease remained undetected, but when the symptoms finally appeared, it was too late. My father tried various treatments, but none worked. Eventually, he needed a liver transplant.

When I learned about his diagnosis, I felt an overwhelming mix of emotions: sadness, anxiety, frustration, anger, determination. But above all, I felt gratitude we'd been lucky to have him in our lives for so long. I felt hopeful that he would get through this if it was the Lord's will.

"We'll get through this." I gripped Daniel's hand and kept my voice steady though I had tears in my eyes. I had always been taught by my parents to trust in the wisdom of God. I knew He loved me and that whatever happened would work out for the best. "I never questioned God. I just don't want them to suffer."

As we celebrated Pedro's first birthday, our joy was muted. We had a small cake while both of my parents were in the hospital—my father waiting for his transplant and my mother undergoing surgery for her cancer. That moment served as a stark reminder of life's unpredictability and the importance of faith in the face of adversity.

A Journey Through Grief and Faith

In January 2012, shortly after New Year's, my father and mother were admitted to different hospitals. My father went to a facility specializing in liver care, while my mother was fighting her relentless battle with cancer at a hospital specializing in cancer.

With my children being just one, three, and five years old, it was incredibly difficult for me to juggle everything. My siblings and I worked tirelessly to coordinate schedules, ensuring our parents always had someone by their sides. As the only one married with kids, I often felt overwhelmed by my limitations in providing support. Thankfully, my aunts stepped in, offering invaluable help during this challenging time.

On my mother's side, I have my aunts Mara and Eliane, who are her sisters, and the aunts married to my mother's brothers: Cláudia, Glória, Regiane, and Eliane.

When my mother got sick, all my aunts rallied around her to provide support and care. Aunt Mara in particular was a constant presence by my mother's side. With her more flexible schedule and no children of her own, she was able to devote the most time to my mother during this difficult period.

All my aunts and uncles lived in the same building in the same neighborhood, while our family lived a bit farther away. Still, we were always together. Whenever we gathered, there was an abundance of food, celebrations, and festivities, including many Christmases and New Year's celebrations filled with dancing and joy.

The bond between my aunts and cousins created a strong sense of family, and those moments spent together are some of my fondest memories.

Aunt Mara and my mother's siblings were not the type to openly express their feelings. They were strong individuals with formidable personalities, yet they each possessed a soft heart hidden beneath their tough exteriors.

Growing up, they had a hard time demonstrating their emotions, largely due to our grandmother's upbringing. She was a busy woman who believed that if she didn't show affection, none of her children would compete for her attention. As a result, they all grew up with a scarcity of hugs and tenderness.

* * *

One day, I visited my mom when Aunt Mara was there, helping her with baths and everything she needed. Mara's eyes were filled with a longing for my mom to get better, even though there was little she could do beyond providing support.

I leaned in and asked Mara, "How is Mom doing?"

She paused for a moment, her voice gentle yet tinged with worry. "We just need to pray for a miracle, and we hope your mom doesn't have pain."

Aunt Mara was always by my mother's side during chemotherapy, a constant source of strength. "I'm so thankful for you, Mara," I said to her one evening, watching as she helped my mom settle back into bed.

"Oh, honey," she replied, her eyes welling with tears. "I'm just doing what any sister would do."

Despite their stoic nature, the bond between my mother and her siblings was beautiful to admire. They may have lacked the outward displays of affection, but their connection ran deep.

During our discussions, Aunt Mara often reminded me of how they faced challenges together. "You know, we might not say it out loud, but we feel it. When something needs fixing, we just get it done."

"Straight to the point, right?" I laughed, recalling how my aunts would say, "Just go and resolve it! Don't waste time!"

"Exactly! We're all practical." Her eyes twinkled with amusement. "That probably comes from the Libyan side of the family. They say our great-grandmother Maria had a tough personality, while her husband, Miguel, was the sweetest man."

"Wasn't Miguel a pioneer in Guarulhos?" I asked, intrigued.

"Yes, he was," Mara nodded. "There's even a street named after him in our hometown."

My mother's siblings were a constant source of strength, always rallying together to support one another, whether the challenges they faced were financial, emotional, or health-related.

The Relief Society also played a crucial role, with many sisters staying with my mother, keeping her company, helping her shower, and offering comfort. The unity and love within our family, and that which we received from the members of the Church, moved me to tears, and I often reflected on how deeply my mother connected with those sisters.

My mother served as the president of the Relief Society in her area for many years. When she was diagnosed with cancer, she was released as president, but the new president asked her to stay on because of her example. So my mother agreed to continue serving as the Relief Society second counselor until her last days, embodying steadfast faith and unwavering support.

After so many years of witnessing service performed by the ward members, we weren't surprised that they would offer us support, but they did so much more than that. The outpouring of love and affection from the members during this trying time made me feel as if heaven were descending upon us to lift us up. We felt their love as they prayed for us, fasted for us, brought us meals, sat with my mother or father in the hospital, and comforted my whole family.

* * *

My father was the sweetest, most selfless person I knew. He always served and helped others. Everyone around him adored him. But being in a different hospital at the same time that my mom was getting ready for surgery was really difficult for him. He wanted to be near my mother. He always took her out to eat so he could spend time with her. They would go to church meetings together and regularly served together. They were always doing everything together, whether it was with family or friends. Being in separate hospitals made it harder for them to spend time together.

But that wasn't the only thing that made communication between my parents difficult. Whenever they attempted to speak, the emotional weight often left them in tears, prompting them to avoid the conversation altogether.

Meanwhile, my father was awaiting a liver transplant, and I could see his condition deteriorating. One day, as I sat at the kitchen table, my phone rang. I answered to hear his voice, shaky and filled with emotion.

"Hey, sweetie," he began, trying to sound cheerful but failing. "I wanted to talk to you about something important."

"What's on your mind, Dad?" I sat up a little taller.

"I'm just worried." His voice trembled. "I fear that your boys won't remember me. With everything going on, I might not have much time left." I could hear my dad crying as he spoke the words.

My heart sank, and I tightened my grip on my phone. "Dad, they love you. They think you're the coolest grandpa in the world. But I understand. I want them to see you."

"Really? You think that would help?" Hope flickered in his voice.

"Yes. I'll find a way to get special permission for them to visit," I promised.

The hospital policies didn't allow young children to visit where my father was waiting for his transplant, but I called the hospital and asked to speak with the management. It took a few minutes, but after a transfer or two, and a heartfelt conversation, I managed to get permission to bring my boys so they could visit their grandfather.

On the day of the visit, I felt a mix of excitement and anxiety as I drove to the hospital with my boys in the back seat, chattering eagerly about seeing their grandpa.

"Do you think he'll be okay?" Miguel asked, his brows furrowed.

"He'll be so happy to see you," I tried to reassure him.

As we walked down the corridor to my father's room, a knot formed in my stomach. At his room, I peeked around the frame and then quickly led the boys in. Dad lay in bed, his belly swollen and his face pale. Yet when he spotted us, a broad smile broke across his face.

"Meninos!" Excitement lit up his eyes. He beckoned for them to come to him, arms outstretched. "Come here."

They rushed to his side. He dug into his bedside drawer and pulled out a pack of crackers. "Look what I have."

"Crackers!" they squealed, delighted by the unexpected treat.

He handed them out like treasures. To me, they were.

I cherished the bond the boys shared with my father. He was always expressing his love for us. My father had always been very loving and generous with us as children and was now the same way with his grandchildren. He was always involved in our lives and supported us no matter how inconvenient it might have been for him. It was easy for me to love him, and it was easy for my boys to love him too.

My father's eyes sparkled as he watched them enjoy their snacks, and I couldn't help but smile at the memories of how he always showered my boys with presents and treats. He would take them to the "Loja de Um Real"—a Brazilian store similar to the Dollar Tree— and let them pick out little toys and trinkets.

Some Saturday mornings, he would knock on our door, beaming with joy as he handed us fresh, warm bread from the bakery. That was my father—always thinking of us, always showing his love for our family. And oh, how he adored my boys.

As they nibbled, my father shared stories, his voice growing stronger as he animatedly recounted adventures from his youth. The room, usually heavy with worry, became filled with laughter and light.

"This is the best day ever!" Miguel shouted.

My father chuckled, and the sound filled my heart with warmth. Here we were, creating precious memories that would linger in my boys' hearts long after my father was gone.

After some time, my father turned serious, his gaze focused on my boys. "You know, boys, your grandpa loves you very much. Always remember that, okay?"

"Yes, Grandpa!" they chimed in unison from their spots crowded around the edges of his bed.

As we prepared to leave, my father took my hand and squeezed. "Thank you for bringing them. You don't know how much this means to me."

I smiled and ran my thumb over the back of his frail hands—the same hands, once so strong, that had lifted me up, sheltered me, given me blessings, and more. "I think I do. We're all in this together, Dad."

The following day, we received news that he needed to be sedated.

Sharing the news with my mother that the doctors planned to turn off the life support machines was one of the most painful things I've ever done in my life.

But she looked at me with her unwavering calm and said, "My child, while there is life, there is hope. Be strong." That was my mother—grounded in faith even in the darkest moments.

After my father passed away, my mother returned home, but I could sense her deep sorrow from missing him. Just a month later, she was back in the hospital. My siblings and I gathered to say our goodbyes.

Each night, I called my brother to check if she had passed, but she lingered on. After three days, our dear friend and Relief Society president, Terezinha, knocked on my door. I opened it to find her smiling, her energy brightening the room.

"Hey! I just had to come by," she said, stepping inside. "I had a dream last night, and it kept nagging at me."

"Oh? What was it about?" I asked, curious.

"I dreamt that you needed to spend some time with your mom, go to the hospital, and be with her today," she replied, her expression sincere. "I want to offer to babysit your kids."

I was taken aback for a moment. "Wow, Terezinha, that's so thoughtful of you! I hadn't even thought about going to see my mom today."

"I'm here for you to go," she said. "Family is everything, and I know how much you cherish those moments with her."

"Thank you so much. That means a lot to me." A wave of gratitude washed over me.

"Great. Just let me know when you're ready, and I'll keep the kids entertained. They'll have a blast." She rubbed her hands together and grinned.

As we chatted a bit more, I realized how blessed I was to have leader friends like Terezinha—people who not only supported me but also acted as a guiding light during moments when I needed it most.

As I arrived at the hospital, I invited my mother's siblings to join us for one final goodbye. My mother was so weak that I was surprised she hadn't passed yet. I wondered what she was waiting for. I didn't want her to suffer anymore. I knew my mother was still breathing because I could see the gauze near her oxygen mask moving up and down.

Gently, I ran my fingers through her hair and was inspired to sing:

> Come, take a little hand, and wipe away a tear.
> This love will last throughout eternity.
> A mother's call is holy, ordained by God above
> To help, to teach, and bless with charity.[5]

As I finished singing the hymn, I noticed a single tear rolling down her cheek. Though many believe that those who are sedated can't hear or feel, I knew she was listening.

I leaned in close and whispered in her ear. "I promise, Mãe . . . Jacqueline, Henry, and I will stay faithful in the gospel, and we'll never fight over material inheritance." In that moment, the rise and fall of her breath ceased. I felt her spirit leave her mortal body, free from pain.

---

5. Jayne L. Brown and Robert F. Brunner, "Come Take a Little Hand," The Church of Jesus Christ of Latter-day Saints, accessed Nov. 5, 2024, https://www.churchofjesuschrist.org/media/music/songs/come-take-a-little-hand.

In that moment, I knew I was by myself. Where I had felt companionship a moment before, my mother was no longer by my side. Yet I was astonished despite my pain. As I tried to process what was happening, peace came over me. I felt as though just out of sight, my mother was being welcomed back with loving arms. In our faith, we believe our family members wait to welcome us as we step away from mortal life. I could feel that and was reminded of the temple and our family members who had already passed away. It was a great comfort to feel as though my father was receiving her and hugging her as they would walk into a new life together, never again to be separated.

I whispered softly, "My mom is gone." After that, I stepped out of the room. With a heavier heart, I announced to the corridor, "My mom is gone," urgently seeking a nurse to inform her and to find out what to do next.

My father passed away just three days after my birthday, on February 17, and my mother followed on April 21, 2012. Interestingly, my father's birthday was April 22, and we like to think he welcomed her as a precious gift on the other side and that they celebrated like they never had before—with other loved ones who had gone on before them. My siblings and I imagined a welcome home party, filled with joy that my parents were together again in that eternal realm.

A movie was released that year predicting the end of the world, and I thought, "This is the end of my parents." But it wasn't the end of our eternal family.

At their separate funerals, the crowd was overwhelming, with many coming to comfort my brother, sister, and me. Yet despite the sorrow, I felt an unexplainable strength enveloping us—a peace that came from knowing they were together and free from pain.

I held fast to the knowledge that the gospel assures us we will be together again. That's why I cherish the temple; it holds the promise of forever. Though we know this truth, the everyday reality is a constant reminder of how much I miss them, yet I find comfort in the Holy Ghost, guiding me through the void they left behind.

Spreading the Good Word: Podcasting

Two years after my parents passed away, Daniel wanted to get his MBA, and so we moved to Utah to try to apply for BYU. When he got accepted to Tampa Bay University instead, we relocated to Florida. Those years weren't the easiest, but the Church members in Tampa welcomed us and loved us, for which we will always be grateful. Daniel graduated and got a job in Florida, and we lived there for six years before moving back to Utah for another job.

I had the opportunity, back in Utah, to participate in the TV program *Come Follow Up* by BYU TV. On the Church website, they have an application to cast audience members. So I applied, and they chose me. *Come Follow Up* is a live discussion with a religion professor where people are invited to ask questions about the gospel of Jesus Christ. The guest responds to their questions and discusses how viewers can apply the Bible and the Book of Mormon in their lives. It was a wonderful experience to be able to participate in that.

I was so excited after that experience that I wanted to find more resources to help me with my daily study of the scriptures. I found a plethora of YouTube channels and podcasts in English but very few in Portuguese. I realized then how blessed the English-speaking work is to have so many gospel-based resources available, and I wanted to share those with my fellow Brazilians. I began brainstorming what I could do to help create more gospel resources for Portuguese speakers.

There were a handful of men who were making videos in Portuguese, but I noticed there were very few women. I wanted to make something that would help motivate women in the Church to study their scriptures and feel like they weren't alone. In many places in Brazil, The Church of Jesus Christ of Latter-day Saints doesn't always have a large congregation for its members to feel supported. I wanted to make something that would help those women feel like they had a resource they could go to. I wanted them to know that someone was thinking of them. I wanted to connect with them and help serve my home country.

While Daniel was getting his MBA, my brother and sister moved to England. After several years of being apart—partially because of COVID—my sister and I were finally able to reunite when she came to Utah to visit with her husband and son. It was the first time I got to meet my nephew, and it was such a special time. The bond between my siblings and me has grown even stronger after the loss of our parents, and it's something we want to preserve for the rest of our lives.

During this visit to Utah, I decided to host a tea party at my home and invited some friends from our youth who now lived in Utah. It was a beautiful sunny afternoon. We made pão de queijo and cakes, and I set out my best china. We all sat around the table, enjoying each other's company, laughing, and reminiscing.

As we gathered around the table, I shared my thoughts about the abundance of English-language resources for scripture study and Church materials, expressing my desire to create something for the Portuguese-speaking community. This longing resonates deeply within me, especially since I didn't serve a mission and share with others the joy and blessings that the gospel has brought to my own life.

At one point, we started discussing our plans and things we wanted to do. I mentioned that I had this idea of starting a podcast. That's when Laís, one of my sister's friends with a bold and lively personality, jumped in. (She was a mother of three, and it amazed me how much energy she had.)

"I'll do it with you!" she said in her raspy, energetic voice.

"Really?" I asked, a bit surprised. "You'd be up for it?"

"Yes! Let's make it happen!" She brushed her beautiful brown hair behind her ear, her eyes sparkling with enthusiasm.

Then Letícia, another friend at the table, chimed in. "Well, if you're serious, you should set a date for the meeting and start planning for next year." Her smile never failed to light up a room.

I looked at them both, a little overwhelmed but excited. "Okay, let's do it."

Laís smiled and nodded, "It's set. We'll make it happen."

* * *

The day I met Laís at her house, I was excited for our meeting. It was a calm afternoon after my part-time job, and I headed straight to her place, eager to get started. When I arrived, Laís greeted me at the door with her usual warm smile and energy.

"Oi amiga, thanks for coming!" she said, giving me a quick hug. "You won't believe what just happened. Ana dropped off her kids earlier, and before I even mentioned the podcast, she gave me this." She held up a large New Testament book, filled with pictures and study notes. "Can you believe it? She said she brought it for me without even knowing what we were planning!"

I raised my eyebrows, surprised. "Really? That's amazing! Especially since Sunday School next year will be focusing on the New Testament."

Laís nodded enthusiastically. "Exactly! It felt like more than just a coincidence."

Shortly after, Ana arrived. She looked radiant with her blond hair and green eyes. "Hey Laís! Hey Caroline!" Excited energy came off her in waves. "I just dropped off the kids."

"Perfect timing!" Laís replied. "I mentioned you might want to join us for our podcast meeting."

Ana's eyes sparkled with excitement. "Oh, I would love that! I actually have some ideas I'd like to share."

"Great! We'd love to have you," Laís said, leading Ana to the living room.

The three of us settled in and got to work while the kids played quietly in the background. We already knew we wanted to base the podcast around *Come, Follow Me*—the Church's home-centered study program that encourages families to study the scriptures together at home—focusing on next year's study of the New Testament. But now, with Ana on board, we were brainstorming even more ideas.

"You know," Ana started, leaning forward, "I've worked on some of these types of projects before. I could help with creating the vignette for the podcast, like an intro. I even recorded a few sample voice-overs. Let me show you."

She pulled out her phone and played a clip. Her voice was smooth and professional but still warm and inviting—the perfect tone for our podcast introduction.

Laís and I exchanged a look of approval. "Wow, Ana, that's amazing!" I said. "This is exactly what we need!"

Laís nodded. "Yes, it's perfect. You're so talented. This is really going to elevate the whole thing."

With the vignette taken care of, we moved on to another important detail: the name. Laís turned to me and said, "Now, we just need to figure out what to call this thing. It has to be something that really reflects what we're trying to do."

We all started throwing out ideas, brainstorming names that captured the spirit of the podcast. We wanted it to be simple yet meaningful—something that would resonate with people who would participate in *Come, Follow Me* with us.

"I think it needs to reflect how we want to guide others in their spiritual journey," I said. "Something that's both uplifting and relatable."

As we brainstormed ideas, we discussed the familiar biblical story of Martha and Mary. I recalled the verses where Jesus gently tells Martha, "Martha, Martha, thou art careful and troubled about many things: But one thing is needful: and Mary hath chosen that good part, which shall not be taken away from her" (Luke 10:41–42).

This story resonated deeply with us, highlighting the balance that we as women often need to find between being busy and being present. Martha, busy with preparations and overwhelmed by her responsibilities, represents the struggle many of us face in our daily lives. We often fill our schedules with tasks, believing that productivity equates to worthiness. Yet Jesus reminds us that amidst our busyness, we must not lose sight of what truly matters—being present and nurturing our relationships.

Mary, sitting at Jesus's feet, embodies the essence of choosing the "good part." Her focus on spiritual nourishment and connection serves as a powerful reminder that there are moments in life that deserve our undivided attention. In a world that often celebrates busyness as a virtue, this scripture calls us to reevaluate our priorities. Are we so caught up in our to-do lists that we miss the chance to engage meaningfully with those we love?

As we discussed this story, it sparked a rich conversation about our own lives. Each of us shared our experiences of juggling responsibilities—work, family, and community commitments—and the challenge of carving out time for what truly matters. We recognized that choosing the "good part" often requires intentionality and sometimes even sacrifice. It calls us to slow down, to listen, and to be present in the moment.

In a moment of inspiration, we decided on our new logo and vignette, symbols of our shared mission and vision. The logo beautifully encapsulates our values, serving as a reminder of the community we were building together.

Ana and I chimed in unison, "Let's call it 'Marta Maria: A Boa Parte do Dia Podcast.'" We burst into laughter, thrilled by our shared vision.

We were more motivated than ever, and with Ana now part of the team, our vision for the podcast was coming to life.

It felt like everything was falling into place. The excitement in the room was undeniable. We weren't just creating a podcast; we were building something that would help connect and uplift others. And we were doing it together with shared faith and purpose.

I won't deny that doubts about my abilities crept in, and I worried I might not be good enough. However, my desire to bless the lives of others far outweighed those concerns. I felt a strong calling to contribute positively, and that drive pushed me forward, encouraging me to embrace this new venture with enthusiasm and hope.

Before our first recording, I reached out to a man named Lucas in Brazil who had been creating videos and podcasts in Portuguese about the Church, and I told him about our meeting and idea.

"I'm transitioning my channel, Videira Verdadeira, to Scripture Central," he explained over the phone. "They're looking to amplify their content, and I think that more women talking about the gospel might be a great fit."

"That sounds amazing!" I replied, excitement bubbling up in my chest. "What do you need from us?"

Lucas continued, "I'm in talks with Dale, the board member responsible for Scripture Central in Portuguese. If you could send me a copy of your podcast, he and I will listen to it and see if this project aligns with what they want in their portfolio."

"Absolutely! I'll get that to you right away," I assured him. As we hung up, I felt a surge of hope. This could be an amazing opportunity!

* * *

Our first recording session took place in a random conference room, and I remember setting up with a borrowed microphone and basic resources. The room was a bit cramped, but we made it work. As we huddled around the table, excitement buzzed in the air.

"Can you believe we're actually doing this?" Ana adjusted her chair.

"I know! It feels so real now." I glanced at the microphone. "Let's just give it our best shot."

Despite the humble setup, we recorded our first episode, pouring our hearts into every word.

After wrapping up, I sent it off to Lucas. A few hours later, my phone buzzed with a message that made my heart race.

"He loves it!" I exclaimed, showing my friends the screen.

"Wow, that's amazing!" Laís said, her eyes wide with excitement.

"This could be our big break!"

A few days later, I received a message from Lucas and Dale, and they proposed a meeting to discuss working under the umbrella of Scripture Central. When I shared the news with my friends, we gathered in my living room, each of us buzzing with anticipation.

"Imagine having access to a real studio!" Ana said, practically bouncing in her seat.

"They offered us everything we needed—microphones, lights, the works!" I grinned from ear to ear.

Letícia's eyes sparkled with enthusiasm. "This is the next step up. This could become big."

With our hearts full of hope, we prepared for our meeting, excited about the possibility of elevating our project and sharing our faith with a wider audience. This was just the beginning, and I could already feel that something special was unfolding.

It was hard to express just how happy I was. What had started as a simple desire during a tea party had blossomed into a real opportunity. We were diving into discussions about what we loved most—sharing the precious truths of the gospel of Jesus Christ. Each brainstorming session became a chance to reflect on our faith, connect with one another, and create something meaningful for our community.

As the weeks progressed, our excitement grew. We began planning our next recordings and mapping out topics we wanted to explore—stories of faith, personal experiences, and the challenges women face in their spiritual journeys. Each episode felt like a labor of love, and the connection we built as a team deepened with every conversation.

Finally, the day came for our first studio session. Stepping into the Scripture Central studio in Springville felt surreal. The building, with its three levels, had a charming, rustic quality that contrasted beautifully with the polished, professional atmosphere inside.

When we reached the studio, I marveled at the spacious setup. It wasn't big, but the walls were soundproof and the room was filled with professional-grade microphones and cameras and soft lighting that made everything feel more official.

As I joined my three friends around the polished table, I couldn't help but say, "Can you believe we're here? This feels like a dream!"

Laís, adjusting her microphone, smiled back at me. "It really does. It's incredible to think about how this all started from our tea party discussions. Look at us now!"

Letícia chimed in. "I'm so excited. It feels like we're stepping into a new chapter of our journey together."

I nodded, feeling the excitement in the air. "Exactly! We have this amazing opportunity to share our faith and connect with so many people."

With each recording, we weren't just sharing information; we were building a community of people connected by our stories of faith. As we began our first official episode in the studio, I felt a profound sense of purpose, hoping our journey would resonate with many and bring the gospel's light into their lives. Our podcast has gained remarkable traction, especially in Brazil, and it's inspiring to see how our message sparks conversations and connections. Each story shared adds depth to our collective journey, reminding us that we're never alone in our struggles. This exchange not only strengthens our faith but also encourages others to embrace their spiritual paths with renewed vigor.

As my husband and I sat together on the couch one evening, our kids sleeping in their beds, he turned to me with a warm smile and said, "I love seeing you so passionate about the podcast. It's incredible how much you're growing through this journey."

I nodded, feeling a swell of gratitude. "There are days when we head to the studio in the afternoon, and before we know it, the sun has set and we're still recording—sometimes even three episodes back-to-back. But it doesn't feel like work. It feels like we're creating something meaningful together."

"I'm really glad we can support you in this work." He leaned back, his gaze reflecting pride as he swung an arm around my shoulders and pulled me close. "I can see how much you're growing spiritually as you study the scriptures. It's amazing to witness, and our whole family has been blessed by it."

His words reminded me that this venture is a collective effort, intertwining our lives and deepening our connections. Every recording session feels like a new adventure, filled with laughter, shared struggles, and deep discussions about faith and the challenges we face as women today. As our audience grows, we've received touching messages from listeners who share how our discussions have impacted their lives, reflecting the profound blessings that come from seeking and sharing the teachings of Christ.

"I adore these beautiful women," I told my husband. "They explain everything so well. I listen to them while I'm doing things at home, and I learn so much. Our Heavenly Father is wonderful, always using different means and His angels to help us learn more about the gospel." I leaned into my husband's side.

He planted a kiss on the top of my head. Everything in my world felt just right.

* * *

"This week's study of *Come, Follow Me* felt like a warm embrace—a direct hug from heaven—where I could feel the love of Heavenly Father speaking to my mind and heart. Right at the beginning, you began to describe everything I'm going through, but I felt that the Lord is watching over me and preparing something very special for my life. I need to trust Him and then do what I can, and things will improve. [. . .] Christ lives, He loves us, and Heavenly Father has prepared all things for our happiness. I am grateful."

"Hey girls [. . .] I just listened to this week's episode, and it did me a world of good. Yesterday, I had an experience with the family of my Relief Society president that left me a bit sad. Listening to you in today's episode inspired me to pray for this brother and for my president—not just as my partner in leadership but as my sister in Christ."

"Our friend Regiane in Japan was baptized yesterday, the 16th. Thanks to your online channel, she was able to learn about the Church. I was so happy to hear her story and the path she took to make this possible: you in the USA, she in Japan, and I here in Brazil. "

In moments like these, when I read the kind things people have to say about our podcast, I remember why we started it in the first place: to uplift and connect with others on their spiritual journeys.

Looking ahead, I'm excited about what's to come. We have plans for special episodes featuring guests from various backgrounds, each bringing unique perspectives to our conversations. I believe these stories will enrich our podcast and inspire our listeners even further, just as the gospel has inspired and blessed my own life after everything I've been through.

CALLINGS AND CAREER

When we moved back to Utah, we were unsure which ward to attend—our geographic ward or our native language ward, the Portuguese one. After attending the Portuguese ward, it quickly became clear that this was where we needed to be. It felt like home, filled with familiar faces and shared cultural values.

Shortly after, my husband received a calling as bishop of this ward, a tremendous blessing for our family.

Matthew 16:25 became a guiding principle for us: "For whosoever will save his life shall lose it: and whosoever will lose his life for my sake shall find it."

I could see kindness flourishing within our family, and our children truly felt the Savior's love through these acts of service. This journey taught us that as we lose ourselves in the service of others, we ultimately find a richer, more meaningful life—one filled with purpose, connection, and the profound joy that comes from sharing love with those around us.

This verse reminded us of the importance of serving others and being actively engaged in the work of the Lord. Though there were days when my boys didn't want to participate, they often found joy in the service and camaraderie that came with being involved. Helping with church events and sharing moments with fellow ward members fostered a sense of belonging and reinforced our commitment to each other and our community.

In 2024, devastating floods struck Rio Grande do Sul, Brazil, marking one of the most severe natural disasters in the region's history.

Triggered by relentless rainfall in late April, the floods affected 1.45 million people across 417 cities, which is about eighty-four percent of the state.

Water levels in Guaíba Lake near Porto Alegre surged to 5.3 meters, breaking a record from 1941. The floodwater swept through towns and cities, leaving over 100 people dead with hundreds more injured or missing. A partial collapse of the Rio das Antas dam forced further evacuations and put downstream communities at risk, adding to the widespread damage.

In Utah, our Brazilian community felt a strong desire to help. A member of our Church, together with two others, organized a donation drive, and over two days—Friday and Saturday—we gathered at our chapel, with people from all over Utah (and not just Brazilians) contributing supplies.

The whole chapel became filled with clothing and boxes, creating a powerful scene of generosity and unity. The gym, the classrooms, and even the hallways were piled high with life-saving supplies like food, clothing, personal hygiene items, blankets, and more.

On Saturday, we stayed until 2 a.m. tirelessly sorting, packing, and stacking boxes to ensure everything was prepared for transport.

As I stood in the middle of the cultural hall, surrounded by the incredible outpouring of donations and the hum of busy hands, I thought to myself, *This is more than just donations—this is love in action.*

Watching people arrive, some bringing tape and boxes, others simply ready to roll up their sleeves, I couldn't help but feel overwhelmed. Everywhere I looked, people were working together, packing and sorting with such care.

This is what community looks like.

The chapel had transformed into a hub of hope. Families, friends, and even strangers came together doing something that would reach far beyond this hall, all the way to those waiting in Brazil. Despite the exhaustion, there was such a deep, shared sense of purpose.

As I walked through the bustling gymnasium, surrounded by boxes and bags piled high with donations, I was filled with gratitude.

In that moment, I realized that our efforts were about more than just collecting donations; we were also caring for one another in every possible way. We were not just sending supplies; we were sending hope.

Together, we collected ten tons of donations at our chapel and a total of sixty tons across Utah. With the support of Azul Airlines, these donations were transported to Florida and then sent to Brazil. A truck made two trips to move everything to a warehouse for shipping, and as we worked, it was inspiring to see the outpouring of support. Despite our exhaustion, our knowledge that these supplies would bring relief to countless families affected by this historic disaster kept us going.

Joseph Smith, the prophet of the Restoration of Christ's Church on earth, once said that a person who is filled with the love of Christ will not be content to serve their family alone but will have a desire to bless the whole earth. I felt like this was my way of being able to reach out to the world and offer help, support, and love to those who might not have many people buoying them up.

* * *

After three years of dedicated service, my husband was released from his calling as bishop. In sacrament meeting, during his release, the stake president shared that our ward had accomplished in three years what many wards take five years to achieve. His words filled me with pride over the hard work we had poured into our community.

Our Brazilian immigrant community in the Church is vibrant and resilient, full of individuals at different stages of building a new life in the United States. Every day, people arrive from Brazil with dreams and challenges, often hoping to pursue studies, find work, or reunite with family. Some are young students navigating a complex immigration process while balancing school and adapting to a new culture. Others have been here for years, working diligently to support families, either here or back in Brazil, but still facing the unique challenges of life as immigrants. Many are unable to work legally due to visa limitations, so they rely heavily on community support, contributing their time and talents to help each other and strengthen bonds in creative ways.

When the stake president finished speaking to the congregation, he invited us to share our testimonies.

As I approached the pulpit to share my testimony, an unexpected wave of emotion washed over me. I had prepared a few simple words to express my gratitude, but as I looked out at the familiar faces before me, the words caught in my throat. The room brimmed with love and memories, and my heart swelled with appreciation for this community that had become our true family. Taking a deep breath to steady myself, I felt tears begin to well up.

Standing before the congregation, I found myself reflecting on the remarkable journey we had shared—the countless hours in meetings, late nights planning activities, and the joy of watching our children thrive within the ward. I wanted to convey how the gospel had transformed our family and how the friendships we cultivated had become the very fabric of our lives.

"We came here just a few years ago, feeling like newcomers," I began, my voice trembling. "But each of you has woven yourselves into our story, into our family." My heart swelled as I recalled the countless ways they had uplifted us, supported our children, and shown us love, especially as my husband took on the weighty responsibilities of bishop.

In that moment, I felt the incredible bond we shared—one built on service, friendship, and the love of Christ. It was humbling and beautiful, and I was overwhelmed with gratitude for the way we had helped one another through life's ups and downs.

I found it challenging to say "I" instead of "we," as I felt deeply intertwined with my husband's service.

I shared a poignant quote from Elder Neal A. Maxwell, who said, "None of us ever fully utilizes the people-opportunities allocated to us within our circles of friendship. You and I may call these intersectings 'coincidence.' This word is understandable for mortals to use, but co-incidence is not an appropriate word to describe the workings of an omniscient God. He does not do things by 'coincidence' but instead by 'divine design.'"[6]

To conclude my testimony, I shared part of the poem "The Train of Life" by James Tippett, which deeply resonated with me:

> As time goes by, other people will board the train . . . our siblings, friends, children, and even the love of [our] life. . . . [Many] will step down over time and leave a permanent vacuum. Some, however, will go so unnoticed that we don't realize they vacated their seats. This train ride will be full of joy, sorrow, fantasy, expectations, hellos, goodbyes, and farewells. Success consists of having a good relationship with all the passengers, requiring that we give the best of ourselves.[7]

As time goes by, other people will board the train—our siblings, friends, children, and even the love of our lives. Many will step down, leaving a permanent vacuum; others will depart so quietly that we won't even notice.

This train ride is filled with joy, sorrow, dreams, expectations, hellos, goodbyes, and farewells. Success lies in nurturing good relationships with all our fellow passengers, giving the best of ourselves. As I finished reading, I felt profound gratitude for each member of our ward—each an integral part of my journey. This experience enriched my life in unexpected ways, and as I stepped away from the pulpit, I felt blessed by the divine design that brought us together.

Over those three years, I watched my boys grow into curious young men, and with their increasing independence, my husband and I made it a priority to engage in meaningful conversations about dependability and values. I hope they treasure these discussions as they navigate their teenage years.

---

6. Neal A. Maxwell, "Brim with Joy" (Brigham Young University devotional, Jan. 23, 1996), 2, speeches.byu.edu.

7. James Tippett, "The Train of Life: A Poignant Funeral Poem by James Tippett," Celebrant Marc, July 2, 2024, https://www.celebrantmarc.co.uk/category/original-funeral-poems/page/2/.

During this time, I embraced my career as a real estate agent, supported by my husband. It was the perfect moment to dive into work while being present at home, especially with my business degree from Brazil. Earning my real estate license in Utah opened up many opportunities, and I've been fortunate to work with wonderful clients.

I also ventured into podcasting about real estate, sharing insights and connecting with others in the field. Despite my busy schedule, I prioritized leisure activities, enjoying concerts and daily gym sessions with my husband, who is a great partner in both fitness and life.

Balancing motherhood, career, and personal time brings challenges but also immense joy. Each day is an opportunity to learn, grow, and strengthen my family bonds. I find inspiration in the wisdom of coaches and motivational speakers, and the teachings of our Church leaders also resonate deeply, guiding me toward a healthier way of living.

Eternal families and the bonds we share are central to the plan of happiness established by our Heavenly Father. As we navigate challenges, the gospel of Jesus Christ provides strength and resilience. President Gordon B. Hinckley once said, "The great plan of happiness is designed to bring us home to our Heavenly Father." This truth reminds us that covenants and commandments guide us and that this life prepares us for eternal joy.

Reflecting on this journey, I'm reminded that life is not just about milestones but about the relationships we cultivate. Through all the ups and downs, I remain grateful for the divine design that has woven our lives together.

7

KERRY OWEN
The Philanthropist and Advocate

While waiting at the traffic light of a busy four-way intersection, I noticed a disheveled man hobbling awkwardly along the sidewalk. His tattered clothing and unclean appearance, along with a half-filled trash bag hanging over his hunched back, suggested he was homeless. His face had a gray pallor with deep wrinkles, and his eyes remained fixed on the ground. With every step he took, he grimaced. His right leg was limp, heavy, and twisted.

My mind flooded with questions. What could have caused the injury? What had led to his current sad state? Did he need help?

As the questions swirled around my mind, I was struck by an image of him as a precious newborn baby. No longer was I seeing an unkempt homeless man on the sidewalk but rather a beautiful child of God. Pure love filled my soul. This image made me wonder whether he had been loved and nurtured in his formative years. Had he ever been told that he was of great worth?

I thought back to my childhood in England and how my parents had opened our family home to children from troubled backgrounds.

Some children confided in me about their traumatic experiences, which left me feeling sad and had me thinking of ways I could help them feel better—whether it was by hugging them, holding their hand, or sharing my toys with them.

Perhaps this homeless man grew up in circumstances similar to the children who stayed in my family home. Had he needed a place to feel safe and loved, like I had grown up with?

The light turned green for the vehicles coming from my left. As the cars passed this homeless man on the sidewalk, a black pickup truck slowed down and rolled down its windows. The young male occupants threw their open soda cans at the man while shouting obscenities. As he pulled his arms up to protect his face and head from the heavy blows, his trash bag fell to the ground.

The young men laughed hysterically at each blow.

I gasped at this cruel injustice and cried out, "No! No! No!" but my window was closed and no one could hear my cries. I tried to catch the truck's plate number, but it sped off too quickly.

The traffic light for my lane turned green. I desperately wanted to abandon my car, run to this man, comfort him, and see what I could do to help, but there was nowhere for me to legally pull over. Honking sounds from multiple impatient and angry drivers made me hit the accelerator. I had no choice but to drive on.

I got one more look at the homeless man who was now crying out to the heavens with his arms outstretched. I burst into uncontrollable sobs as I left the scene.

"God," I cried, "why did you show me him as a baby, only to see him be hurt, ridiculed, and demeaned when there was nothing I could do to help?"

This was not the first time I had experienced images like these, but on those previous occasions, I had been able to take action and use my hands to serve those in need and use my voice to advocate on their behalf. Yet here I was, unable to help this man. It was similar to the feeling of helplessness I feel when I see images on the news of people suffering in far-off lands and know there's nothing I can do about it.

My family and I had been living in the United States for sixteen months. I was busy directing a local nonprofit (charity) called Reach Out Today in a voluntary, non-paid role and was still involved in the New Zealand charity I had founded years earlier called Feed the Need. Being a wife and a mother to five children, while also living with a chronic health condition that required regular immunoglobulin treatments, was not easy.

Despite all this, I knew that the image of that man as a newborn baby was inspired. I had been given a glimpse into how Jesus saw this man. That night, I prayed about what He would have me do.

A burning desire to learn about homelessness in America, which I now called home, kept me up late that night. Bleak statistics surrounding youth aging out of foster care and ending up homeless were disheartening! Once again, I was reminded about those children who had stayed in my childhood home all those years ago. Now, as adults, were they also homeless?

In the subsequent weeks and months, I visited local homeless shelters and safe houses, asking youth and adults if they would be willing to speak with me about how they ended up homeless. Thankfully, my British accent with a New Zealand twang seemed to intrigue them, and they agreed.

"My mom put her addictions before us kids," one youth said.

"My dad would beat my mom really bad, then he would come into our room and do the same to us," said another.

Time and time again, they told me about being exposed to trauma, suffering neglect, and being placed in and out of foster care as children. They desperately wanted stability, safety, a place to call home, and a family who would love them and meet their physical and emotional needs.

My heart broke listening to their stories. Often, my emotions got the better of me, and these individuals would reach over to comfort *me*!

Soon more images entered my mind through dreams, confirming that I was on the right track. I felt inspired to begin a project to advocate for more transitional housing for youth who were aging out of foster care or experiencing homelessness. I also began developing a program to help children who were entering foster care or being reunited with family.

Eagerly, I began connecting with local government agencies and other nonprofits where I got to meet like-minded people who wanted to help with this project. I was labeled "The Fairy Godmother" by one agency, but funnily enough, I hadn't done anything yet.

Next, I sought out speaking opportunities to advocate for these vulnerable youth. Public speaking is one of my biggest fears, and despite having spoken a lot in New Zealand for Feed the Need, it never got any easier.

One opportunity presented itself from Rotary, a global network of clubs whose mission is to bring people together to improve communities and the world through service. They asked me to speak, and I was thrilled to have the opportunity. I sat at the kitchen table and switched on my computer. A few moments later, a large crowd came into view.

My body shook and my face burned, as it always does with public speaking. "Thank you, Rotary, for inviting me to speak with you today." Even though the meeting was via Zoom, it was still intimidating. I glanced over the sea of faces on my screen and reminded myself to breathe.

Although I'm a natural introvert, I have seen, through past efforts, that using my voice to advocate is effective and can bring about change. I would just have to give it my best.

As I shared some of the stories from the youth and adults I had met with, I struggled to keep my emotions in check yet again. (This is a habit of mine.)

"While talking with a nineteen-year-old young woman who had recently aged out of foster care, I witnessed her anxiety, nervousness, and social awkwardness. I saw her constant compulsion to scratch her arms until blood appeared. It was clear she was broken. Broken by her family. Broken by society. She may have looked like an adult, but the reality is that she was still a child, trying to process her trauma in a teen body." As I spoke on her behalf, my nerves calmed somewhat at the rightness of what I was doing, or trying to do, which was to make young people's lives, like hers, better.

"She was living in compromising conditions, with no support or wraparound services . . . How can we expect vulnerable young people transitioning into adulthood to thrive? We need to do better than this. We are in a race against time." I could practically hear the ticking clock counting down her opportunities, her future, her hope. "A race to help the next set of vulnerable youth *not* become another set of bleak statistics!"

To my great relief, the Rotarians saw the value in this project and took it on.

Meeting with corporate businesses, builders, city planners, community leaders, and anyone else who would listen and get behind this transitional housing project was no small feat.

Every step of the way, my husband, Matt, continually supported me in my endeavors. He would listen to me ramble on, even in the middle of the night, about the project.

I rolled over in bed one night and whispered, "Are you awake?"

From beside me came a hesitant "Uh-huh."

That was my go-ahead. "I just can't sleep thinking about all those youth and what they've been through." Tears welled in my eyes and choked me up. "What if this project fails and all this work and heartache will be for nothing?"

Matt turned to face me, putting his hand on my arm in a comforting gesture. "Kerry, you are doing everything you can. I know it will work out because you never give up." In our dark room, there was a lull, but even though I couldn't see him, I knew he hadn't fallen back asleep. A moment later, he added in a worried tone that I'd gotten used to, "But please try to get some sleep. Because otherwise, you'll be no good to anyone."

He was right—my immune system was already compromised.

If someone had told me it would take six years from start to finish to get this project done, I think I may have been deterred, but as the saying goes, "Good things take time," and this was a good thing!

Wiping at my eyes, I let out a long breath, let my mind quiet, and eventually fell asleep.

* * *

"Finally, we're here!" said Spencer, the committee chairperson who led the Rotarians on this housing project. He had experienced brief periods of homelessness and substance abuse issues while in his youth. Now, as a successful businessman and philanthropist, he was a force to be reckoned with!

His passion and commitment were remarkable and key to making this project a success.

We stood side by side, glancing up at the beautiful apartment complex in Millcreek, Utah. Spencer had a look of absolute contentment on his face.

A crowd gathered to see the opening of our project. A big white ribbon with a large red bow had been placed over the front entranceway.

"Yes! It feels so surreal," I replied. It was good to finally be at this point.

The camera crews took position and began filming. City leaders, Rotarians, and even youth who had aged out of foster care or experienced homelessness spoke to the crowd.

After the ribbon had been cut, the beautiful apartment complex was now officially open for those youth who needed a home. Inexplicable joy filled my soul and—you probably guessed—my tears began to flow. I felt a mixture of emotions: gratitude to those who had helped make this happen, a sense of pride and relief that we were finally here, and excitement for those youth who would be calling this place home. I went around hugging anyone who would accept a hug, including strangers!

One person asked my husband, "Is Kerry going to finally sit back, put her feet up, and relax now?"

Matt grinned as he glanced over at me and shook his head. "Not a chance! She'll be on to her next project before long."

I chuckled. It was most likely true because I knew there were other dreams to follow and more work ahead. But for now, I let myself enjoy this special moment.

As the cameras, journalists, reporters, and community leaders toured the complex, I took myself off into one of the apartments. Every room had been carefully thought out: the furniture layout, bedding, window dressing, artwork, and framed uplifting quotes. Knowing that this building would house hundreds of youth over the next few years, and thousands over the decades, delighted my soul.

"Kerry. Kerry! I was trying to find you." Mina hurried into the room where I stood admiring the decor. She had been managing a program called Milestone for many years. This was the organization that would be providing house managers and wraparound care for those housed in this apartment complex.

I smiled, tears still in my eyes.

Mina was a firecracker with a big heart. She put her arm through mine. "I wanted to show you something."

She walked me into one of the apartments and pointed to a framed quote, all lit up, which read "Remember why you started." She gave me a look, a wink, and a long hug. If I was going to hug strangers, I was certainly going to hug Mina. And once again, the tears welled up, and I cried in Mina's arms.

Before leaving the apartment complex, I reflected on that homeless man by the roadside. Oh, how I wished he could be here today to see this building! Then I would embrace him, tell him about the image of him I'd seen, the love I felt, his great worth, and how God had led me on a journey to alleviate and prevent homelessness for generations of youth. Something good—amazing even—had come from the injustice he had endured that day on the sidewalk.

Childhood Experiences and Lessons

I may have been only four years old, but I watched with much anticipation as my parents busily prepared to host a large gathering on our back lawn to celebrate the royal wedding of Prince Charles and Princess Diana. The sun shone and the sky was blue on this beautiful summer's day.

There was a sweet aroma of freshly cut grass still in the air as I watched my dad hang the red, white, and blue British flags around the patio area.

My mum had been busy preparing a feast. There were platters of quarter-cut sandwiches, scones with strawberries and cream, sliced fruit, and homemade cakes and cookies. She had even made her own orange and lemon cordial and large bowls of party punch with a ladle to serve.

Everyone had been saying this was the "Wedding of the Century." Our family had watched the wedding unfold on our television earlier that day. It was magical! There were horse-drawn carriages, finely dressed guards, bridesmaids, and page boys, and Princess Diana's dress was everything I had dreamed of. I decided then and there that I wanted to reenact this royal wedding so that I could dress up and look just like her!

When all the guests arrived at our party, everyone was buzzing about the royal wedding and discussing every detail. The celebration was everything and more. The food was delicious and there were plenty of friends to play with. While my childhood friend, Nicolas, and I were waving British flags around the lawn, I told him of my plan to reenact the wedding.

A few days later, while at Nicolas's house for a playdate, I began emptying all the drawers and wardrobes, trying to find something I could wear for our reenactment of the royal wedding. Bedsheets and towels were all I could find. Nicolas would be Prince Charles, and his sister Vanessa would be the bridesmaid.

Like the day of the real royal wedding, the sun was shining and there were no clouds in sight (which is rare in England). *This wedding was going to be perfect*, I thought. However, things went downhill fast.

Vanessa was not holding the bedsheet (the improvised wedding dress train) high enough off the ground, and it was getting dirty. Then Nic ran off, leaving me standing at the altar! Maybe he was grossed out at the thought of having to kiss the bride? Especially because I was just his playmate.

Very quickly, all three of us were crying and Nic's mum had to intervene.

It was hard to accept that my plan had failed miserably. It was a good lesson though. Life rarely unfolds as planned. In fact, my life would take a 180-degree turn from the direction I had planned to go in. Learning to change my mindset has helped me find joy in all those twists and turns.

I was reminded of this when, at seven years old, I had set all my hopes and dreams on my next sibling being a girl!

I was anxiously waiting at my bedroom window for my dad to arrive home from the hospital. My mum had delivered another baby, and my dad was driving home to announce if it was a baby boy or a baby girl.

Please be a girl! I repeated it over and over in my mind. I already had three brothers, two older and one younger, so I felt I was owed a sister!

As soon as my dad's car pulled into the driveway, I ran downstairs to hear the news as fast as my little legs would carry me.

He entered the front door, smiling from ear to ear, joy radiating from his face. "It's a boy!" he announced.

My brothers cheered while a feeling of disappointment swept through my body. I burst into tears and ran back upstairs.

Moments later, my dad entered the room and asked, "You know what this means, Kerry?"

I shook my head.

"You'll still be my favorite daughter!"

His words reminded me that being the only daughter wasn't a disadvantage; it was a unique bond that made me feel special. I was also reminded that I could realign my mindset to find joy.

Once my baby brother arrived home, I instantly became the doting sister. My parents went on to have yet another boy, and I became like a second mum to him. I was content having just brothers and being my dad's "favorite" girl. The power of perspective!

Around that same time, I was about to learn another lesson.

There was a girl in my class at school who had eczema. Her whole body was covered in flaky, dry skin. When she scratched herself, her skin flaked off and bled, which caused quite a racket in the classroom.

Everyone, including me, would say, "Ew! Gross!"

When it came time to play sports in the school hall, none of us would want to pair up with her, and she would always be the last person chosen. My classmates and I wrongly believed that if we sat next to her or touched her, we would catch her eczema, so we stayed away.

This girl was always alone and would often cry. Not only was she struggling with severe eczema, but she was also dealing with the pain of being excluded.

My mum must have noticed this and felt for her. One day, she talked to this girl's mum at the school gate and invited her over to our house for a playdate.

I gulped as fear set in.

She began coming to our home on a regular basis and we did have fun, although I kept her at arm's length and discouraged her from playing with my toys. One day, however, I was taught an important lesson at church.

My Sunday School teacher held up a picture of Jesus with a leper. The leper had been pushed out of the community and had begged Jesus for help. Jesus stretched out His hand and touched him. The Savior had compassion on him, and the leper was healed.

I was reminded of my friend with eczema and decided that when she came for playdates, I would let her touch and play with my toys. I couldn't imagine then how happy this would make her.

Seeing her joy at being treated like she was the same as everyone else really touched me. This lesson was a valuable one, and one that would prepare me for the work I would do as an adult.

When I turned eight years old, I was excited about being baptized a member of The Church of Jesus Christ of Latter-day Saints. I had been attending this Church my whole life and had seen my older brothers get baptized and was happy it was finally my turn. Knowing that my dad would be the one baptizing me made it all the more special.

I had been taught that by being baptized, my sins would be forgiven. So all those times I hadn't let the girl with eczema play with my toys would be forgiven. There were many other things I needed to be forgiven for too! It would be like starting all over again, which felt good.

Both my dad and I were wearing white clothing when we entered the baptismal font, which was full of warm water.

I glanced up and smiled at my family and friends who were excitedly looking on.

"Are you ready?" My dad glanced down at me with a warm smile.

I nodded, eager to be on with it.

He placed his hand around mine and my other hand on his arm. Then he said, "Having been commissioned of Jesus Christ, I baptize you . . ."

I can't remember any other words he said—only how excited I was. When he finished the prayer, he dipped me beneath the warm water and lifted me back up. The water ran down my face and I felt so happy. I embraced my dad, wishing I could do it all over again!

I feel fortunate that I had a good, kind, and gentle father who gave me a positive view of men, especially given the events that transpired a year later with my first male teacher.

One day, while sitting in an exam at school, my classmate leaned over and in a low whisper asked, "Can you help me understand this question?"

I quietly explained the question to her. Unbeknownst to me, my schoolteacher assumed I was cheating, picked up his metal ruler, and walked up behind me.

All of a sudden, I felt a sharp, loud smack on my back and spun around. My teacher raised his ruler and with great force struck me again and again. I would never have expected this of him; he was strict, but I hadn't thought of him as heavy-handed and cruel.

The shock left me spluttering and gasping for air.

"Stand up!" he shouted.

I stood, in complete fear of being hit again. He grabbed me by my school tie and dragged me to the corner of the classroom.

Once I caught my breath, I buried my face in my trembling hands and began sobbing uncontrollably. The pain was excruciating.

"Take your hands off your face and stop that noise!" he shouted.

As hard as I tried, I could not quieten down my sobs. He pulled my tie again, this time with greater force, toward the floor.

It stopped me from crying but also left me gasping for air.

He faced the class. "If anyone else cheats during the test, you can expect the same treatment!" he threatened.

I remained in the corner trying to stay quiet and control my frantic breathing. I was terrified, in shock, and in pain, and I didn't know how to handle the situation.

Once the school bell rang for lunch break, I couldn't get out of there fast enough. I began searching desperately for my older brother, Chris, on the playground.

I found him playing football, his laugh calling to me above the crowd of his friends. I ran over to him, and the tears came again as he turned and looked at me.

He rushed to my side. "What's the matter?"

I told him what happened.

"It's going to be all right." He put his arm over my shoulder, giving me a big brother's comfort. "Come with me."

He led me to the head teacher's office and knocked on her door, planning to tell her all about the incident. But after a while of waiting and getting no response, he took me back to the playground.

"The head teacher must be at lunch. Let's go out and play. You can watch me play football if you want," he said as we headed back.

Chris didn't usually let me hang around him and his friends— this invite was huge! It was reassuring to be near him during that lunch hour. When the bell rang, my heart skipped a beat, but Chris rubbed my arm and said, "It's going to be okay."

Even though this incident was never reported, my brother's comfort and protectiveness did me a lot of good.

I experienced how it felt to be wrongly judged and sorely mistreated. I didn't want to ever look into my teacher's eyes again. My trust and respect for him was completely gone. For the remainder of that year, I was fearful and careful to not set him off again.

During the next school year, I was subjected to another injustice at the hands of a man who had been entrusted to watch over me. What happened left me feeling completely vulnerable and alone and would change my life forever. I was so ashamed of what had happened that I decided to keep it a secret. I would tell no one—*no one*. It wasn't until I was to be put in this man's care again that I finally spoke out. While justice was later served, the damage could never be completely undone.

Later, when I transitioned to senior school at around age eleven, the bullying began. A group of girls, much older than me, decided I was an easy target. I dreaded every school day, fearful of what they would do to me next. What bruises would I be left with? What else would they say to damage my already fragile self-esteem?

Nine months later, when the bullying had escalated to new levels, I plucked up the courage to report them to the school office. The staff took swift action. I only wished I had done it earlier. The daily torment was over, but my self-confidence had been sorely damaged.

This fast influx of rude awakenings gave me some insight into the pain of injustice and the harm others can inflict on you, not just physically but also mentally and emotionally. It seemed to increase my sensitivity to others' suffering and the need to find a voice when something just isn't right.

The next time I would use my voice was in a religious study class at my local public school when I was fourteen years old.

The religious studies teacher had announced that the next class would be on the "Mormons."

As soon as that was announced, dread seeped in. My plan, leading up to that class, was to stay quiet. None of my friends knew that I attended church, let alone the "Mormon" church, and I was inclined to let it stay that way. I had no desire to draw any unnecessary attention to myself, especially after the things I'd been through.

The day arrived for the class, and my nerves hadn't eased. I made my way to my desk and found a printout sitting on it that said "Mormon Cult." My stomach went into a free fall as I fell to my desk chair and picked up the printout.

As I read the false and misleading information, I felt more and more uncomfortable. My teacher started a discussion, but I remained quiet. I was a fairly shy girl who blushed easily, so I told myself to keep my lips shut.

After the class discussion, the teacher put on a short film about the "Mormon cult." As the film played, tears began streaming down my cheeks, and without any planning on my part, my hand went up.

I guess my inner voice wanted to speak up, despite all my fears.

The teacher noticed me and paused the video. "Yes, Kerry. Do you have a question?"

What am I doing?

I cleared my throat and nervously spoke up. "Miss, I am a 'Mormon.'"

Gasps sounded all around the room.

"Most of this information is not true," I stated.

You could have heard a pin drop.

Thankfully—and to my huge relief—the teacher was very respectful, and in a very kind manner, she said, "I'm sorry. This is the information I was given by the education board. Would you feel comfortable telling us a bit about your religion, clarifying what's true and what's false?" Her gentle invitation helped me find the courage to continue.

"The film said that Mormon fathers dominate their wives, but my dad doesn't dominate over my mum. If you knew my mum, you would know she is not someone who could be dominated."

My teacher gave me an encouraging nod.

I continued. "My dad is a great example of what a husband and father should be."

The classroom was still quiet, and I could feel everyone's eyes on me.

This was uncomfortable, but I had to say one more thing. "Also, the printout says that we're not Christians, but we are! I have been taught about Jesus Christ for as long as I can remember, and I believe that He is the greatest example for us to follow."

"Thank you, Kerry," my teacher said. "I appreciate you sharing with us. Do you think you could bring me some literature that I could use in the future when teaching about the Mormon religion?"

I nodded, feeling as though a weight had been lifted off my chest. That was a pivotal moment for me . . . learning to speak up even in front of my peers.

* * *

My brothers and I were raised by good, faithful, hardworking parents. We never went without. Our Saturdays were often spent outdoors, our Easters and Christmases were spent with extended family, and our summer holidays were spent camping all over Europe. One summer vacation sticks out in my mind—because we narrowly escaped death.

The car was tightly packed, with little room to move, but we didn't mind one bit! We were excited about this adventure. My younger brothers, cousin, and I were sitting in the back seats while my mum sat in the front, next to my aunt, who was driving.

We had been driving since the crack of dawn from our home in England to France via the Channel Tunnel. Our plan was to make it to the campsite within twenty-four hours to avoid stopping the night somewhere.

As it began to get dark, we became anxious to get to the campsite as quickly as possible. We were tired.

My mum had been following the travel directions provided by the campsite, but another map showed a much quicker route. She decided to follow the map rather than the one recommended by the campsite.

As we turned onto the quicker route, we began to feel a bit nervous because the road we had turned onto was pitch black. There was no lighting or road lines to guide us.

"I've got a bad feeling about this route," my mum said after some time.

My aunt stopped the car and asked, "How long do you think it's going to take on this route?"

"Maybe two hours," Mum said. "The route suggested by the campsite is five hours."

They agreed that we would continue the way we were going.

Within a few minutes, my mum put her hands up and yelled, "Stop the car! We cannot go any further! We have to turn around and go back into the town!"

Despite being a bit frustrated with my mum, my aunt turned the car around and headed back into town. We ended up staying the night there.

The next day, when we went back onto that same road, we realized that the point when Mum had put her hands up in the air and asked my aunt to stop driving was the point of no return.

The road we were on, we soon discovered, hugged tightly to an extremely steep mountainside, up in the Pyrenees, one of the highest mountain ranges in Europe. There were no safety barriers, and some parts of the road had fallen away, making it a treacherous drive.

At times we even came across wild animals on the road, and at other times we spotted some smashed cars at the bottom of a rugged ravine. Had we tried to traverse that route in the dark, we likely would have ended up there as well. It was a terrifying journey.

When we got to the other side, we offered a prayer of thanks that we were able to safely cross this dangerous pass. Once at the campsite, my mum relayed the experience to the campsite manager.

"Oh, my goodness!" the campsite manager gasped. "That pass is a perilous route, and that's why we don't recommend it."

We all knew that my mum's impression to stop the car at the point of no return was inspired.

This experience taught me the importance of listening to your intuition and the impressions that come to your mind. This would be a good training ground for the future impressions I would receive.

Dating and Marriage

Not long after that experience, Matt walked into my life. He was one of my brother's friends who had recently returned from serving a mission for the Church in Leeds, England. Matt was tall, with silky dark hair, hazel eyes, and olive skin. Prior to his mission, I had thought him good-looking, but because he came across as arrogant and had completely ignored me, I wasn't interested in him at all. But yet here he was now, a changed man! He was friendly, helpful, thoughtful, kind, and still handsome.

One evening, Matt and I found ourselves sitting alone in my aunt's kitchen, talking about what we hoped for out of life. It was refreshing to have a deep and meaningful conversation with one of my brother's friends.

We discovered that we enjoyed a lot of the same things—like walking in the countryside and visiting villages and national trust properties (historic buildings like churches, cathedrals, castles, manor homes, and mills)—plus, we shared the same faith. It was after that conversation that my feelings for Matt grew. I had no idea that he had feelings for me too until one day, he surprised me at my front door.

The doorbell rang, and I took my time answering it, thinking it was for one of my brothers. "Matt?" I said, startled to see him there.

He was smartly dressed in a suit and a bow tie and gave me the biggest smile.

I smiled back. "Are you here for Steven?"

He shook his head and handed me an ice cream tub full of *ice,* not ice cream, and a little toffee hammer.

I pulled my chin back. *What on earth?*

He turned to leave.

"Wait!" I called after him. "What am I meant to do with this?"

He glanced over his shoulder and smirked. "Smash the ice," he said and went off.

I sat down on the kitchen floor, hitting the ice with the little hammer, wondering what I would find inside. It crossed my mind that he and my brothers were possibly pulling a prank on me, and I looked out the kitchen window several times to check if anyone was laughing at my expense.

Eventually, I found a little plastic container in the ice.

With trembling fingers, more from intrigue than the cold I felt from the ice itself, I opened it. Inside was a note that said, "Now that we've broken the ice, how about a date?"

My heart did somersaults! It wasn't a prank—Matt wanted a date with me! And how flattering that he'd spent time putting all of that together for me.

One date led to another and another and many more. Matt put a lot of creativity and thought into them. He would pick me up with a picnic basket full of my favorite foods—which included pork pies, "Marks & Spencer" sandwiches, Cadbury's chocolate trifle, prawn cocktail skips (crisps), and sparkling grape juice—along with a picnic blanket. Then he would take me out to a beautiful spot in the countryside.

He decorated my bedroom with balloons and hearts several times to surprise me after work. And he led me on treasure hunts many times. I wanted to try to be creative too, so I emptied out our garden shed once and converted it into a little French restaurant and served him dinner in there.

All these dates were nice and fun, but what impressed me most about Matt was watching him at his grandparents' farm.

It was evident his grandparents adored Matt, and they had a close mutual bond. Matt would tease them, make them laugh, be affectionate, and play cards with them, and he would even wear his nan's knitted jumpers—sweaters—with pride. Without being asked, he would wake up early to help his granddad on the farm and come back to the farmhouse with his sleeves rolled up in farm dirt.

Then there was how Matt cared for and treated the animals on the farm. I watched him once helping a lamb, who was struggling in labor, and another who had gotten caught in the fencing wire. These instances, and others, endeared me to him.

After a year of dating, we knew we wanted to spend the rest of our lives together. We began talking about marriage and our hopes and dreams for the future. We wanted to buy a home in the English countryside and have ten children (ha!) and maybe some animals too.

I knew I wanted to be a mother, but I also wanted to do something else to help people. Maybe I would train to be a nurse or a teacher. Matt was thinking of being a Chartered Surveyor or going into business.

Little did either of us realize that despite all our planning, life would go very differently than planned.

For example, I never thought I would ever ask myself the question "Would Matt still love me if I lost my hair?" Yet on a family vacation in Europe, while we were still dating, I found myself having clumps of my hair coming out in my hands while washing it in the bath.

That morning, my family had gone into the local town to the farmer's market. I had decided to stay back and swim in the vacation rental property's pool. It was a beautiful sunny and hot day, the perfect time to lighten my hair, or so I had thought. Chemistry in school was not my strongest subject, and I was about to prove that by unknowingly causing a chemical reaction!

I had a bottle of Sun-In, a hair lightener, which I liberally sprayed on the top of my scalp. I had used Sun-In before and had been pleased with the blond highlights it produced, but I had never gone into a chlorinated swimming pool afterward.

I lay out on the patio sun lounger, letting the sun lighten my hair while I was reading. I wanted to look good when Matt and I reunited after the holiday. (Matt had recently gone on a vacation to Cyprus and had come back with a deep bronze tan and looked so handsome.)

After about twenty minutes, I was getting too hot, so I jumped into the swimming pool and enjoyed a lovely swim.

Once out of the pool, I ran a bath in the vacation property, got in, and began washing my hair . . . off my head.

What is going on? I had huge clumps in my hands, and panic started to swirl in my stomach.

When I rubbed my shampoo on my scalp again and pulled my hands away from my head, there was more hair. I went under the water to wash the shampoo out, but when I sat back up and saw the water filled with hair, that's when I knew my hair had fallen out! I had wanted to impress Matt, but here I was, looking in the bathroom mirror and seeing large bald patches on my scalp. This was a complete disaster for an eighteen-year-old! I cried and cried.

While still on holiday, I called Matt on the phone to tell him about my hair loss. I said we couldn't see each other for at least six months so that my hair would have time to grow back. Despite all his reassurances over the phone that he loved me with or without hair, I was not going to risk it.

Once back on English soil, my mum and I went into the local city to find a wig. I felt relieved to cover up my unsightly scalp.

Matt was really keen to see me again, saying he had missed me. With much persuasion on his part, I agreed he could come over. *At least I had a wig on.* I thought.

Within an hour of being with Matt, he had somehow talked me into showing him my scalp without the wig. And when I did, he leaned over, kissed me, and said again that I was beautiful with or without hair.

Matt's reassurances helped me realize that he genuinely loved me. The saying "Beauty is in the eye of the beholder" really was true! As time went on, and as my hair grew back, our relationship deepened.

The night Matt proposed was not what he had envisioned, but it was perfect to me.

He had planned to propose in a hot-air balloon or something else rather grand. However, here we were, both kneeling down in the loft above the converted garage at my family home.

The loft area was a popular place to hang out with friends. Even though there was no room to stand, it had mattresses, blankets, and a skylight window where we could lie down and watch the stars. While looking up into the night sky, Matt and I talked again about marriage. Up until this point, I wanted to marry Matt, but I hadn't felt ready because I had only just turned nineteen.

"Oh, it's gone midnight. I had better go to bed," I said. I was about to crawl out of the loft when Matt pulled me back in for one last hug.

While hugging, on our knees, something happened . . . I suddenly felt I was ready to marry him and began to cry. "I want to grow old with you," I blurted out.

"Same." He wiped away my tears.

Then it was almost as if I could read his thoughts: *Is Kerry saying she's ready for marriage?*

Without any words being said, I nodded in response to that unasked question.

Matt blinked, understanding dawning on him. "Will you marry me?" Traditionally, the man is the only one kneeling during a proposal, but hey—I guess traditions can be broken.

More tears followed as joy filled my heart. "Yes!" I wrapped my arms around his neck and kissed him.

When the happy tears and kisses stopped, he pulled back and frowned. "I had wanted to ask your dad for his blessing before I proposed! This is all so different from how I had planned."

"I don't need any grand proposal—this was perfect. Plus, my family loves you, so my dad will give his blessing instantly!"

"I'll go knock on your parents' door and see if I can speak with your dad."

It was midnight, but Matt was already crawling out of the loft. I followed him as he made his way up to my parents' bedroom and knocked.

"Uh-huh?" my dad groggily called out from the other side of the door. The lights were all off.

"Can I come in?" Matt asked in a stage whisper.

"Hmm, okay," my dad said.

Matt walked in, leaving me in the hallway. He took a few careful steps in the dark and knelt next to my dad's side of the bed.

"George, I would like to ask your blessing to marry Kerry," he said.

My dad sat bolt upright, rubbed his eyes, and then looked at his watch. "It's almost one o'clock in the morning! Let me get some sleep first, and then we can talk after breakfast, okay?"

"Of course," Matt said. He tiptoed out of the room.

Matt met me back in the hallway and relayed his conversation. This was not the response I expected from my dad.

Maybe he thought me too young, I thought.

Maybe George doesn't like me as much as I thought! Matt questioned.

We then went our separate ways, Matt to the loft and me to my room. But neither of us got much sleep that night.

After breakfast, Matt asked my dad if it was a good time to have that chat.

Straight-faced, Dad stood from the table. "Yes, let's go into the back garden."

I wrung my hands as they exited the side door, and for the next twenty minutes, they walked several laps around the back lawn in a seemingly deep discussion.

What on earth could they be talking about all this time?

My family loved Matt, so why wasn't Dad just giving his permission? But being his "favorite daughter," I shouldn't have been surprised. Eventually they stopped walking and talking and embraced.

Finally! I thought with a tinge of relief.

Later, Matt filled me in on the conversation. My dad gave him some pearls of wisdom on marriage and also asked him some questions, like how he intended to provide for me and take care of me as his wife. Once satisfied, my father had given his blessing.

* * *

The day finally came when I would be marrying my Prince Charming. I may have only been nineteen years old, but I felt ready.

The sun was shining and there were no clouds in the sky, similar to that of the royal wedding reenactment all those years ago, but this wedding was not going to end in tears. Well, maybe—but they'd be tears of joy.

My wedding dress was on, my hair had long since grown back and was done to perfection, and I was ready to go.

My dad took my hand and helped me into the wedding car. On the drive to the chapel, Dad was quiet and thoughtful as he stared out the window.

I wanted to thank him profusely for being the best dad ever, but I also wanted to keep my emotions in check. I didn't want to have mascara all over my face on this special occasion.

Once at the chapel, Dad and I waited for the musical piece to begin. It was by Ennio Morricone from the soundtrack "The Mission." This was our cue.

Walking down the aisle, I made eye contact with family and friends and felt their happiness reflected back at me. Seeing Matt's beaming smile warmed my soul. And it was a forerunner to the next time I would walk down an aisle, many years later, on the other side of the world in New Zealand. That time, though, would be for very different reasons—to receive an insignia awarded by Queen Elizabeth II.

Motherhood, Adoption, Loss, and Empathy

"Okay, it's time." The social worker let out a long breath.

The birth mother nodded, took a deep breath, and tenderly kissed her three-day-old son goodbye. Slowly, she walked across the hospital room toward me and carefully placed her baby into my outstretched arms.

As my hands cradled this newborn baby, an immense love washed over me. I made a silent promise that I would cherish, love, nurture, and protect him for all my days. It was the same promise I had given to my firstborn son five years earlier.

The birth mother stepped away and shakily sat herself down in the same worn-out hospital chair where she'd been nursing her baby for the past three days.

The first few days with my firstborn baby were a happy time that I spent marveling at every facial expression and movement. I wondered how this time had been for this birth mother, especially knowing that she was about to say goodbye to him.

Although this mother had chosen Matt and me, I felt guilty for being the one holding her baby! I couldn't take my eyes off this mother. My heart went out to her, and an intense sadness filled my soul. This only intensified to the point that I could literally feel her grief and loss flow through me. *Is this how it feels to "mourn with those that mourn"?*

Now, as a twenty-six-year-old woman, mother, and wife, I saw another side of adoption: the sacrifice of a birth mother who was putting the needs of her baby above her own wants.

How could I help this mother feel better? Was there anything I could do or say to help her?

Quickly, I turned to Matt, who seemed to know exactly what I was thinking. He took this precious baby into his arms so that I could go and comfort her.

Although this birth mother was settled on her decision, it did not change the fact that she had just embarked on a difficult journey of pain, loss, and grief. The only thing I could do was embrace and reassure her that I would love her baby with all my heart and that Matt and I would take good care of him.

When the social worker gestured to us that it was time to leave. I didn't want to take her baby! I stood there motionless.

"Can I walk you to your car?" the birth mother asked.

Relief filled me, knowing we would have a bit longer with her. Maybe that was why she asked.

There was no easy way of saying goodbye to her. We were literally taking a piece of her, and it was painful to witness.

Matt and I had always talked about adoption, but the plan was to have our own biological children first.

Shortly after he and I were married, we ended up expecting a baby and were very excited. But instead of having "morning sickness" for the first trimester, it was "all-day sickness" that lasted the whole nine months. Our plan to move to the countryside was put on hold so that we could stay close to family for support.

After a challenging birth, our first child, Lewis, entered the world. The moment he was placed in my arms, I knew that motherhood was the most beautiful gift.

When he was six weeks old, his breathing issues began, along with regular hospital visits and stays. He was diagnosed with a hiatal hernia and gastroesophageal reflux disease (GERD).

Watching our infant struggle to breathe was petrifying and took an emotional and physical toll on us. I had to sleep with our son in an upright position, to clear his throat when he vomited, for several years. But when he turned four years old, he was finally able to manage his own symptoms.

When Lewis was five years old, I experienced a painful miscarriage. It was during this time that I felt strongly that we were meant to start the adoption process rather than continue trying for a baby ourselves.

Matt, however, was not ready. "I don't know how I feel about adopting right now."

We had always worked well as a team, and it seemed strange to me for us not to be on the same page.

One afternoon, I knelt in prayer. "If we are meant to adopt, then please have Matt feel right about it." Within minutes of this prayer, he phoned me.

"Kerry! I had a call from Richard today," Matt said, his enthusiasm practically bouncing through the phone to me. Richard was the best man at our wedding. "He and his wife just adopted a large sibling group!"

My heart started to beat faster as he spoke. *Could this be an answer to my prayer?*

Matt continued, "As Richard was telling me about their experience, I suddenly felt that we too were meant to adopt right now!"

I could not respond because I had started crying. Tears streamed down my cheeks, and I wrapped my free arm—the one not holding the phone trembling at my ear—around my midsection.

"So I went ahead and called the adoption agency and set up the interviews to start the adoption process for us."

My heart was full. I knew that God listened to prayers, but to have this particular prayer be answered so quickly was yet again another confirmation of His love for me and my family and that this was His will.

Before long, we had been approved, and in time, we were chosen by a birth mother. Toward the end of her pregnancy, she wanted to meet us.

As we entered the room, the expectant mother and I locked eyes and smiled.

It was as if we knew each other. She was a pretty and gentle-natured young woman. Her parents were there to support her during this process along with the social worker.

"I have a list of questions for you," the expectant mother said, her voice uncertain. We took our seats across from her in the meeting room.

"Fire away," Matt replied.

She shakily opened her piece of paper and began. "Why did you decide to adopt?"

Matt looked to me to answer this question.

"When I was a teenager, I decided I would like to adopt in the future. And after having a miscarriage, Matt and I felt this was the right time," I said.

"How does your son feel about you adopting?"

This time, Matt took the lead. "He's about to turn six years old and has been asking for a sibling. He's excited!"

Her posture relaxed, and her nerves calmed the more we spoke. "Can you send me photos and an update each year on his birthday?"

"Yes, absolutely."

We settled more and more as she asked her questions, and we seemed to be giving her the answers she wanted to hear. Finally, she said, "I like that you already have a child and that my baby will have a brother."

"We're excited for Lewis to have a brother too." I smiled, feeling my heart grow.

"And I like that you're both so young too and will have the energy to run after another little one." The contentment in her voice made me feel like this was right. Everything was as it should be.

Yet having had that positive interaction with the mother, I still wasn't prepared for the moment she would hand over *her* baby to me twelve weeks later—the baby she had carried for nine months in her womb, had given birth to, and had tenderly nursed for the past three days and formed an attachment with.

Having experienced a miscarriage, I was no stranger to loss or heartache, but this was different. I felt out of my depth to know how to handle this situation. Holding *her* baby and then feeling her pain, loss, and grief. And then driving off with *her* baby.

I sobbed my heart out for this young mother as we drove away from the hospital. I knew that life would never be the same for her—or for me. I vowed to myself that if or when we adopted again, I would pray to try to find more ways to help the birth mother through that difficult transition.

Once we were home, Lewis came running out of the house and up to the car window, desperate to get a glimpse of our new family member, who we named Jacob. As he looked at his new baby brother, his bottom lip quivered. The brotherly love was instant, and Lewis never left Jacob's side for the rest of the day.

Before long, we had extended family over, eager to meet him, hold him, and welcome him into the family. The union was beautiful, and this time, I cried for joy.

It would not be the last time I promised a birth mother that I would love her baby with all my heart—except the next time, it would be 11,000 miles away in New Zealand.

New Zealand, Sickness, and Comfort

"Kia ora!" the customs officer said with a big smile. We later learned that *kia ora* means *hello*. "Welcome to New Zealand."

His detection dog was sniffing my carry-on bag. The officer asked to look inside, which I willingly agreed to. I knew there was nothing of consequence inside, or so I thought. All he found was a banana peel, which I had forgotten to dispose of on the plane.

In a friendly but bold manner, he proceeded to inform me why fruit, even banana peels, can carry pests and diseases that could threaten New Zealand's environment and food industry.

I had only just stepped foot onto this new land that I would call home, and I was already causing trouble! I frowned and could feel my brows pinching together.

"You are still welcome!" the officer rushed to reassure me with a wink, raised eyebrows, and a laugh.

Our young family of four soon discovered, similar to that of the customs officer, that "Kiwis" like to tease, have a great sense of humor, and use their eyebrows a lot to communicate.

It would not take us long to make many new friends who included us in their family gatherings, picnics at the beach, and camping, fishing, and boating trips. We might have been far from our land of birth, but we quickly felt at home in this beautiful part of the world.

We had never imagined living anywhere other than England, but just prior to adopting our son, I woke up with this feeling that we were meant to move to New Zealand. When I told Matt, he was initially stunned, but similar to the adoption situation, it soon felt right.

Within a year of living in New Zealand, I found myself sitting in our doctor's clinic, absolutely stunned. *Could it be true?* The last time I was pregnant was when I had that miscarriage.

"Am I really pregnant?" I asked the nurse again.

The nurse chuckled. "Yes! Your test came back positive. Must be something in the New Zealand water." She smiled.

Matt and I were delighted that we were expecting a baby, but when the morning sickness became "all-day" sickness again, it became a difficult time for us all. Before long, our family doctor sent me to the hospital because I wasn't able to keep even water down.

"You have something called hyperemesis gravidarum," the hospital nurse said as she put the IV line in my arm, ready to administer the saline fluid drip.

These hospital stays became a common occurrence throughout my pregnancy. I was very grateful to our neighbors and friends, including our family doctor's wife and daughter, who stepped in to take care of my boys when Matt was at work.

"You may as well move in, you poor thing," said the hospital nurse as I was being wheeled back to the hospital ward yet again.

This stay, though, would prove to be a more difficult one.

One night, I rang the nurse's bell because I needed help going to the toilet.

A nurse who I had never seen before flung open the door to my room and angrily said, "What do you want?"

I explained. During my pregnancy, I had lost my hearing in my right ear, causing vertigo, and along with my very low blood pressure, I was unsteady on my feet.

She snapped, "You'll have to wait!" then banged the door shut on her way out.

While waiting, I wet the bed and then fell back to sleep.

When the nurse came in and found I had wet myself, she woke me up, shouting, "You stupid girl!"

She stripped my clothing and the bedsheets off the bed, wheeled me to the shower, and washed me down heavy-handedly, which caused me great physical pain.

I was reminded of the schoolteacher who hit me with the metal ruler and pulled me to the ground by my tie. Despite being an adult, I could not stand up for myself. I was too weak, and all I could do was cry.

The nurse replaced the bedsheets, placed me back in bed, put the new bag of saline liquid on the drip, and left without a word.

I wept myself to sleep thinking about all the other patients under her care that night, praying that they would not be treated as badly as I had been.

The next time I woke up needing the bathroom, I realized I had only slept an hour and that the same nurse was still on duty. I was not going to ring the bell, so I prayed that I could hold it in this time and go back to sleep. I did drift off but only to wake a few minutes later, needing the bathroom again.

This time, however, there was a woman standing next to my bed who had soft facial features and a warm smile. She was maybe in her late forties or early fifties, with a fair complexion and sparkling, deep-set blue eyes. She seemed to read my mind and said, "I can help you to the bathroom."

I thanked her profusely.

She was not dressed in a nursing outfit, but her offer of help in my hour of need was an answer to prayers. She stayed by my bedside all night, taking me to the restroom regularly and showing me some much-needed tender, loving care. At times, she stroked my hair and told me she loved me. There was something familiar about this woman, which made her care feel all the more special.

Multiple times, I couldn't help but wonder if she was an angel sent from heaven.

Fifteen years later, when a cousin shared a photo of my paternal grandmother, Flo, in her younger days, I recognized her as the woman by my bedside that night. Flo had passed away twenty years before she'd come to my aid in my hour of need. I burst into tears and called out her name, thanking her for her love and for being my angel in my hour of need.

In The Church of Jesus Christ of Latter-day Saints, we believe that our loved ones who have passed on aren't far from us and are there to help and buoy us up in our times of need. This experience only increased my faith in that.

* * *

The morning I went into labor, Matt received a phone call from the friend who was watching our boys. She said that our youngest son, Jacob, had been rushed to hospital with a severe asthma attack. Matt held back that information from me until our son, Levi, was born. I didn't have long to enjoy this special union with Levi before Matt broke the news.

"Kerry, I don't know how to tell you this," Matt said. Then he hesitantly continued. "Jacob was rushed to hospital with an asthma attack, but he's fine now."

"What?" I asked. *Did I just hear right? My little Jacob is in the hospital?* I began to panic and cry, thinking how hard it must be for him not having me there to comfort him. Jacob was in a different hospital than we were.

I became so emotional that I turned to prayer for comfort as I often did. "Please, Lord, comfort my Jacob! I can't be with him, and I don't want him to be alone and scared."

Matt went to the other hospital to check on Jacob and found him being entertained by the nurses there. Jacob may have had tubes up his nose and experienced a severe asthma attack, but he seemed oblivious to it all. Incredibly, he thought that one of the nurses was me!

When Matt came back to relay that to me, I was so relieved!

"The strange thing was," Matt said, "that the nurse who Jacob was calling mum didn't look anything like you!"

That was a miracle in itself and an answer to a desperate prayer.

DREAMS, IVF, ADOPTION, AND CHARITY WORK

My three young boys kept me active and on my toes. Life was fulfilling, idyllic, and fun! But then one night, I had a dream—a lucid dream that would change the trajectory of my life and impact the lives of so many.

I saw thousands and thousands of children going hungry. Some children reacted to their hunger pains with anger and aggression, while others were sad and withdrawn. They were all worrying about where their next meal would come from, and for a number of children, a feeling of hopelessness had crept in.

For a moment, I felt their emotions flow through me. The hopelessness was the most distressing. Desperate to help, I began searching for food, only to find a basket overflowing with it at my feet! I quickly handed the food out to each of the children and also took the opportunity to tell them they were loved. Soon the children in my dream stopped fighting and being sad; instead, they hugged one another and were happy. I cried joyful tears as the scene changed from a distressing one to a joyful one.

I woke up knowing that I had been given a calling that night to find and feed those children from my dream—to be God's hands.

How do I begin? How do I juggle this with being a wife and mother to my three young children? Plus, we were going through the process to adopt again. *Where were the children from my dream? How would I provide the food they need?* So many questions filled my mind that I couldn't see a way forward—until my next dream.

In my second dream, I was shown the same children with the same struggles.

This time, guilt kicked in. I felt so sorry that I had not found and fed them yet.

This was a good lesson. Sometimes we think we're too busy to help or that it's not the right time, but my dream reminded me that it *could* be done, even if it meant having three young children in tow and using our family savings to make it happen.

In the middle of building a commercial kitchen, my husband and I got the news that a birth mother had chosen us and that we had a baby girl waiting for us.

We jumped up and down with joy.

"A girl!"

I had thought that I was destined for a life surrounded by brothers and sons, but here I was, being told this baby was a girl.

The questions began again. *How could I be His hands, finding and feeding the children from my dreams, with the arrival of our new daughter? How can I be an attentive mother to four young children if I'm busy with charity work?*

During a prayer, a peaceful feeling came over me, and I knew I needed to take one day at a time.

When it came time for us to bring our daughter home, I prayed about her birth mother and how to help her with this difficult transition.

Two clear impressions came to my mind. The first thought was to invite the birth mother to stay with us in our home for a night or two so that she could witness our sons interact with their new baby sister and see her get settled in. The second impression was to keep in contact with the birth mother via text and send her regular photos and updates to reassure her that all was well.

When I extended the invitation to the birth mother, she happily accepted. These impressions proved helpful as the birth mother began her journey of loss and grief.

Another dream came, which reminded me I had work to do! It was time to make a start. So my little baby girl, Abigail, joined me in a baby carrier in the kitchen so that we could stay close to each other as I began the journey to feed the children from my dreams.

The charity work took perseverance, commitment, hard work, a lack of sleep, and sacrifice to "feed the need"—a phrase that eventually became the name of our charity. And we received the help of many friends!

I busily prepared and served food over many years, and sometimes I had the special opportunity to hold children's hands and embrace them, being God's hands in His work.

One of the boys I had the privilege of meeting had been one of the children I had seen in my dreams years earlier. Our brief but special interaction was a gift from above. The love I felt for him was that of a mother for her child—I wanted to scoop him up and take him home.

During these busy years, Matt and I also did IVF (a fertility treatment), which took its toll on my body. In the end, we were blessed with a son (yes, another son!) who we named Samuel. Motherhood has been—and still is—my greatest joy in life.

The charity work in New Zealand came with trials and difficulty, but it also came with valuable lessons, miracles, love, and joy. It was a better life plan than Matt and I could have ever dreamed up.

There is much, much more to this story of "feeding the need," but that is for another time. What I want you to know is that this story has a happy ending: I found and fed *all* the children from my dreams and used every opportunity to tell them they were loved. These interactions were incredibly special and a highlight of my life.

The charity work came to the attention of Her Royal Highness Queen Elizabeth II, who signed her name to award me a Royal Honour, followed by an investiture ceremony in New Zealand where I received an insignia (award) for my services to children.

The New Zealand government then stepped up and introduced a free lunch program!

The Feed the Need charity still operates today, providing breakfast packs, snack packs, weekend packs, and family food boxes.

Over the Christmas season, The Church of Jesus Christ of Latter-day Saints has "giving machines" in many countries, including New Zealand. These machines are vending machines with a twist—instead of getting a soda or treats out of them, the public can donate to a specific cause. The one in New Zealand includes Feed the Need as one of the charities the public can donate to. Last Christmas, we were able to deliver 2,227 food packs to those in need because of the donations received via the giving machines.

My dreams gave me an insight into how food insecurity negatively impacts a person's overall well-being—mental health, physical health, and emotional health—and that by being *God's hands* when serving the hungry, we can bring relief and restore hope. Through this service, I learned the truthfulness of Matthew 19:26: "With God all things are possible."

Being His Hands and Voice

"What would be your dream job?" the man asked the young refugee woman named Sa, who had six of her ten children huddled up next to her in her dark and musty apartment.

"My dream job?" Sa asked with a look of confusion on her face.

The man nodded. He represented the local refugee resettlement group in Salt Lake City. He wanted to help Sa get a job that she could hold down. So far, she had only been able to get cleaning jobs, but because of multiple serious injuries to her spine, physical work caused her significant pain.

Sa was young yet looked so old because her back was twisted and hunched over. Her previous employer told me, "Sa was in agony as she cleaned. We had to let her go."

"I do not dream," Sa eventually replied. She looked at her hands in her lap as tears began to run down her cheeks.

I reached over and took her hand.

Sa had suffered so much in her short life. She could not remember her parents—only being a homeless child living alone in a busy and dirty city in Myanmar. One night, around the age of seven or eight, Sa remembered being taken by a group of men, thrown into the back of a van, and driven off into the dark night.

She was subsequently sold into human trafficking. At the age of eleven, she became pregnant, and at twelve, she gave birth to a baby who died within hours. This was just the beginning of a horrific story. The fact that she had survived, and had six of her ten children alive and with her, was a miracle in itself.

I had not experienced what she had, not even close, but I'd experienced enough in my youth to feel great empathy for her.

Sa's eyes widened, and she glanced up, her countenance brightening. "Wait, I did have a dream! When I was a little girl, I wanted to grow up, be a doctor, and help people!"

This memory seemed to bring her joy, but it caused me great pain. She had wanted to grow up and help people, yet people had been so cruel to her and had literally broken her body, mind, and spirit. My heart broke for her.

When I first met Sa, my family and I had only been living in America for six months. Moving to America was never part of our plan, but we had learned by now to follow the breadcrumbs the Lord gave us.

For the months leading up to our move, I cried on a daily basis. I loved New Zealand and its people. It was a huge burden to say goodbye. It reminded me of the time we had to say goodbye to our family and friends in England all those years earlier. Here we were, moving again, thousands of miles away from everything that was familiar and from everything we loved.

As I saw Sa's damp and infested living conditions, I was dismayed—broken windows, no window coverings, dirty mattresses on the floor, water dripping through the roof, and her family covered in bite marks from the infestation issues. I couldn't help but mourn for her—and get to work.

Ironically, her landlord was on the "Good Landlord" list. Not that he was actually good, but he had paid money to be on that list so that he could continue getting the rent subsidized by the government for the refugees he housed in his awful housing complex.

Within weeks of that initial visit, I knew what I needed to do. I gathered a team of volunteers and once again recruited Matt to support the cause. Matt always had my back—and those of the people I wished to serve.

We sent Sa and her children out for the day. Then we got to work. We assembled new beds and laid out new bedding, fixed broken windows, and made and hung curtains. Even the pest control guy did the job for free (and subsequently said it was the worst infestation he had ever seen).

Later that day, Sa and her children returned home and were thrilled to see the transformation. She held my hands tightly and cried happy tears.

Sa would be the first of many refugees I would meet, love, and cry for. She was also the first person I had met who had been trafficked, and sadly there would be others.

Reach Out Today was the registered nonprofit I had been directing ever since moving to America. It had been set up by my cousin and his friend.

When they asked if I could direct the charity in a voluntary capacity, I prayed about it.

There were already a lot of charities going about doing good. "Was there a need for another charity?" I asked in prayer.

The answer I received was "Yes, there is still so much need."

After that prayer, I knew my work here had just begun in this land so far from home.

Then the dreams started coming again, just as they had back in New Zealand. I knew there were people, from a variety of backgrounds, who I needed to find and serve. I needed to make a start.

Sometime later, I sat with a team of counselors in a school district office around a boardroom table. Clenching my hands in my lap, I took a deep breath and then spoke up. "Do you have any students with needs that aren't being met?"

"Some of our students don't have access to hot water, shampoo, or professional haircuts," one of the counselors said. "And it's often these students that stand out and get targeted by the bullies."

I knew what it felt like to be bullied and wanted to quickly come up with a solution.

That day, I worked with the counselors to come up with the idea of a "pop-up salon."

"Could your charity provide spare clothing for children who are dealing with trauma and wetting themselves at school?" another counselor asked.

I quickly scribbled down notes. That request started the clothes drive in my neighborhood.

"What about toothbrushes and deodorant?" a third counselor asked.

I nodded and jotted that down: *Hygiene packs.*

And this was just my first meeting with one group of school counselors. It taught me that if we want to find opportunities to serve, we just need to ask.

In time, the program Just Serve, a service provided by The Church of Jesus Christ of Latter-day Saints, became a valuable resource for Reach Out Today. The Just Serve website lists many charities and organizations and the many ways the general public can help serve or volunteer. Most of our food packs and hygiene packs come from the public who found us on Just Serve.

When the day of the pop-up salon arrived, I grabbed clean towels, hair dryers, and anything else I thought might be useful. Things might not go as planned, as I had learned time and time again, but my hope was that the children would enjoy the experience.

When I walked into the school restroom, where we would be washing and cutting hair, I came to an abrupt halt as I took in the scene before me.

One of the social workers had put up fairy lights around the mirrors, plug-in air fresheners to help improve the smell, and cute signs on the walls saying things like "You are amazing" and "You are loved."

She had worked hard to make the restroom feel more like a salon. It warmed my heart and made me misty-eyed. She knew that these children were of great worth and deserved some TLC.

My job was to bring professional hairstylists who would be willing to do hours of free labor, along with volunteers to help us welcome the students, put them at ease, and wash their hair, plus assemble hair care kits for them to take home.

The students arrived dressed in old and dirty clothing with greasy, unkempt hair. They were visibly apprehensive as they huddled in on themselves, kept their eyes on the ground, and stayed silent.

One girl shook. "I've never been to a salon before. I'm excited but very nervous," she said.

A volunteer and I tried to help her feel more comfortable by showing her the sinks, describing how we would wash her hair, and introducing her to the hairstylists.

After that, she took a deep breath and said, "I'm ready!"

As we washed her hair, she gradually became more relaxed, even enjoying it by the end. When she sat in the stylist's chair, the stylist knelt next to her and made conversation. The next minute, she was laughing.

Once her hair had been cut, she turned to us and asked if anyone could braid her hair.

A volunteer willingly put her hand up and quickly went over to do so.

As I watched this girl lean back and soak in the feeling of her hair being braided, I felt a sadness come over me that caused me to wonder about what this young girl had experienced in her life and her current situation.

After the pop-up salon had finished, I asked the social worker about this girl's story.

"It's very sad," the social worker said. "Her mother died of an overdose when she was young, and her dad is in prison for life. She currently lives in the local trailer park with her grandfather, but that's not working out. I feel so sorry for her!"

As I drove home from that event, I had an impression come to my mind that this girl was yearning for a mother's touch. The volunteer who'd braided her hair had filled that void, if only for a few minutes. Even a makeshift salon in a cold school restroom can provide an opportunity to care for someone in need.

News of the pop-up salons spread fast, and requests ended up coming from other schools, teen group homes, and safe houses for vulnerable young girls.

It was at one of these pop-up salons, in a safe house, where a young teenage girl cried as I washed her hair.

Once again, I had this sad feeling come over me.

After her haircut, she disclosed that she had been trafficked by her own mother when she was only nine years old.

By her own mother! I could not even begin to understand.

We cried together.

As I drove away, I thought about Jesus Christ's example to us when He washed the feet of His disciples. And the pope's example, who also washed the feet of people in prisons and refugee centers and people of different faiths. I had not washed anyone's feet, but I had seen the impact of washing someone's hair. And *because I cared*, they felt loved.

Other requests from the schools were to organize a "winter shop-a-thon" and back-to-school shopping events for children who came from impoverished backgrounds.

I approached a local business that agreed to provide the cash for these children to use during these events. A store agreed to open its doors to us a few hours before it opened to the public.

Volunteers came to help the children during their shopping experience. Having that in-person experience proved powerful for both the volunteers and those they were serving—including myself.

In the first "back-to-school shop" I'd ever done, a young boy, maybe nine or ten, made a beeline for me with a huge smile on his face.

I had never met him before, but he wanted a hug and asked me, "Are you an angel?"

I smiled and shook my head. "Only human."

He nodded and got a decisive look on his face. "You must be a princess then!" He ran off.

At the end of his shop, he came to me again asking for one last hug.

"Did you have fun?" I asked.

"Yes! It's been the best day of my life!" he exclaimed. "I have had a lot of sad days." He proceeded to tell me, and two other volunteers, his heartbreaking story. His name was Michael.

As I was cleaning up inside the store, Michael's social worker came to find me. "Are you Kerry?"

I nodded.

"Michael wants to share his free Burger King breakfast with you," his social worker said with a smile. "He's refusing to eat without you."

My heart warmed as I agreed. We walked outside to the parking lot.

As soon as Michael saw me, he gave me a huge smile and threw himself on me, saying, "I want to give you half of my breakfast so that we can eat together!"

Here he was, having had so many "bad days" in his young life, wanting to split his breakfast with me.

"That's so sweet of you," I said, "but that breakfast is just for you."

He frowned and looked at his feet.

"But how about I sit with you while you eat?" This did the trick, and we sat together while he ate.

He talked the whole time. I can't remember what was said, but I do remember how I felt sitting on the floor in the parking lot together. A peace came over me, confirming that this was exactly where I was supposed to be and who I was supposed to be with.

When it was time for him to leave, he handed me his Burger King cardboard crown. "Here, this is for you."

I shook my head. "No, I couldn't take that." I didn't want to take anything from him that might bring him joy.

He kept insisting. "But you're a princess. You have to have it."

This time, I felt I could accept it.

After this event, I got in touch with the school district where Michael was a student, and I asked about him. Matt and I wanted to offer our home to become his home if needed, but I was told that his grandmother had stepped in to take care of him.

To this day, I keep the crown Michael gave to me next to my immunoglobulin infusion supplies (needles, tubing, etc.) to remind me that if Michael can do hard things, so can I. Michael never realized that this crown would actually help me seven years on. He had, in fact, served me.

I sometimes find myself thinking about Michael even today. He would be seventeen years old by now . . . almost an adult. Has he managed to heal and move on from those bad days? Has he found the angel he was looking for in people? I hope so.

Then there was thirty-three-year-old Keith, who at the age of eighteen had aged out of the system. His story, along with other stories, would help me "prove" to our community that this marginalized group of youth needed more housing and wraparound care.

I was grateful that Keith was willing to speak to me.

We sat in his friend's living room, across from one another, with a coffee table in between. With a pen and notepad, and butterflies in my stomach, I took a moment to breathe.

It has always been nerve-racking for me to ask questions of complete strangers, especially when they could trigger bad memories. I said a silent prayer and began.

It was best to start the interview by asking about their happy memories—this usually helped the interviewees relax—but when I asked Keith about his happiest times, he sat there staring at the coffee table and was quiet.

After a moment, he replied, "I can't remember any good memories. Sorry."

"No family gatherings?" I asked.

He shook his head.

"No day trips?"

He shook his head again.

"What about warm embraces?"

One more head shake.

At that moment, I found myself trying to contain my emotions and wishing that I could have stepped back in time and hugged him as a boy.

The abuse and neglect Keith had suffered from his mother had been hard, but it got even harder when the system "took over." He was moved from place to place, living in group homes, shelters, foster homes, homes of extended family, and back to foster homes.

"I never felt like I belonged anywhere. I felt unlovable," he said.

It didn't surprise me he'd felt that way.

"Sadness became a constant feeling during my teenage years. When the kids in the neighborhood were playing sports or riding their bikes, I stayed inside, choosing to be on my own."

When Keith aged out of foster care, he had no support or anywhere for him to go, and he became homeless. Before long, he found himself addicted to opioids, which he said "took away my sadness at first, but the addiction only led to more sadness."

After the interview, Keith said that he appreciated being listened to and that I made him feel of value.

He *was* of value! He had great worth!

He was happy that his story would give a voice to so many like him. So was I.

We embraced and said our goodbyes.

As I drove away, it dawned on me that maybe using my hands to write stories—and raising my voice to speak up for people like Keith—in order to advocate might be just as important as packing up hygiene kits or washing hair. It could potentially bring about change—not just for "the one" but for whole groups who have been marginalized, neglected, or rejected.

My mind turned to the refugees. *Maybe, just maybe, I could do something more for the refugees* . . . I was reminded of one of my dreams.

In this dream, I could hear wailing and crying coming from a dark tunnel. As I looked into this tunnel, refugees streamed out of the entrance. Worn-out women were holding their crying babies, and men were carrying children and their family's belongings on their backs. They were cold, tired, and sad, and they seemed like they had lost all hope. Their clothes were torn and their shoes had holes in them.

They must be hungry! I thought.

I ran over the road to a local restaurant and ordered a hundred portions of fries to take to them.

The owner of the restaurant refused my order and said, "We don't want to encourage the refugees to stay here."

I was stunned and asked him, "Can you not hear their cries?"

He turned around and walked away from me.

I was dismayed that another human being could turn their back on those who are suffering. It was beyond my comprehension. The next thing I remember was Matt waking me up . . . He'd heard me crying in my sleep.

I had always interpreted the dark tunnel as being a place they had come from—the wars they had fled from, the horrors they had seen and had endured, and the difficult journey they took to get to safety.

One time, we helped a refugee family move into an apartment. I wondered how they would move without our help. They often had no means of transporting their items and families.

As we moved the items, we couldn't help but think that it would be easier to throw away these things and buy new ones for them. However, it was evident that the few belongings they had were far more than just objects to them. These items were all they had left of their former lives, and to them, they were priceless. Each item held memories, hopes, and a sense of identity that the chaos of displacement threatened to erase.

Once we had moved everything into their new apartment, the father let out a huge sigh and said something in his own language to his wife and children. His children excitedly hugged their father and cried happy tears.

Smiling, I asked, "What did you say?"

He replied, "I told them we are safe now."

As I drove home, I wept knowing that Jesus, having once been a refugee Himself, would have wanted this family to feel safe, have their treasured belongings with them, and have their needs met.

* * *

"Five months to walk here? Did I hear that right?" I thought as I looked upon a tired, young refugee family of four in dire need of supplies while trying to keep my jaw from dropping.

"This family walked a perilous and arduous journey for five months," the interpreter told us, "to reach the U.S. border seeking safety. They only carried with them the clothes on their backs, a few belongings, and refugee status documents."

They clearly needed a lot.

I could not shake the fact that this family looked like one of the families I had seen in my dream, walking out of that dark tunnel.

The other volunteer and I piled into the car with this family and went to Walmart.

We ran around the store, putting much-needed items into the cart.

When we were in the nappy (diaper) aisle, the mother was trying to tell us something. Eventually, she pulled down the baby's clothing, and we saw a nappy rash but a whole different level. Layers of skin had literally fallen off—it was no wonder the baby cried constantly. Through the help of an interpreter, the mother explained that on the journey, they had no access to diapers or hygiene supplies. We were soon able to get help from the pharmacist.

When we were finding clothing for their son, who was five years old, I couldn't help but think about how the journey was for him. The interpreter told us that he had walked the whole five months.

My heart went out to him.

When we dropped this family back at the interpreter's home, who was providing this family some shelter overnight, I couldn't help but tell the interpreter about my dream of seeing refugees walking out of a dark tunnel.

The interpreter shocked me when he said, "This family *did* walk through a tunnel."

"An actual tunnel?" My brows shot up, and so did his.

"Yes, an actual tunnel, with no lighting. It was wet, damp, and dangerous inside."

I had never thought the dark tunnels in my dreams could be actual tunnels that refugees went through to find safety. Both of us could hardly believe what we were hearing.

As I drove home, I sensed that this was just the beginning of my work with refugees. Helping them move home and source furniture, food, hygiene items, and other much-needed items is all important, but I knew that there was so much more to be done. I could feel it. I would need to pray for guidance.

My prayers and dreams had guided me in the past: first, with the charity work in New Zealand, specifically Feed the Need's food and youth programs, and next, in America, with the images and dreams that led to the housing project for youth aging out of foster care or experiencing homelessness, among other programs.

The dream about the refugees remains at the forefront of my mind and in my prayers. For now, their immediate needs are the focus, but I suspect I will have another dream and more images to lead and guide me on a new journey to better serve their needs.

Wherever we turn in the world, there is need. It's just a matter of opening our eyes and remembering that when we serve, we are God's hands here on earth.

I am sometimes asked how I do it all, with having a large family to take care of and a chronic health condition. I have learned that when we are on the Lord's errand and striving to be His hands by offering comfort, compassion, service, and love, we are given strength from above.

Whether it's using our hands to serve the hungry, wash the hair of the poor, pack up and deliver essential items to the needy, assist those who have been displaced, or embrace someone experiencing grief, pain, and loss, we can be a conduit of God's love for them.

Dr. Larry Nelson, an author and professor in the human sciences, said, "Caring for those who are poor is of temporal importance to them, but it's of spiritual importance for us."[8] I believe this whole-heartedly. Whenever I serve those in need, I feel closer to our Savior and hope to be more like Him.

Some words from the song "His Hands" perfectly describe Jesus Christ's example and my hope for the rest of my days:

> His hands would serve his whole life through
> Showing man what hands might do
> Giving, ever giving endlessly
> Each day was filled with selflessness
> And I'll not rest till I make of my hands what they could be
> Till these hands become like those from Galilee[9]

---

8. Hank Smith and John Bytheway, interview with Larry Nelson, "Episode 38 Part II: Dr. Larry Nelson, 2 Corinthians 1–7," followHIM: A *Come, Follow* Me Podcast (podcast), September 6, 2023.

9. Kenneth Cope, "His Hands," Invubu, accessed Nov. 5, 2024, https://www.invubu.com/music/show/song/Kenneth-Cope/His-Hands.html.

8

ESTHER JACKSON-STOWELL
The Broker

BEGINNINGS

Some days, you just need a soda run.

After hours of cleaning, organizing, and preparing for the birth of our second son due in two months, I was ready for a break. So when my husband, Rich, asked if I wanted to step out to grab a drink with him, I was out the door before he'd finished his sentence.

We left our son, Joseph, with his grandparents and made the two-block drive to our local gas station.

I waited in the heated car, bundled in my warm winter coat that bulged a little over my baby bump, and listened to a country song Rich had chosen while he went in to get his Pepsi. I was glad for five minutes to myself where I was not surrounded by prospective things I thought I needed to clean, arrange, or throw out.

Rich entered the store and passed a guy sipping from a Big Gulp–sized cup—he was just shy of Rich's 6'1" height and rocking a shaved head and a full beard. I recognized him immediately. He and his wife were new to our ward and had given talks in church last Sunday. In the Church, we often invite new members of the congregation to give talks and introduce themselves during sacrament meeting. It's a way of helping the members get to know one another.

And it had worked. "Oh!" I said to myself as I perked up—as much as a seven-months-pregnant woman can perk. "It's the couple from church."

I enjoyed their talks, especially the wife's. The moment she'd stepped up to the pulpit, she'd caught my attention. She spoke with an impediment that I'd later realize was due to hearing loss, but that wasn't what stuck with me. Her aura was different from the crowd I had become accustomed to since we'd moved here, with her relaxed, unbothered personality and her not-afraid-to-make-mistakes vibe. When she spoke, she reminded me of myself, and her humor resonated with me. She'd been sincere, funny, and not afraid of unapologetically sharing her story with those who needed to hear it.

Needless to say, I made a mental note to connect with her and get to know her. I was new to Utah and wanted to surround myself with people who enjoyed life the way I knew how to live it—with humor. So I took seeing her husband at the gas station for exactly what it was—a sign.

I waved.

He didn't see me. So I waved again—and again—until my waving was almost frantic. Finally, his gaze locked on mine.

"Hi," I mouthed.

His lips fell away from his straw.

"Hi!" I tried again.

This time, his eyes went wide.

"Hi!" I tried a third time, continuing to wave.

He panicked and abruptly did an about-face. I let out a peal of laughter. Clearly, he didn't have a clue who I was. Well, he would soon enough.

Not long after, he and his wife stepped out of the store, and I slumped out of our blue Subaru Outback and waddled over to them. "I'm Esther Stowell—from the ward."

The wife took the lead. "Oh, nice to meet you!" She smiled wide and reached out her hand to shake mine. "I'm Megan, and this is my husband, Joey."

I told her about how I'd waved at her husband through the window and even mimed how he'd turned away from me. Soon we were all laughing.

"I know," she said. "He told me there was a crazy Black woman outside waving at him."

That had us in hysterics—more Megan and I than Joey, or Rich for that matter when he finally came out with his drink, wondering what I'd gotten into now. He once again realized I couldn't be left alone, lest I make new friends and turn a short trip to anywhere into a long interaction that he had to peel me away from.

Megan and I exchanged phone numbers, and sometime after the birth of my second son, Gabriel, we started working out together. We would wake up at 5 a.m. and I would go to her house to do P90X. Meg lived two blocks away from us, which was convenient. We'd jump around her living room, with her hearing husband in the next room who never once questioned our passionate attempt to exercise.

Over time, Megan and I became great friends. I loved her tenacity and love for life. Soon we went on trips together, would do impromptu dances (most times, reenacting our P90X moves) whenever we would meet, and exchanged text messages about our highs and lows. Those consisted mostly of humor-filled memories of our children, whether it was the time her son stumbled upon his dad's razor and proceeded to give himself a fantastic haircut, or the time my toddler smeared poop all over my husband's feet while he was sound asleep.

Becoming friends with Megan was easy. After all, making friends was a skill I had a knack for. Since moving to Utah, I'd made lots of friends—from Clarissa, my party-planning buddy, to Debbie, my go-to cupcake person who will make time to bake with my children at the drop of a hat, to Emily, my husband's cousin who's always ready to hang out and watch *The Mentalist* with me, and so many more that it would take too long to name them all. But it hadn't always been that way. Life had taught me a lot about friendship.

* * *

As a child, I never saw myself as affluent, but we were—something I realized as I got older.

The sun, a fiery orb, painted the sky in hues of orange and pink as I entered the world in the vibrant Nigerian city of Eket. Nestled along the Atlantic coast, Eket was a symphony of sights, sounds, and smells.

The rhythmic beat of drums, the spicy aroma of jollof rice, and the infectious laughter of children filled my early years.

My father was a chieftain—a chieftaincy title he received for the significant work he did for our community. He was a revered leader in our region, very embedded in politics, and a founding father for our state, and he had a very community-centered outlook. He established a school in our village, a bank, and other businesses. His wealth and involvement in politics often had governors coming to him like he was some kind of kingpin when they wanted or needed something.

And me? For lack of a better way to describe who I am to the people in that community, my husband's family has not-so-loosely applied the term "princess." It's not exactly wrong—my family in Nigeria had hired labor, like chauffeurs, chefs, and assistants who planned out our days and picked up after us. The Jacksons are well known in the community and have social standing and prestige, but still, "princess" has never been a term that's settled well with me. It's so far removed from my life—a life that involves getting sodas with my husband after a day of hard labor I did with my own two hands—that I find it laughable.

As a child, wealth wasn't the lens I used to view equality, but it was the lens used by my siblings and other kids in town. I spent much of my youth wanting to build friendships with children that my siblings teased and harassed for being poor. I didn't understand why those kids would in turn antagonize *me* when I tried to befriend them. Or why the very next day, they'd turn around and want to be my friends again—a turnaround I always welcomed.

Growing up in Nigeria, I experienced the vibrant tapestry of African culture. I learned the intricate dance steps of the Efik people, savored the flavors of traditional delicacies like fufu and egusi soup, and listened to the enchanting melodies of highlife music. Yet amidst the beauty and richness of my homeland, I also witnessed the challenges and inequality that plagued many communities. These experiences ignited a spark within me—a desire to bridge the gaps and create a more equitable society.

It was in Nigeria that I took the first steps on the path to learning to be a middleman. For me, being a broker has always been more than just a job—more than my company, Ekot Real Estate. It's also been a way of life.

A New World Awaits

On a warm weekday afternoon, my father, Sunday Jackson, led two men—one of European descent and the other Chinese—down the hall to our parlor, which was situated on the front-facing portion of our two-story home. Dad was dressed in a fine light gray kaftan, a traditional outfit with a top that goes past the knee, which felt like a crisp dollar bill to the touch. He wore his best smile full of teeth, and despite his imposing posture, he seemed inviting. The two men, also dressed in their western business best, greeted him warmly.

I might have only been seven years old, but I knew what this meant: one, Dad was having a business meeting, and two, I could get out of doing chores.

Sneaking away from our maid, I rushed into the parlor and to my dad's side, the maid close on my heels. Dad was already showing the businessmen to their seats. "Please, sit, sit. Make yourselves at home." In the same breath, he hollered out to the cook, "Ekwere, bring these men food." He didn't ask his guests if they were hungry. In a Nigerian home, we don't ask—you're expected to eat. Why else would anyone pay someone a visit if not to eat?

They all took their seats, my dad taking his on the red sectional couch in the center of the room. It had throw pillows, was made of leather, and depicted the crest of the Nigerian flag on it. I made my way over to him and sat on the ottoman. He gave me a big, sunny smile and patted my cheek. My dad traveled a lot, so when he was home, it was such a treat for me.

The maid rushed in and beckoned me with a wave to come with her.

I glanced at my dad, then stood.

"Where are you going?" Dad patted the cushion next to him. "Come back here."

Smiling, I sat back down and shrugged at our maid. *What? I can't go. Dad said.*

Shaking her head, the maid backed out of the room and closed the door behind her.

Dad gave me an encouraging nod. He paid people to parent us, to feed us, to make sure we brushed our teeth and got to bed on time, but he believed kids should be kids. He didn't mind us rolling on him, goofing around, hanging out—even if it was during important meetings. But it wasn't just that. My father was a charismatic entrepreneur with a heart of gold, and he instilled in me a love for adventure and an unwavering spirit of determination. His entrepreneurial ventures, from small-scale businesses to community development projects to politics, ignited a spark within me—a desire to make a tangible difference in the world. I was interested in his meeting, even though I couldn't always understand what was happening.

As Dad and his partners got talking about business, I couldn't help but think how different it was to have a white guy and an Asian guy in our home. Dad normally had his meetings at his factory, but for these men, he had to have this meeting in his house . . . to share himself.

They talked about manufacturing carpets. The white guy from Europe was Dad's partner, and the guy from Asia oversaw the raw materials and machinery.

Much of the meeting was casual. Dad served them drinks from the bar that my brothers liked to sneak alcohol from when they thought no one was looking. (They didn't worry much about *me* seeing, though I did sometimes wonder what would happen if I told on them . . .)

My dad cracked a joke, and his partners responded with big, manly laughs. All the while, Dad kept me involved by wrapping an arm around me or patting me on the leg.

Much of what took place in his meetings was over my head, but there were some clear takeaways. The first thing I learned was the value of diversifying.

In that space, I witnessed what I would come to know as the norm—working with people from all walks of life and races for a common goal. In that parlor that day, their goal was to finalize the manufacturing process for my father's carpet factory. Dad showed me that life was full of opportunities if you were willing to work for them and take risks.

My father was a man of ambition and vision. He was, and had always been, an entrepreneur; he dreamt of business ventures and pushed the boundaries of what was possible. His entrepreneurial spirit taught me the value of perseverance and the importance of thinking outside the box. From our living room in Calabar, I witnessed my first business meeting.

*   *   *

In Nigeria, I was surrounded by a rich culture and a strong sense of community. Family was everything, and the values of respect, hard work, and faith were instilled in me from a young age. I came from a family of plural marriages, which was the norm for affluent men in my community. My mother was my father's second wife. My parents, though separated, were both strong figures in my life, each contributing to the formation of my identity in different ways. (My dad remained with his first wife, Jenny, who was the mother figure I was raised to know.)

My mother, Cecilia Ikpe, was a devout Catholic her whole life. She nurtured my empathy and instilled in me a deep sense of spirituality. Her unwavering faith and selfless service to others shaped my moral compass and inspired me to use my talents to help those in need.

According to my dad, my mother decided to leave him when I was about three months old, striking out on her own. My mother has a different view of what happened, and from the stories I overheard as a child, and having become a mom of three children myself, I tend to rely on her account.

She shared with me, in my adult years, that during my birth, she lost her womb, leading to excessive bleeding. As a nurse, she understood the implications and knew she needed time and space to care for herself, lest she lose her life in trying to keep up with her healing and the tumultuous relationship she had with my father. As a chief, and probably ill-advised, my father refused to allow her to leave with her children—a punishment for daring to leave a man of his standing, I suppose.

Divorced and living a life in Nigeria, outside of the norms of what most perceived as fitting for a woman in her forties, she embraced her independence and excelled in her life's work. She was a nurse, and her dedication to her patients was inspiring.

I keep a picture in my home today of my mother in her traditional nursing outfit—a white dress, cinched at the waist, with a matching

241

bonnet on her head, the likes of what you'd see in the older movies depicting nurses in Europe. Prior to her career as a nurse, my mother studied in the UK, another major feat for a young woman from Nkana. She was a trailblazer in her days and continues to carry that spunk with her today. She believed that her work was a calling, and she approached it with a sense of duty and compassion I deeply admired, albeit from afar. Her example taught me that serving others is one of the highest forms of purpose.

In our household, faith was not just a belief system—it was a way of life. We attended church regularly, and prayer was a constant presence in our home. My mother made sure that I understood the importance of a personal relationship with God.

One evening, when I was eleven years old, my father took me on an unexpected trip to the village. This trip was different from our usual holiday trips to the village, which occurred mostly during Christmas. I left my father's compound and made the short walk—though at that time, with my child-like sense of distance, it was quite far—over to my mom's home to visit with her.

It was something of a surprise to us both, but we were grateful for the time together. Her dark, wavy hair was pulled back into a tight bun like she arranged it when she was on duty at the hospital, and she wore an Ankara buba top with a wrapper tied around her waist that matched her top. She was so beautiful and had a light in her dark eyes that always made me feel safe and loved.

Taking my hand, Mom led me into my grandmother's room at the back of the house and up to her bed. Grandma was bedridden and had been for some time after breaking her hip riding a bike. (Bicycles were the mode of transportation for many in the village.) She never could walk again, but she got around with help or by scooting.

Mom nudged me over to the bed, then leaned down closer to my grandmother. "This is your granddaughter," she said. Every syllable was enunciated with a deep Ibibio accent with a British undertone.

Slowly, and with some effort and help from Mom, Nne (meaning grandmother) sat up in bed and looked me over. She stroked my cheek with papery-thin skin, and her countenance changed, warmed—one moment, it had been cold and lost, and now it was focused and happy. She didn't speak much, but her expression said it all as she ran her fingers over my face. *Wow, look how beautiful she is. This is my granddaughter. Aye-yin mmi, welcome—how are you?* Translated, *aye-yin* means my child's child, or grandchild.

I felt the awe in every tender caress, in each sweep of her gaze over my face. I felt loved.

As this went on, Mom went out to the veranda from Nne's bedroom, down the few steps, and to the outside firepit to tend to the fire where she made food for us to eat. The scents of yam and meat wafted my way, as she worked on the traditional fufu, a dough-like food made of yam, and afia efere soup, made of goat meat. She used the yam to thicken the soup, then added spice leaves and okra.

Mom finished making the meal and came to help Nne over to the veranda. We ate slowly, savored the delicious meal while we visited, and laughed in the warm night air. All too soon, we'd finished our food, and Mom helped Nne back to her bed.

My mom's apartment ran vertically to the veranda, and we headed there after getting Nne situated. Mom's kitchen was straight through the door. To the right of the counter, crates of mineral drinks—or soft drinks—were stacked high. She was always ready for any opportunity to visit with her children and knew to have our favorites available—cabin biscuits, Fanta, Dr. Pepper, peanuts, and other snacks children would like. I grabbed a Dr. Pepper and immediately took a swig, the bubbles from the carbonation tickling my nose as I did.

Mom and I headed up the stairs to her room where we knelt in front of one another. "Put your drink down," she instructed.

I did as I was told.

"I'm going to teach you the Hail Mary prayer," she said.

I didn't get to spend much time with my mom, but it was as though she wanted to make sure that the time I did spend with her was spent on what was most important in life. And for her, that was her faith.

She recited the prayer. "Hail Mary, full of grace, the Lord is with thee. Blessed art thou among women and blessed is the fruit of thy womb, Jesus . . ." After finishing, she said, "Now it's your turn. Repeat after me."

We went line by line, over and over, until I too had it memorized. I didn't know it at the time, but this was a pivotal moment in my life. I'd loved being with her, feeling her love, and learning what was important to her.

She gave me a proud smile as we finished up, and she tenderly cupped my cheek. "Yes, Esty-girl. Good. Never forget that God has a plan for your life. He has placed you on this earth for a reason, and it is your job to seek out that purpose." She stroked her thumb over my cheek. "Do you understand?"

I nodded. "Yes." It wasn't the first time she said this to me, and it wouldn't be the last, but it was definitely significant.

To her, it was important for me to understand that message. Internalize it. And I did.

Later that night, my dad sent the driver to get me.

Three days later, unbeknownst to me and my mom during our meeting, my dad moved us out of the country. My father had decided that we were to immigrate, seeking new opportunities and a better future. He brought me and my older sister, Ekaete, to the United States. It would be eleven years before I would see my mother again in person, and though my heart ached at the thought of losing her, I kept her message in mind.

It was in America that I found my purpose.

* * *

The transition from Nigeria to the US resulted in a whirlwind of emotions. I left behind the familiar comforts of my childhood home, the warmth of my immediate and extended family, and the vibrant streets of Calabar. As I stepped onto the plane, a mix of excitement and apprehension filled my heart.

Arriving in Oakland, California, as our final destination was like stepping into a different world. The bustling city streets were wider, filled with more cars than the number of people I was used to seeing in Calabar, and the unfamiliar faces were both overwhelming and exhilarating.

Shortly after arriving, I was enrolled in a local school where I quickly became the "new kid"—a label that carried with it both curiosity and a sense of isolation. In school, I stood out in ways that made me uncomfortable.

"Why do you have an accent?" a girl with long, light brown hair asked me one day. It was recess, and I sat outside, soaking in the mid-day rays with my face to the sun and my eyes closed.

I opened my eyes and frowned, thinking she was the one with the accent. "I am from Nigeria."

While I could speak English, my accent and lack of knowledge of American idioms often led to misunderstandings and feelings of inadequacy.

Another girl came up beside her, this one with bright green eyes. I wasn't used to seeing so many pale-skinned, pale-eyed people. "Why do you have a boy's haircut?"

Without thinking, my hand drifted to my short haircut. "We don't grow our hair out in Nigeria until after we graduate secondary school." It was common for girls to keep their hair shaved short until college.

"What's secondary school?" the first girl asked.

I gave it a thought. "High school?"

They laughed.

"That's weird."

"You should grow your hair out." They walked off.

In the distance, I heard someone shout my way, "African booty scratcher!" I didn't know if it was those girls, but it wasn't the only time I'd be called that. I didn't even know what it meant, but I knew how I felt when I heard it—confused and singled out because the de-livery was meant to sting. My shoulders sank with my heart.

I felt like an outsider, constantly trying to fit in but never quite succeeding. The transition was difficult, made all the more difficult when my dad and stepmom returned to Nigeria almost immediately upon arriving here, leaving my sister and me with our aunt.

I did eventually make friends, and junior high became a much better experience for me. Luckily, acclimating to a new environment as an eleven-year-old served me well. Learning through play was a big help.

So when a new student arrived from Mexico, I seized the opportu-nity to help reduce her acclimation time. Like me, she had an accent, but unlike me, she'd escaped the buzz cut and had a head full of beau-tiful, silky dark hair that flowed to her waist.

One day at lunch, I noticed her curled up in a corner as other kids played in groups and ran around her. I recognized myself in her and knew what she must be feeling. Only a year earlier, I'd been in the same place. It felt like being thrown into the deep end of a swimming pool as the perpetrator watched with a gleam in their eyes, hoping you'll sink and not swim.

I got up from my spot on the bleachers, made my way over to her, and sat down. "Hey, what's your name?"

She glanced up at me, her amber-colored eyes wide. "Karen," she answered.

"It's good to meet you, Karen. I'm Esther. What school did you come from?" Junior high, I learned, received kids from several surrounding elementary schools.

"I went to school in Mexico," she said.

My accent was mostly gone by now, but I was proud of my heritage and wanted to share. "I'm from Nigeria."

She smiled as we jumped into topics like our favorite classes and what we were having for lunch. Soon I was introducing her to my friends, and they were welcoming her into the group. Looking back, I can see that my experience with Karen was my first time acting as a broker.

And I learned a lot from Karen as well. She was my first introduction to Spanish culture, which is very family-oriented and loving. Her family took me in immediately. They cooked for me, never asked many questions, handed out tamales like they were going out of style, and loved a good party.

Friends come easy when you're the rich kid in school—I'd learned that back home. But when the tables turned—after living through a year in elementary school as the unpopular "African booty scratcher"—I realized that friendships were earned, not bought.

Because Karen and I had similar histories, being her friend gave me the foresight to recognize a need and consider what I needed to do to meet it. Karen is the reason I have a knack for making friends and connections. From her, I learned how to tell when someone was uncomfortable and needed some support, and eventually, I learned how to tell when they were ready for me to back off and let them stand on their own.

As I navigated the challenges of adolescence in a foreign land, I found strength in my faith. I began to see myself as a bridge between two worlds—Nigeria and the United States, tradition and modernity, faith and exploration. This duality became a defining feature of my identity, and I started to embrace the unique perspective it gave me—a perspective I hoped everyone would have the opportunity to experience in this lifetime.

FALLING IN LOVE AND FINDING FAITH

Years later, I ended up in college at California State University in Hayward. While studying business for my undergrad, I sat in the Union Building one day during lunch, devouring a teriyaki bowl.

I glanced toward the offices on the top floor, where TVs were perched on the wall below for easy viewing. I'd been watching music videos when some movement above suddenly caught my eye. My gaze wandered to the faces of the people there, and I saw *him*.

Our gazes met, and my fork stopped halfway to my mouth. He was one of the most handsome guys I'd ever seen, with a nice smile and medium brown hair with hints of a copper tone in it.

I smiled back at him, then quickly returned my attention to my chicken and rice, reasoning it was much more likely he was smiling at someone behind me than at me. I'd never seen this man before; he definitely wasn't part of my usual crowd. My cheeks warmed at the possibility he'd been looking at someone behind me and that I'd just embarrassed myself by thinking it was me.

I continued eating, trying my best not to let the almost disastrous blunder overwhelm me. I had just crammed in a few more bites, including a rather large piece of sauce-covered broccoli, when I caught sight of him again. He headed down the stairs and made his way in my direction.

Panic rushed through me like a tidal wave as I began ransacking my brain for information—I'd acknowledged this guy, made eye contact, and now it seemed I'd have to talk to him. The question was, Had I ever *met* him before? I was pretty sure we didn't share any classes. Or maybe he really was headed to the group seated at the table behind me.

I glanced back at the group, but they were all busy in their own worlds, completely oblivious to the handsome stranger headed this way. Turning back, I sucked in a breath as he made a beeline—in a slow, confident manner—right to my table.

He reached out a hand to shake mine and smiled again. The man had dimples. Dimples! "Hi, I'm Rich. Do you work at Olive Garden?"

I furrowed my brow. Yeah, he definitely didn't know me, but he was *so handsome* that I could easily forgive him for that lapse.

I almost opened my mouth to speak, but then I stopped. *Make sure you do* not *have food in your teeth!* I quickly ran my tongue over my teeth, hoping that piece of broccoli wasn't hiding in there somewhere, and then cleared my throat. "Nope." I did *not* work at Olive Garden.

"Ah." He nodded. "I thought maybe I'd seen you there before. What's your name?"

My heart fluttered in my chest. *He wants to know my name? Heck yes!* "It's Esther," I replied with all the cool confidence I wasn't feeling.

"Good to meet you, Esther," he said. Then he seemed to remember something and grabbed a pamphlet he was carrying under his arm. The flier was for a political forum he had put together on campus. "It's tonight. You should come."

"Maybe I will. Thanks." I smiled as he walked away.

I was absolutely twitterpated with him. I replayed our short inter-action over and over in my head and gushed to a friend about the en-counter. And you can best believe I showed up to the event later that evening. My friend even came for emotional support—and backup in case I decided I wanted to get out of there.

During the event, I couldn't take my eyes off him and his friendly way of interacting with people. Afterward, I couldn't tell you what a single one of the guests talked about, but I could've painted a portrait of every contour of his face (including, of course, the dimples). I'd never felt that way about anyone before. It was a powerful, exciting, overwhelming feeling—one that still hasn't gone away.

* * *

A month went by without seeing him. I'd all but decided our meeting was a one-and-done. I was disappointed, but life went on.

One day, I was heading to my favorite place on campus with a group of friends. "I don't know what you've been told. It ain't the butterfly, it's the Tootsie Roll," I sang loudly.

My friend laughed. "I dare you to do the dance with it."

"Ha! You mean this one?" I said while doing the move.

My friend covered her eyes. "No, no—I never should've dared you."

"It's fine." Seeing that everyone was watching, I did the Dougie. Mid-move, I glanced up—and there stood the man of my dreams!

He smiled wide, clearly amused. I, however, wanted to hide under a rock. And wouldn't you know it, but that man disappeared again! My embarrassment was quickly replaced with an onslaught of disappointment.

A few months later, a friend showed up waving a piece of paper in my face.

"Here," she said.

I took the paper and saw a phone number on it. "What's this?"

"You know the guy with the dimples?"

"Yes," I replied, amused by her fitting description.

"I ran into him at work." She grinned. She worked at the used bookstore down the hill from campus. "He gave me his number to give to you." She knew who he was because she was the same friend who'd gone to his event with me.

Needless to say, I called him, and he invited me to *another* event, this time with John Stossel. I went, but by the end, even after he walked me to my car, I couldn't help but think that he was just trying to fill seats. It was a disappointing thought, to say the least.

I tried to forget about it, but shortly after we parted ways, I got a call. My heart went from calm to fluttering all over the place again as I answered.

"Hi," he said. "I was hoping we'd have more time to talk after the event."

"Yeah?" I was driving back to campus to the Warren Hall parking lot, a smile taking over my face. I guess he wasn't trying to fill seats after all. He was interested! Right? Maybe. I hoped.

"Yeah," he said.

Stay calm! Taking a deep breath, I parked my car and stared through the windshield at the view over the valley. At night, it was almost like looking at a reflection of the stars in the sky. There wasn't a more fitting place to have a conversation with Dimples.

"Tell me about yourself. What are some things you like?" He hesitated, then added, "Where do you shop?"

I chuckled. It was such a specific question. I didn't want him to think I was some super poor girl because I shopped at Ross, though "some poor girl" was exactly what I was at that time. My family had money, but I was on my own. Their wealth, their titles, didn't hold sway in my world. I was a real riches-to-rags story . . . but I was proud of it! I worked hard for every penny I had, and someday, I'd run my own successful business that I built from the ground up with my own two hands. For now, I was scraping by, but I still wanted to show some class, so I said, "Marshalls."

"Oh, that's great. I shop at Ross," he said.

"Oh, perfect." I laughed at how silly I'd been. "Me too!"

We talked for a long time, and at one point, he admitted to trying to catch my eye multiple times at the library. I couldn't even remember ever seeing him there. I'd been so focused on my destination—on my purpose, like my mother had told me—that the last thing that had been on my mind was boys. Not to mention that most of the boys I knew and dated were from Nigeria and only interested in me because of who I was—or rather, who my *father* was. They were interested in my power, my wealth, my prestige, and my social status. But Rich . . . he saw *me*.

Rich confessed that his Olive Garden gambit had just been an excuse to talk to me. Again, that twitterpated feeling—the one I'd never really experienced before—came back in full force. I liked him. A lot. He was sweet. Down to earth. Straightforward. So different than what I knew.

"You should know . . ." he said, pausing for a moment. "I'm Mormon."

My gaze darted around as I tried to think of how to respond to that. "Okay," I finally said. *So you go to church—why are you telling me that? But I guess that's nice because I go to church too.*

"Just thought you should know." He sounded solemn, but I couldn't comprehend why.

Later, at home in bed, while I replayed our conversation in my head, my mind veered to his "confession" of being religious. No one else I'd ever known—friends, boyfriends, often even family—had ever been that up-front about possible issues in a relationship. I wasn't used to such honesty; it was strange yet refreshing. As I drifted off to sleep, a smile firmly planted on my face, I thought, *You're a little weird, but whatever . . . you're cute.*

* * *

The first time I went to The Church of Jesus Christ of Latter-day Saints was with my aunt, but I don't remember it very well. The next time I went was with Rich.

When I walked into the chapel, it felt like I had come home. The peace within the walls of that building really resonated with me. We made our way inside and sat down among rows of other young people. Rich later explained his ward was a "singles ward," or a congregation made up of young, unmarried people from nearby universities. This particular one was the Berkeley Ward, situated near UC Berkeley. These wards are a way the Church helps young people make connections and, hopefully, find their future spouses.

Sometime later, when he got up to speak, I watched him go, eyes wide. *You get to talk? That's cool, I guess—and weird. But whatever . . . you're cute.*

In the Catholic Church, or the various other congregations I'd had the privilege of being a member of or visiting, members of the congregation didn't give talks, so this was all new for me. I liked it. I liked all the talks, all given by members of the ward.

* * *

Not long after Rich invited me to church, we planned another date. I'd just parked my car at my apartment complex when I spotted him lying on the grass on the little island between the uncovered parking and the covered parking. He looked like he was loitering, with his hands behind his head, his face turned up to the sun—a very clean vagrant. He rocked a white dress shirt and tan pants.

I slowly walked up to him, taking in his features, and wondered what kind of guy would just lie down in a spot like this. So weird. *But whatever . . . you're cute.* That was quickly becoming my motto for him.

"Hey there," I said.

His hazel eyes popped open, and he smiled up at me, showcasing those fantastic dimples, and I became mush. "There you are."

We headed inside my apartment so I could finish getting ready, but before I could, I ran into one of my two roommates, Jenny. She handed me a piece of paper. "We're being evicted."

My heart nearly pounded out of my chest. "What?"

"Laurel didn't pay her portion of the rent," Jenny said. "We have three days to vacate."

She stepped out, leaving me in a wake of fear and frustration. What was I going to do now? Where would I go?

"Are you all right?" Rich asked.

I was on the verge of a panic attack, so on the whole . . . not so much. Not only was it hard to find decent housing in this area, especially in the middle of a quarter, but it was also expensive, and I barely had enough to cover expenses. I forced a smile and pointed to the couch. "Yeah, just give me a minute. I need to finish getting ready."

Rushing to the restroom, I contained my panic until I shut the bathroom door behind me. I took my time getting ready, trying to calm down and figure out what my next move would be, when a light *tap, tap, tap* sounded at the door, knuckles on wood.

"Esther, there are two men waiting at the door for you," Rich said.

I scoffed. No one knew where I lived. Rich was lucky I'd given *him* my address. I continued taking my time, and when I felt ready, I stepped out.

The last thing I expected was to actually find two men sitting in my living room, talking with Rich. They were young, younger than me, dressed in suits and ties, and wearing name tags proclaiming them as missionaries for The Church of Jesus Christ of Latter-day Saints. I'd met them before. They'd come by to give me a lesson once.

They all stood as I entered the room. Embarrassment sunk in as I thought, *Oh, there* are *people here! Rich wasn't kidding. And I took so long!*

Rich signaled to them. "I let them in. I hope that's okay?"

In that moment, all the emotions I'd been trying to hold back came crashing forward and I started to cry. The tears streamed down my face, and I quickly covered my eyes as my crying turned to sobbing. I was in such a bind, and I really didn't know what I was going to do. In three days, I'd be homeless. The landlord already had my rent for the month and wasn't likely to give it back. And even if he did, where would I go?

"What's wrong?" Elder Spencer asked.

Rich stepped up and wrapped an arm around me, and I proceeded to fill the missionaries in on my predicament.

This time, Elder Ruiz stepped forward. "Can we give you a blessing?"

The offer surprised me. *They want to pray for me?* I was so touched. I nodded. I could use all the prayers I could get.

They had me sit down in a chair from the kitchen table and then came up behind me and asked for my full name. I gave it to them, and they gently placed their hands on my head.

One of them began to speak. "In the name of Jesus Christ, we lay our hands upon your head to give you a blessing . . ."

I had no idea what they'd planned to do. When they asked if I wanted a blessing, I assumed that meant they wanted to pray for me, so this was all so new and unexpected. But as they spoke, I felt the Holy Ghost wash over me, and I knew everything would be all right.

As they finished, I wiped the tears from my eyes and stood to face them.

They smiled at me. Rich too. We could all feel the shift in the room. It was the Spirit.

Then the door swung open as if on cue. It was Laurel, my roommate who hadn't paid rent. She strode in like everything was normal—like we weren't just about to lose our home.

"Laurel, what are you doing? You didn't pay rent," I said.

She looked at me, brows pinched together. "Yes, I did," she said, pointing over her shoulder. "Just now." Then she wandered off.

My gaze shot to the missionaries and then to Rich. Had that just happened? They all smiled. I did too—how could I not? In that moment, I knew God was in control and that He had been the whole time.

The more I went to church, the more I recognized the miracles in my life. The Church helped me put things into perspective and understand principles that I hadn't been able to articulate before but were already a part of me. Suddenly, the doctrine of Christ became a more permanent part of my life.

Soon I understood that when Rich told me he was Mormon, that's what he'd been saying: that this was his life. These everyday miracles were the norm, and he was "all in" with Jesus, living His gospel all the time.

* * *

One day, after about a year of Rich and I dating, I was working at the VP of Student Affairs office in Warren Hall when he sent a bouquet of multicolored roses with a card that said "Meet me where it began."

I was overwhelmed by the gesture, embarrassed that everyone I worked with had seen the delivery, and working up to a good panic attack. Trying to stay calm, I went to my boss.

"Sorry to ask, but may I be excused for a few minutes?"

My coworkers sent a bunch of "oohs" and "aahs" my way—and so did the lady who'd brought the flowers in the first place. (Yeah, she was still there.)

My cheeks heated.

My boss gave me an indulgent smile. "Take your time."

"Thank you." I quickly made my way out of the building, headed for the Union.

The only problem was that I'd entered from the wrong direction, not the one Rich had been expecting. I came in the front, assuming he'd be on the main level, but he wasn't. I made my way farther into the building and noticed a figure standing at the top of the stairs with another bouquet of roses—red this time. My feet felt planted to the floor with my excitement. Rich smiled, beaming with joy, and waved down at me.

With my heart soaring, I waved back.

It was then that I knew this was more than just a note to meet him for lunch.

We met at the top of the stairs and he got down on one knee.

He started to speak, and I wish I could remember what he'd said, but I was in a full-blown panic attack by then and didn't hear a word. All eyes were on us, including the lady who'd delivered the first bouquet. (Apparently she'd followed me, knowing what was going to ensue and definitely wanting to witness it! I later found out that Rich had recruited her from one of the offices where they'd met earlier, and she had willingly offered to participate in Rich's declaration of love.)

"Esther." He gulped, looking more nervous than I'd ever seen him. "Will you be my wife?"

I might not have heard everything he said, but I managed to say the right thing when the time came. "Yes!" I was utterly overwhelmed, but I was thrilled that he'd proposed to me where we first met—where it all began.

He stood then and kissed me for all the crowd to see. Their raucous applause synced perfectly with the rhythm of my heart.

Later, I saw a picture he'd taken of me that day with the flowers. And you know what? My hair was on point! I had just gotten it done. Ha! God really is in the details.

* * *

A few months later, I was still taking lessons from the missionaries. Over the months, I'd had a steady rotation of elders and even sisters teach me. The question of baptism had come up several times, and even though the gospel aligned with everything I believed and made me feel like I was home, I couldn't commit. I was in love with Rich but didn't want to feel like I was getting baptized because I'd met a guy.

During one meeting with the missionaries, Rich's dad, Ben, was in town and joined us. Rich took after his dad in a lot of ways, including his looks; Ben had the same coppery brown hair as Rich, though with a few gray streaks here and there, and he even had dimples! Aside from that, he was a happy-go-lucky guy and fun to be around.

We sat in the living room with the missionaries, Rich at my side, hand lightly resting on my knee, as we talked. The topic of baptism came up again. As usual, I was reluctant and tried to change the topic, but Ben wasn't having it.

He leaned forward in his chair, resting his elbows on his knees. "Esther, do you believe in the gospel of Jesus Christ?"

I was so used to his silly side that his sudden seriousness took me off guard. "Yes."

"Do you believe that the Book of Mormon is a second witness of Jesus Christ?"

I nodded.

"And do you believe Joseph Smith was a prophet of God?"

"Yes." I did—I had for some time. I'd prayed about all these things and received a witness they were true.

Ben looked me in the eye. "Then what's holding you back?"

I didn't have an answer to his question. I realized in that moment it didn't matter what people thought. If they believed I joined because of Rich, then so what? If Rich and I broke up, it would still be true. The Church of Jesus Christ of Latter-day Saints was unequivocally *my* church. It was Christ's church, and I knew it. Ben's direct line of questioning was exactly what I needed.

As time went on, my testimony only grew stronger. Nothing felt more natural than to enter the waters of baptism, with Rich performing the sacred ritual. Like the first time I walked into the chapel at the singles ward, I felt like I'd come home. That feeling has stayed with me all this while—whether I'm at church in Sandy, Utah, or Uyo, Nigeria.

* * *

Rich moved slow, as in S-L-O-W, and that was okay by me. In my mind, I wasn't quite ready to be called Mrs. Stowell. It had taken a year for him to propose, and it was another year before we were married.

It gave us time to deal with my family, who were less than thrilled that I decided to marry so young. In my culture, you got an education first, and marriage came in your thirties—I was still in my early twenties. And to top it off, I was marrying a foreigner outside my race. This had never been an issue for me, from the first moment my dad brought his European partner and Chinese manufacturer to our home when I was seven years old.

I was a friend broker, after all.

The first time someone pointed out that Rich and I were an interracial couple, I was shocked. I didn't see us that way.

I heard about my family's disapproval from all sides—all but one, that is.

In February of 2006, my brother Aniefiok emailed me. Aniefiok was twelve years older than me and had been in college when I'd been at home in Calabar as a kid. Unlike the lower schools, where you spent time in boarding schools, colleges allowed for a more independent living. My older brothers lived at home but spent most of their time in school or out with friends. Aniefiok was away often, but he often carried me along on his escapades with his then-girlfriend, Kuna. I absolutely adored them both.

In his email, he used his nickname for me, Ekot, which is the term used to identify one's occipital lobe. With a buzz cut and a not-so-proportional body frame, my head must have protruded enough to be the first thing my older siblings saw when they looked at me. It was like a chunky baby being called "chubby cheeks." For me, it was Ekot, a term that might have once been literal and had since turned into an endearment.

In one message, in just three lines, he gave me more compassion and comfort than anyone else in my family had even attempted since hearing about my wedding to Rich.

> My sweet Ekot,
>> If you're happy and this is what you want, go ahead.
>> Ignore everyone else.

I sank into my chair, my heart full of emotions that I couldn't fully comprehend. Aniefiok now lived in Abuja with his family, and I was sure he was getting stories from our family in the States about me and Rich, but he still made sure to reach out and check with me. He couldn't have known how much that email would mean to me.

A month later, Aniefiok, having struggled with epilepsy for years, had an episode in his bathroom and fell. By the time his family got him to the hospital, it was too late. His youngest child was only eight months old at the time.

I was heartbroken, but the Spirit spoke to my heart and reminded me of God's plan of salvation—that mortal life is not the end of families. My heart still ached for his wife and children, but the knowledge that families could be together forever kept me going.

Later, my family used Aniefiok's death to try to convince me that I shouldn't marry Rich. They told me it wasn't what Aniefiok would've wanted. Naturally, that made me cherish Aniefiok's email even more.

Three months later, in June, Rich and I were married in Oakland, California, in the hall at the temple grounds. (We would be sealed a year later, making our temporal marriage an eternal one.) We celebrated with a mixture of my culture and his. Traditional food of my country was featured heavily—including fufu and a variety of soups to go with it, jollof rice, baked chicken, sautéed goat meat, moi-moi, puff-puff, and fried plantain.

I wore a traditional Nigerian dress, which was in shades of pearl for the wedding, and I donned a more colorful one in cream and burgundy for the reception. To complete my happiness, I wasn't the only one in traditional dress. My family—and Rich—wore the traditional outfits of my country. The men were in lace kaftans, like my father wore during his meeting with his business partners, but this time the colors were green and white, soft rather than crisp, and the women wore the same colors but styled as buba and wrapper, with the younger cousins in dresses, custom-made especially for the occasion. The wedding hall was filled with all the colors of the rainbow in clothes, flowers, and people.

My experiences in America and Nigeria led me to this incredible fulfillment of happiness that I never thought possible. As Rich slipped the ring over my finger, I saw the guiding hand of God in my life that led me to this point. The joy we felt that day, in the blending of families, cultures, and races, became a symbol of the lives we would lead together.

Embracing My Calling

Three months into our marriage, Rich approached me with a sheepish look on his face. We sat at our kitchen table in our basement apartment. He was full of nervous energy that made him fidgety. His knee bounced under the table.

"There's this thing I've always wanted to do," he said hesitantly. "I want to join the military."

I blinked. Okay . . . In all the time I'd known him—almost two and a half years now—I'd never heard him mention this. He was thirty, and most people who joined the military did it when they were younger, right? He couldn't be serious, could he? But as I looked at him, I could see the sincerity in his eyes. "You want to join the military?"

"Yes."

"Since when?"

He leaned back in his chair and ran a hand through his hair. "Since forever. What do you think?"

I didn't particularly like the idea. But . . . *If I say no, maybe he'll have a midlife crisis later. But if I say yes, hopefully he won't have a midlife crisis.* Comfortable with my reasoning, I nodded. "If this is important to you, do it."

What we couldn't have prepared for was that I would be pregnant during basic training. Or that I would essentially become a single working mom, raising our first child on my own, while Rich was in Kosovo. Figuring out daycare for our firstborn, Joseph, so I could work was practically a comedy of errors, but I eventually figured it out.

I worked as an administrative assistant, or document administrator, for a property management division of an affordable housing coalition in the Bay Area peninsula. I didn't know it then, but so much of what I'd learned in this position would be the foundation of my own business as a broker, real estate agent, and property manager later in life.

Rich's absence was hard, but I always found that when I was at my absolute lowest, God had a way of lifting me back up.

One night, Joseph fell ill with a high fever. He was only three months old, and I was a first-time mom with no clue what to do. I was exhausted, scared, and had to be at work the next day. I didn't have anyone to talk to, and out of desperation, I wrapped my baby up, placed him in his car seat, and took him to the emergency room.

My mind raced as I drove as fast as I safely could with a baby on board through the dark Oakland streets. *What if this isn't the right thing to do? What if I'm just overreacting? What if I'm not?* The point was, I didn't know and just had to do the best I could. So I kept going.

As I pulled up to the ER at 1 a.m., the red lights of the hospital sign guiding me in, I got a call. It was Rich. He never called me at this time—he knew I'd be asleep—but God knew I needed to hear his voice. Rich always had a way of calming me down.

"Hey, how are you?" he asked, seemingly unaware of the hour and just happy to hear my voice.

"I'm at the ER with Joseph. He has a fever and I can't get it to go down." My voice trembled, even though I tried to hold it together. I pulled into a parking spot and let all my worries and frustrations out. Rich just let me talk. Meanwhile, I kept my gaze glued to my sick baby as he fussed in the car seat behind me. "I don't know if I'm doing the right thing."

Once it was all out, Rich spoke up. "It's going to be fine. You're doing the right thing."

A huge weight lifted from my shoulders, and I finally felt like I could breathe. These were the words I needed to hear, exactly in the moment I needed to hear them. He kept up his constant assurances as I picked up our baby and took him inside, not feeling as abandoned and lonely as I had before he called.

The nurses gave Joseph a Tylenol, and by the time the doctor saw him, his fussing had stopped, and he was fine. *And* I had learned what to do the next time.

To this day, I still don't know why Rich called, because it wasn't our normal time to talk, but I guess that doesn't really matter. What mattered was that in my hour of need, he was there—even though he didn't know I needed him. It had become our pattern. I would need him in some way, he'd do a random thing I didn't see coming, and things got better. He was my anchor.

THE BROKER IN ACTION

I squinted out the narrow front window of the cottage-style home as Eddie stepped out of his car. He was an older man, maybe in his early- to mid-sixties, and moved slowly, unfolding himself from the driver's seat, one hand gripping the top of the car door for balance. He made his way to the sidewalk, a sharp limp in his left leg like maybe he had a bad hip, and hobbled his way to the house. A pang of doubt twisted my stomach as I considered all the stairs inside this house. Too many, including the set leading to the front door.

Since starting Ekot Real Estate three months after moving to Utah, I'd made it my goal to make sure people not only found what they wanted but what they needed. This mindset had not only helped me find homes for many people, but it had helped me build a successful business from the ground up that I was proud of.

Eddie's sister-in-law, Porsha, had made the appointment for him a day earlier, but she hadn't mentioned he might struggle with stairs. He hadn't even made it in the house yet, and I was already unsure if this was what he needed.

The house was no grand estate, just a compact Victorian cottage nestled among many other similar ones in Holladay. It charmed with its gables and cozy rooms but demanded endurance to navigate.

As he headed up the front steps, I opened the door.

"Eddie?" I gave him my sunniest smile.

He glanced at me and nodded. "Esther?" He seemed almost guarded in his tone and body language, like he'd expected I would be rude or intrusive. Not that I could blame him. I showed up looking my best in my best black dress pants, yellow blazer, and high heels. That was just part of the job. But I knew very well that the title "real estate agent" came with other attached stereotypes, like we were all pushy, too sales-driven, money-motivated above all else, and more. But that wasn't me.

I showed him around the house and soon had him laughing and smiling, but I also felt increasingly concerned as his limp worsened with every step.

"This is a nice place," he told me, this time with a spark of laughter in his eye.

We stopped in the kitchen. "It is," I agreed, but I already knew this wasn't the home for him. "What are you looking for precisely?"

He glanced around. "Something like this."

Maybe some real estate agents would've gone in for the proverbial kill, but I couldn't. "Aren't you worried about all the steps?"

"I'm used to steps." He brushed off my concern with a wave of his hand.

We headed out, and I closed and locked the door behind me.

"Have you looked at any other places yet?" I asked. Eddie was so nice that I worried he might just buy this place from me because he liked me—and I didn't want that. "Do you have someone who's working with you to find just the right home?"

He gripped the railing to go down the four steps to the walkway, and all I could think was *I can't sell this man this house.* I just knew I would feel absolutely guilty if I sold it to him. I wanted him to have his *dream* home.

We were almost to his car when he finally opened up. "I'd like a place that's all one level."

I sighed in relief. "Have you heard of homes that are for people fifty-five and over?"

"No, I haven't." His eyes grew wide at the idea.

"It allows you to live in a space you can manage every day," I explained. "Here's what I'm going to do. I'm going to look up those places, and then we'll go see them together. Does that sound good?"

He beamed at me. "Yeah, sounds good."

I got his contact information and we went our separate ways with a promise that I'd be in touch soon with a list of houses that would be more in line with what he wanted. Later, I contacted his sister-in-law, Porsha, again to give her an update.

Porsha lived in a different state and wasn't able to help Eddie the way she wanted. But she filled me in on his story. Apparently, Eddie had been working as a janitor in a homeless shelter for years and had managed to save $80,000, but instead of buying, he rented a little apartment on the third floor of a business in Murray, Utah.

Every day, he had to walk up a flight of stairs to get to his apartment—and not just any stairs but narrow spiral ones. And that wasn't the worst of it. His apartment had no parking, so he parked across

State Street, one of the busiest roads in Utah, and had to cross that road, limp and all, during all seasons—even winter, which can be a beast in Utah—to even get to his building.

Thirty years earlier, he'd tried to buy a house in Sugar House, a beautiful residential area in the Salt Lake area, but he was told by the real estate agent that he made *too much money* to buy a house there. Eddie hadn't tried to get a place again.

"If you could help him," Porsha said, "that would be great. Because I would love for him to have something of his own."

I'd decided to grant that wish before she'd even asked. Hearing his story sparked a fire in me—I would make sure he got everything he needed, wanted, and deserved. "I'll take care of it."

"Oh, thank you so much!" Porsha said.

* * *

The first place Eddie and I went to was perfect.

The moment we stepped inside, we both stopped in awe. Instantly, we knew this was Eddie's new home before we'd even explored it.

"This is it," Eddie said, a smile spreading over his face.

I nodded, unable to speak.

"This is my home."

As we walked through each room, it felt like God was in control. Eddie was His son, and He'd led him to me. Not only that, but He'd inspired me to see how I could be of service to him. I felt for Eddie, not just because he had a limp but also because he had limited family in Utah. I knew what it was like to be alone, and I wanted to help in any way I could.

Eddie was ready to sign papers before we'd even seen the whole thing. "Thank you, Esther."

"My pleasure."

It truly had been. I'd come to care for him deeply and was so pleased for him.

Eddie had always been a hard worker—and disciplined enough to save that money so he could have it to pay for his retirement—and I wanted his money to work for him so that he could be in a nice retirement space. The space fit his needs perfectly: a garage for his car, no stairs, and an extra room for family visits. I helped him purchase the property and furnish it, and I connected him with a lawyer to ensure his estate would avoid probate if anything happened.

Now he's living the life he should have lived thirty years ago.

As I watched Eddie drive away from his dream home that day, I felt the rare satisfaction that comes from seeing someone get a fresh start, one they'd long deserved but never expected. Eddie didn't just find a home—he'd found independence, security, and the comfort of a place he could truly call his own. It was more than just a sale; it was the chance for him to rewrite his story, to reclaim something he'd lost along the way.

Our work together had opened up a path, not only to a house but to a new kind of family. Over time, Eddie became a regular part of our lives, weaving into the rhythm of our days with a natural ease. He stopped by for family dinners, visits with the kids, and even the occasional weekend repair project on his old cell phone. I could tell he felt it too—this connection that had begun as business but grew into something much richer.

Forging this unlikely friendship reminded me of why I had started Ekot Real Estate in the first place: to help people. And not just to find houses but to find spaces where they could finally feel at home—an area where they could be part of a community. It was what I'd always wanted for myself and what I'd sought to give others.

Now that I'd achieved my dream, I was eager to share the blessings.

A Legacy of Love

At six months pregnant with my third child, I shuffled into the doctor's office with a practiced ease, the familiar routine of prenatal checkups almost comforting in their predictability. Having been through this with my two other children, I felt confident, even though this pregnancy was being treated differently than the others. There was some concern because of my history of having extra-large babies and possibly gestational diabetes.

Joseph arrived in the world at nine pounds five ounces, and Gabriel, though slated for a December 25th delivery date, was cautiously recommended to arrive sooner with an inducement on December 21st because he was measuring at around twelve pounds the day before during my checkup. He ended up clocking in at ten pounds four ounces after a full day of labor and having the epidural wear off.

Today, for pregnancy number three, I was here specifically for an ultrasound so that they could check on my baby to see how she was faring considering my birthing history.

I wasn't worried. I hadn't even asked Rich to come with me—he was a key leader in our local congregation, serving to help the local members, and was busy, busy, busy with his calling, job, and position as a professor at the University of Utah. This was something I could handle on my own.

The checkup went fast. Vital signs, check. Weight test, check. Physical examination, check. Everything seemed in line. Then came the time for the ultrasound. I always enjoyed them—the moment I got to see the little life growing inside me and hear the fast little heartbeat.

It'd been four years and another deployment for Rich, this time to Afghanistan, since I'd had my last baby, and I was so ready for another one. I wanted a large family, but it seemed as though that wasn't in the cards for us. But we were thrilled to get three—and ecstatic we were finally getting a girl.

The doctor turned up the speaker, letting me hear the subtle *thwap, thwap, thwap* sound of the heart—but this time it was different than I recalled it sounding during my last two pregnancies. It was slower.

"Hang on a second." The nurse took some images. "I'll be right back." She stepped out of the room.

That was weird. I felt a nervous flutter in my heart but disregarded it. Not long after, the doctor came in with a solemn look on her face.

This time my pulse sped up and there was nothing I could do to calm it. "What is it?"

She took a seat across from me, showing me the images they'd taken with the sonogram. "Do you see this here?" She pointed out a dark spot on the sonogram.

"Yes."

"It's a third-degree heart block," she said.

"Okay." I tried to calm my rising worries with my questions. "What does that mean?"

The doctor took a deep breath. "With a third-degree heart block, the electrical signals that control the heart rate don't properly pass from the atria, which is the upper chambers of the heart, to the ventricles, or the lower chambers." She mimed each part with her hands as she explained. "This results in the atria and ventricles beating independently of each other."

I blinked. "Which means . . . ?"

"I'm afraid this is a serious condition," she said. "I'm so sorry, but I'm afraid it's not likely your baby will survive. If she does, she'll probably need a pacemaker for the rest of her life."

If hearts could stop beating, I was pretty sure mine did in that moment. My breath caught and an immediate lump grew in my throat. *How could this happen? How could this baby I'd been carrying for six months—this baby I could feel moving inside me, that seemed so alive—be about to die?*

I left the hospital crying, the worry of what would happen next hanging over me, and crawled into my car. The anxiety and fear I felt in this moment were somewhat reminiscent of that night all those years ago when I'd taken Joseph to the hospital all by myself. Just like then, I didn't know what to do. But I knew what—or rather who—I needed.

I called Rich, knowing that just hearing his voice would calm me, like it always had in times of crisis.

"Hello, my love." Rich's tone was cheery. "How was the doctor's appointment?"

I burst into tears again.

"What happened?" he asked, alarmed.

I told him everything. "Even if she does make it, she'll need a pacemaker."

The line was silent for just a moment, and then, with conviction, he said, "Okay, so we'll get her a pacemaker."

Oh! Okay. As usual, he said exactly what I needed to hear in that moment.

I made the drive home, and when I got there, Rich was waiting for me in the driveway. He opened my door and pulled me into a hug, wrapping me in the security of knowing I wasn't alone in this.

I snuggled in, breathing in the comforting scent of him. If I had a husband who was willing to walk this path with me, I knew we'd be fine.

* * *

Knowing Rich had my back served as a huge relief, but I still had concerns. For one, I had a husband who thrived on roughhousing, teasing, and scaring my kids. Two, I had a father-in-law who also loved those things and who all the grandchildren referred to as the "tickle monster."

I couldn't help but wonder why the Lord would send a child with heart problems into this family. Heavenly Father would have to step up because my baby girl might have a heart attack if they scared her.

The next day, Ben, my father-in-law, came over, and he and Rich gave me a blessing. It was everything I needed to hear. These two silly men that I loved, with sober hearts, placed their hands on my head and blessed me through the power of the priesthood—the authority to act in God's name—that I would have the peace I needed to go through the process. The Lord blessed me, through them, that I would be at peace with the outcome, whatever it was, and that I would have the strength to overcome the obstacles in front of us.

They reminded me of the blessings we already had—that we were in a place with good hospitals, and that we had the support of family and friends all around us who were praying for us. As they spoke, I couldn't help but remember all those years ago receiving my first priesthood blessing from the missionaries, when the rent had come due and my roommate hadn't paid. I had the same feeling now as I did then—that the Lord had this in hand and that everything would work out exactly as it needed to. That I didn't need to worry.

The same weekend as the blessing, we asked our friends and family all over the world—in Utah, California, Nigeria, Europe, and elsewhere—to fast and pray for us. To fast and pray for our baby. And they did.

It felt like a warm embrace extending across continents and oceans, uniting us all in a singular, powerful act of faith and hope. Despite the physical distances, there was an overwhelming sense of community and solidarity that enveloped us, making the challenges seem more bearable and less isolating. Each prayer and act of fasting felt like a thread weaving a tapestry of support, carrying with it wishes for healing and strength. This collective spiritual effort brought not only comfort but also a deep gratitude for the bonds of family and friendship, reinforced in times of need. It was a reminder of the kindness and the potent connections that sustain us through life's most trying moments.

A week later I went back to the hospital. I was to spend the rest of my pregnancy on bed rest there. Their hope was that my little girl would make it to thirty-two weeks, and if she did, they would be able to deliver her. That was three months of hospital bed rest for me, but I was ready to do whatever I had to.

Before they got me settled, they did another sonogram.

"Hang on a second," the nurse said, staring at the images. "This can't be right."

I felt a flutter in my heart. "What can't be right?" I wasn't sure I could take any more surprises.

She stepped out, then came back in and started over with the sonogram. When the new images came through, it was a moment before she spoke. "If I hadn't seen your file, I would not have known this was the same heart I was looking at."

I sat up taller. "What do you mean?"

"Just a minute." She went to get the doctor.

The doctor also couldn't believe what she was seeing. She showed me the images. "I made my tech do this twice. I thought she'd made a mistake, but I don't see the same thing I saw last week. It has to be a fluke."

My entire body warmed as a glow grew inside me, starting in my core where my perfectly healthy baby rested. This was no fluke. This was a miracle.

She was my miracle.

Three months later, our daughter was born—perfect and whole. She had my brown eyes, her dad's dimples, and a heart that loves everyone. I wanted to share the miracle with the world. I wanted people to know that there are modern-day miracles and that our daughter was one of them.

We named her Naomi Utibe.

In my native dialect in Nigeria, Utibe means miracle.

Bringing people together has always been more than just a part of my job as a broker—it's been my way of life. Over the years, my work has given me the privilege of connecting with diverse individuals and communities, not just in Utah, California, and Nigeria but all around the world. So when the moment arrived that I found myself in need, facing the potential loss of my unborn child, it was these same connections who rallied around me.

This support blended seamlessly with the profound faith and prayers from those both in and out of The Church of Jesus Christ of Latter-day Saints, enriching the tapestry of community that enveloped us. The power of our collective faith and unity was palpable as friends, family, and Church members from every corner of the globe joined together to offer their prayers and fast in solidarity. This outpouring of support was not just a testament to the bonds we'd formed but also a profound reminder of the strength that comes from such unity.

It underscored a fundamental truth: Community is not merely a network of relationships to be tapped into but a powerful force that, in times of crisis, holds the unique capacity to uplift, heal, and provide hope.

I felt isolated and alone when I first immigrated to the United States, but I soon discovered there were many people who were willing to welcome me and help me feel at home.

The support of my community has been essential in helping me overcome challenges, achieve my goals, and find a sense of belonging. It has taught me the importance of giving back and helping others in need.

I believe that the power of community is essential for creating a more just and equitable world. When we work together, we can achieve great things. We can break down barriers, overcome challenges, and build a better future for us all.

ABOUT THE AUTHORS

FERNANDA BÖHME

Born and raised in Rio de Janeiro, Brazil, Fernanda Böhme co-founded Böhme, a women's clothing brand, in 2007, and serves as its creative director and designer. The brand operates seventeen stores across seven states, with an online presence that employs over 300 women. Böhme has earned recognition as one of the Top Women-Run Businesses on the Inc. 500 Fastest-Growing Companies list, has been featured in *Forbes*, was a finalist for the Entrepreneur of the Year, and was awarded the 2019 SBA of the Year for the state of Utah.

As a recent winner of the "40 Over 40" award, Fernanda has been an influential keynote speaker worldwide, sharing her inspiring journey. She has also represented the U.S. Chamber of Commerce in supporting women-owned businesses in the Middle East and has been involved in numerous charity initiatives to empower women globally. In addition to her fast-paced fashion career, Fernanda's architecture and design work has been showcased on the cover of *Build Magazine*.

As parents of a daughter with autism, she and her husband are committed to raising awareness. They reside in Utah with their three children.

Shayla Egan

Shayla Egan is a three-time world marathon runner with a passion for racing on behalf of those in need. A dedicated stay-at-home mother, she also manages a social media account, @ldspreppergirl, where she shares insights on spiritual growth and practical preparedness. A lifelong member of The Church of Jesus Christ of Latter-day Saints, Shayla finds joy in homesteading, running, exploring the outdoors, serving others, and cherishing time with her family. She and her husband are blessed with four wonderful daughters.

Shayla grew up in a large, loving family, a foundation that shaped her appreciation for connection and community. In recent years, she experienced what she describes as a spiritual awakening—an eye-opening journey that deepened her faith and transformed her perspective. This awakening has made her more intentional in serving others and living by the teachings of Jesus Christ, guiding her actions both personally and publicly.

ALLISON HONG MERRILL

Allison Hong Merrill is a Taiwanese immigrant with an MFA in writing from the Vermont College of Fine Arts. She is a *Wall Street Journal* best-selling author who writes in both Chinese and English, both fiction and creative nonfiction, for both adult readers and young readers.

Allison's work has appeared in the *New York Times* and *HuffPost*, winning both national and international literary prizes. Her debut memoir, *Ninety-Nine Fire Hoops*, won over sixty book awards, including the grand prize for the Millennium Book Award in the UK and the grand prize for the Shelf Unbound Indie Best Award. In 2023, the *Focus on Women Magazine* awarded her the title "Woman of Impact." Besides sitting on the executive board of the Calliope Writing Coach Program and being a permanent staff at Writing Away Refuge, Allison is a keynote speaker, an instructor, and a panelist at writer's conferences nationwide and in Asia. She appears on TV, radio, and podcasts and in magazines, newspapers, and journals. She is also available for interviews, teaching, and speaking engagements.

Allison lives in Utah with her husband, their children, and a grandchild.

Kimberly DowDell

Kimberly DowDell has been married to her high school sweetheart for twenty-four years, building a life full of laughter, love, and a lot of dancing. A graduate of Utah Valley University with a bachelor's degree in integrated studies, Kimberly lives in a suburb of Salt Lake City, Utah, with her husband and their four children, each bringing their own joy, adventure, and sometimes surprises to the mix. Named a top instructor in *Zumba Magazine*, she has spent nearly two decades sharing her love of movement, inspiring others to stay active, and building connections through her popular fitness classes.

As a well-known YouTuber and influencer on Instagram and TikTok, Kimberly's content has amassed over 350 million views, inviting audiences into her journey as a wife, mom, and believer. A dedicated advocate for families of children with special needs, Kimberly finds purpose in showing the unique joys that her youngest child, born with Down syndrome, brings to their family. Her story and mission have been featured on KSL, *Newsweek*, WFLA, and *People Magazine*, spreading messages of faith, resilience, and real family life. Rooted in her faith as a member of The Church of Jesus Christ of Latter-day Saints, she aims to bring joy and remind others they're not alone in the ups and downs of life.

When she's not teaching or online, Kimberly is all about family time, whether that's a movie night, a day at the beach, or just sipping a Diet Coke while listening to her favorite country tunes. Her faith, family, and love for community are at the heart of everything she does, and she's grateful for each chance to lift others—one story, one dance, and one laugh at a time.

Ganel-Lyn Condie

Ganel-Lyn knows all is possible with God. As a popular motivational speaker, Ganel-Lyn is known for inspiring others with her unique honesty, authenticity, and spirit. She is dedicated to her family, faith, and inspiring others. As a graduate of Arizona State University with a BS in elementary education and a minor in psychology, she became an award-winning journalist and was editor of the *Wasatch Woman* magazine.

Since losing her forty-year-old sister Meggan to suicide, Ganel-Lyn has become passionate about mental health education. As a lupus warrior, she is the mother to two miracle children. Ganel-Lyn loves dancing to Abba, watching *Gilmore Girls*, and growing older with her supportive husband Rob. She is a regular television and radio guest, and her books, talks, and social media platforms have encouraged thousands of people all over the world.

Caroline Melazzo

Caroline Melazzo is a dedicated real estate agent and podcaster, passionate about exploring the intersection of faith and everyday life. With a bachelor's degree in business administration from Brazil, she brings a fresh perspective to her writing and work in real estate. Her experiences as a Relief Society president and her husband's calling as a bishop in their Utah ward have deepened her understanding of community and service, enriching her insights into the lives of modern women and wives. The profound loss of her parents also shaped her perspective, reinforcing her belief in the importance of eternal families and the comfort that faith provides during challenging times.

In addition to contributing to this book, Caroline has shared her thoughts on faith and family dynamics through articles and her podcast, where she discusses real estate, community engagement, and the challenges of balancing career and family. Her engaging approach resonates with listeners seeking inspiration and guidance.

Residing in Utah, Caroline enjoys spending her free time pursuing fitness, attending concerts, and engaging with the vibrant community around her. As a mother of teenage boys, she understands the demands of motherhood and the importance of nurturing strong family bonds. Her journey reflects a commitment to uplifting others through the gospel's teachings, and she hopes to inspire readers to find joy and purpose in their own lives.

KERRY OWEN

Kerry Owen is an advocate, visionary, and mother of five whose commitment to tackling issues like poverty and food insecurity has inspired communities in New Zealand and the United States.

As the founder of Feed the Need in New Zealand, Kerry developed innovative programs to address food insecurity, including a free school lunch program that gained national attention and paved the way for a government-funded school lunch program. She has a knack for bringing large corporations and other nonprofits on board, creating dynamic collaborations that amplify the impact of these critical initiatives. Her dedication to being in the trenches and working directly with those she serves has garnered widespread support, establishing her as a respected influencer in the field of social impact.

In Utah, Kerry leads Reach Out Today, a nonprofit dedicated to empowering vulnerable children, youth, and refugees as they navigate life's critical transitions. Through Reach Out Today, she spearheaded a successful transitional housing project for youth aging out of foster care, providing stability and opportunities for those at risk of homelessness. Her unique perspective and fresh ideas have positioned her as a trusted voice in her field, leading her to share her insights through guest lectures and other platforms.

Awarded the Member of the New Zealand Order of Merit (MZNZ) by Queen Elizabeth II for her contributions to children's welfare, Kerry is passionate about the power of community to uplift those in need. She strives to balance her charity work with a deep-rooted commitment to family life, always keeping her loved ones at the core of her mission to create lasting change.

Esther Jackson-Stowell

Esther's extensive experience spans several years, primarily in property management, with a portion spent working for a real estate coalition in the vibrant San Francisco Bay Area. In 2010, she founded Ekot Properties Inc., and later, in 2015, Ekot Real Estate, LLC emerged as the sales division, focused on assisting clients in building generational wealth. Esther's journey, which began with a background in the real estate sector, took a transformative turn to better serve property owners and potential tenants.

Academically, Esther honed her expertise by earning a master's degree in public administration, with a specialization in public management, from California State University, East Bay. In addition to her academic achievements, she holds a real estate management license and is a proud recipient of the Certified Occupancy Specialist certification, awarded by the esteemed National Center for Housing Management (NCHM).

For three years, she contributed her expertise to the Salt Lake City Historic Landmark Commission. In 2022, she held the pivotal role of chair of the Salt Lake City Human Rights Commission. The same year, she also held the position of chair for the Poplar Grove Community Council.

Beyond her impressive professional portfolio, Esther embraces her role as a dedicated mother to two wonderful boys as well as a charming daughter, and she is a source of inspiration for the foster children welcomed into her home. Her husband proudly acknowledges her as the "best wife ever."

To learn more about these amazing women, connect with them on social media, or support their businesses and charities, scan the QR code below:

ACKNOWLEDGMENTS

EMILY CLARK IS THE ACQUISITIONS EDITOR AT CEDAR FORT Publishing and Media. She has published nineteen books across various genres, including thriller and romance. Besides being a successful author and a great coworker, she is a woman dedicated to truth who celebrates women and loves their stories.

Emily is personally responsible for finding and inviting each of the women in this book to participate. She is also responsible for working with each of the authors to craft their story in their own voice while simultaneously bringing them all together into this great book.

In honoring each of the women who participated in this project, and the women in their lives who helped shape them, we also wish to use this page to acknowledge the woman who brought it all together, Emily Clark.

Book Club
Discussion Questions

1. Whose story in this book did you find most touching, and why?

2. What does the book suggest about the societal expectations placed on women regarding work-life balance?

3. How does the book address the mental health challenges associated with maintaining a work-life balance?

4. How do the women in the book redefine success through their career choices and personal sacrifices?

5. How do personal relationships influence and impact the career paths of the women featured in the book?

6. In what ways do the women prioritize their roles and responsibilities, and what can readers learn from this?

7. Are there any moments when the women had to make significant compromises? How did these decisions affect their happiness or personal fulfillment?

8. How does the support—or lack thereof—from partners and family members influence the work-life balance of the women featured?

9. How do the women's personal faith experiences influence their professional decisions and practices?

10. What role does prayer and divine inspiration play in the decision-making processes and crisis management moments mentioned in the book?

11. Can you identify a moment in the book when faith led to a pivotal change in a character's life or career? What can we learn from this?

12. How do the women in the book use their faith to influence and inspire others?

13. Discuss how the community and support structures within their faith helped these women overcome personal and professional challenges.

14. How do the women in the book clarify what it means to be a woman of faith?

15. How do the experiences of the women in the book reflect the challenges and opportunities facing women in modern society?

16. In what ways does the book address the evolution of women's roles both in the workplace and at home?

17. How do the women in the book navigate traditional gender expectations?

18. How do the personal stories in the book contribute to our understanding of women's resilience in facing personal and professional challenges?

19. What do the successes and failures of all the women in this book have in common? And how does the background they each come from shape who they become by the end?

20. Reflect on how the women's personal values and goals align with the changing societal views on gender roles and expectations.